Christian Faith, Justice, and a Politics of Mercy

Christian Faith, Justice, and a Politics of Mercy

The Benevolent Community

James E. Gilman

LEXINGTON BOOKS
Lanham • Boulder • New York • Toronto • Plymouth, UK

Published by Lexington Books
A wholly owned subsidiary of Rowman & Littlefield
4501 Forbes Boulevard, Suite 200, Lanham, Maryland 20706
www.rowman.com

10 Thornbury Road, Plymouth PL6 7PP, United Kingdom

British Library Cataloguing in Publication Information Available

Library of Congress Cataloging-in-Publication Data

Gilman, James Earl.
Christian faith, justice, and a politics of mercy : the benevolent community / James E. Gilman.
pages cm
Includes bibliographical references and index.
ISBN 978-0-7391-8685-5 (cloth : alk. paper) -- ISBN 978-0-7391-8686-2 (electronic)
1. Compassion--Religious aspects--Christianity. 2. Mercy. 3. Benevolence. 4. Christianity and justice. I. Title.
BV4647.S9G55 2014
261.8--dc23
2014000854

∞™ The paper used in this publication meets the minimum requirements of American National Standard for Information Sciences Permanence of Paper for Printed Library Materials, ANSI/NISO Z39.48-1992.

Printed in the United States of America

To my wife Rosemary

Contents

Preface

Justice and mercy capture the imagination like few other moral subjects; and for good reason. They inspire many of the religious and political dramas of history and shape the way most societies identify, or would like to identify, themselves. In Western traditions, justice has attracted more attention than mercy, especially amongst philosophical and religious ethicists. If mercy is discussed at all by Christian ethicists it is usually under the rhetoric and rubric of "love" or *agape*, and rightly so. Most commonly, however, justice is set forth as the primary social and political extension of Christian love, while mercy, as a powerful moral force in its own right, is often marginalized or neglected. What troubles me about contemporary Christian ethicists is their habit of thinking about justice in ways that almost completely submerge the moral significance of mercy, a habit strangely at odds with a religious tradition whose founder says very little *per se* about justice and a great deal about mercy. This is not to say that Jesus is not interested in promoting justice, but it is to say that he apparently feels that justice is somehow rooted in mercy, that in a fallen world justice is unlikely to germinate unless sown in the soil of mercy, unless the followers of Jesus practicing the same mercy toward others that he embodies and practices toward them.

This neglect of mercy, even by those ethicists who write a great deal about love, has for some time interested me. I've wondered why it is that Christian ethicists preoccupy themselves so much with justice to the neglect of mercy; especially since mercy and not justice is the axis of their theology. Since for me Christian ethics, both personal and social, begins with mercy, I've wondered what its connection is to justice. Why is it that Jesus markets mercy while his listeners crave justice? Might there not be an organic, moral link between them? If so what is it? Why and how is it that for Jesus practicing mercy somehow makes practicing justice a reality?

My own encounters with mercy are both personal and professional. The chapters of this book encapsulate my professional encounters, while in this preface I recall a couple of ordinary personal encounters. From one encounter, I learned in a personal way that and how grace, mercy, and forgiveness are available to me as remedies for healing. In 1961, while a young boy in middle school, my father, for professional reasons, moved his family of eight from Boise, Idaho to Seattle, Washington. Up until this time, the family had lived entirely in white communities—in Portland and Cove, Oregon, and in Boise. Prior to arriving in Seattle, I don't recall ever personally encountering an African American. In Boise, I had viewed from a distance across the Boise River, a small ghetto of blacks who lived in shacks along the banks of the river. That was it. Not even on TV, since the family did not have TV at home. When we arrived in Seattle we moved into an "all black" neighborhood. My father, a pastor, took a job as pastor/counselor with the Union Gospel Mission on Seattle's skid road. The Mission owned an apartment building in Seattle's Central District, an all-black enclave. Along with siblings I attended for a while public schools that were primarily black; indeed, often I would be the only, or only one of a few, white faces in a classroom. Although this was something new and different, it was of no personal concern. Daily I would walk the three quarters of a mile to Washington Junior High. It happened that on my way to and from school I would meet up with a classmate, Thomas. We became friends and would often play together during recess. One day, when the bell rang to return from recess to the classroom, I instinctively, without thinking blurted out what white kids in Boise sometimes yelled "Last one in's a nigger baby." That day I was faster than usual to the classroom. I knew immediately that what I had shouted was despicable and hurtful. I knew it was wrong. No one had to tell me; I knew instinctively. It was something we "whites," growing up ignorant and arrogant and racist, would say routinely and thoughtlessly and derisively. When Thomas arrived in the classroom after me, he slid into his seat behind me and whispered, "Wouldn't you want to be born a nigger baby?" I said nothing and had nothing to say. I knew I had hurt him with my words; but I did not have resources enough to say "I'm sorry" or "forgive me." But what struck me then and has stuck with me until now is not only his question but the grace and mercy Thomas nevertheless showed me. He never said another word about it; he never expressed animosity or bitterness or the kind of retaliation I fairly deserved. Instead, he continued to walk with me to and from school; the mercy and forgiveness he practiced healed me and a relationship that I had otherwise shattered. He continued to be a companion on the school yard and always a faithful friend. This was one of my first self-conscious encounters with mercy. From it I began to learn that mercy, instead of anger and retaliation, is available to me as a moral resource and as a response to injustice. I had attended church for thirteen years but only from Thomas and other such encounters did I begin to know grace and mercy and forgiveness as practical realities and not just religious jargon.

From a second unremarkable experience I encountered the great power of mercy. It is unseemly to awaken a sixteen year old before noon on any Saturday? Or so it seemed to me one Saturday, as mom tried to awaken me to certain household tasks I had promised to complete before I left home for the day to meet friends in downtown Seattle. With six kids in the house, it was important that we all finish certain routine chores on the weekends. I first ignored, then resisted calls for me to get up and get to work; indeed, I spent my time in bed fabricating cogent reasons for not getting up early; and soon I was "loaded for bear" and prepared to voice my reasons for delaying my chores. But feuding with mom was generally, I learned, to no avail. Instead of fighting me, she began doing the very chores that I promised I would do. She neither argued nor chastised nor punished me; she did not complain or criticize me for my laziness. Indeed, she never granted me the opportunity; with grace and patience and mercy, she set about doing the chores I knew were properly mine; and I hated it. A strange and strangely powerful force came over me and compelled me immediately up out of bed; I started doing the chores as I had promised. Mercy rendered useless my arguments for staying in bed; it nullified the just punishment I deserved; its power transformed and disarmed me and left me defenseless. Quite unexpectedly, I found from this very ordinary encounter that the grace of mercy is more powerful and resilient than retribution and retaliation. Although unremarkable, these encounters with mercy were for me personally extraordinary and, combining with other such experiences, transformative.

Conversations with ethicists and presentations at conferences revealed how volatile the mix of justice and mercy is for some. Reading Stanley Hauerwas's book *After Christendom: How the Church Is to Behave If Freedom, Justice, and a Christian Nation Are Bad Ideas* was disturbing to some when it was first published. And although I don't believe justice and freedom themselves are *eo ipso* bad ideas, I do believe they are routinely misconceived by Christian ethicists; and that's because justice and freedom often "get conceived" independent of the core of their own religious tradition, independent of mercy and benevolence and the community called to preserve and practice them. There are historical, theological, and philosophical reasons for this "misconceiving," some of which I address in this book.

While writing *Christian Faith, Justice and a Politics of Mercy: The Benevolent Community,* I have interacted with many friends and colleagues and students, and have received valuable feedback and insight from them. I used a draft manuscript in a senior colloquium at Mary Baldwin College and benefited greatly from the feedback of students—Aubrey Sparks, Sarah Bailey, Lindsey Leahy, Holly Johnston, and Harriet Melvin-Thompson. This book also benefited greatly from conversations with colleagues Pat Hunt,

Katie Low, Andrea Cornett-Scott, Edward Scott, Roderic Owen, Ken Beals, Sarah Kennedy, and Claudia Bernardini. Others whose lives and conversations over the years have contributed to my understanding of mercy and justice include Edward Leroy Long Jr., Vernon C. Grounds, Charles Courtney, Robert C. Everett, and Jack Hill. Finally, I am privileged to belong to a family that practices mercy and benevolence: my wife, Rosemary, to whom this book is dedicated, my children, Ian and Caitrin, and siblings.

Finally, I owe a great debt of gratitude to Eric Wrona and Emily Frazzette for their patience, editorial advice, encouragement, and direction, for seeing this process through to its completion.

Chapter One

Re-enfranchising Benevolence

A cluster of children approach the Hodja requesting that in his wisdom he settle a dispute. One child speaks, "The four of us have gathered all the walnuts from under a tree; we have all shared equally in gathering them and would like to divide them equally among us. But when we do, three walnuts still remain. It seems that one of us will be deprived of a walnut, but we do not know who it should be. How should we decide?" After some thought the Hodja asks, "Do you wish God's justice in this matter, or man's?" The child replies, "I have seen man's justice, how vengeful and uncaring it can be; I vote for God's justice." The other children agree; they prefer God's justice to man's. "You have chosen well," says the Hodja. So to one child he gives fifty walnuts, to the second child thirty walnuts, to another three walnuts, and to the fourth he gives none at all.[1] That God's justice is not the same as human justice is likewise a point provocatively made by Jesus in his parable of the householder who pays those who labor only one hour the same wages as those who labor all day. When the latter complain that it is unfair to pay the same wage to those working only one hour, Jesus replies that since they have been paid fairly agreed upon wages, they should not begrudge the householder his generosity toward the hourly workers (Matthew 20: 1–16).[2] God's sense of justice, it seems, differs dramatically from the sense of justice devised by humans. In truth, the difference between God's ways and the ways of humans is not really between two conceptions of justice at all but between two different virtues, justice and mercy. God seems to favor mercy over justice, or at least at times to require of devotees mercy and not mere justice. God's preference for mercy may seem from the perspective of moral reason and justice supererogatory; yet it is obligatory in many religious traditions. By exceeding the duties of justice, mercy requires the faithful to live in an extraordinarily benevolent and costly way, a way that from the perspective of justice seems rash, irrational, and even unfair.

My thesis assumes that the primary moral struggle afflicting contemporary societies is neither the so-called cultural wars, nor the clash of civilizations, nor a cosmic struggle between some axis of evil and some axis of good. I do not wish to deny the validity and significance of these conflicts. My assumption, however, is that the most profound and perplexing struggle threatening the health and stability of societies today is not between good and evil at all, but a struggle between two goods, between justice and mercy. I intend to show, however, that there is no bifurcation between these two common virtues, justice and mercy; that although distinguishable they are inseparable. Just as Newton formally united into a single law two separate fields of experience, i.e., the gravity of bodies on earth and the movement of the stars in the sky, so I hope to formally unite into a single principle what are often portrayed as two largely separate moral experiences, i.e., reason's principle of justice in philosophy and faith's principle of mercy in theology. "Benevolence," as we shall see, refers to behaviors and actions that are rooted in mercy, and is a virtue with a substantial philosophical and theological history. Philosophically it refers to qualities like generosity, tenderness, kindness, sympathy, and altruism; theologically it refers to qualities like graciousness, compassion, meekness, mercy, forgiveness, and humility. The former list ascribes benevolence to communities who shape themselves in secular terms; the latter generally ascribes benevolence to communities that shape themselves in religious terms. I do not wish, however, to draw a bold line between these two versions; the two lists of qualities are somewhat interchangeable, although secular communities are perhaps less likely to want to speak of grace, mercy, meekness, and the like because of the religious character of these ideas. So, in using phrases like "merciful benevolence" or "benevolent Christian community" I am suggesting, implicitly at least, that some such parallel secular, humanistic community is possible. Whether in its religious or philosophical iteration, benevolence includes a sense of moral supererogation, although for devotees in most religious traditions mercy and benevolence are nevertheless obligatory, normative behavior.

I often use "benevolence" and "mercy" interchangeably, although they are distinguishable. For my purpose here "mercy" refers to a subjective, moral disposition resulting in objective "benevolent" behaviors, actions, and projects. This disposition and these actions are not self-interested, except trivially. Rather, they are primarily other-regarding and altruistic, intending to redound to the benefit and well-being of others. As we shall see, they situate themselves asymmetrically in relation to common patterns of moral reasoning associated with justice. Furthermore, two general kinds of benevolent projects are distinguishable—amnesty and generosity: (a) Amnesty involves benevolent actions in which justly deserved burdens are withheld in some measure from wrongdoers and undeserving. For example, a criminal found guilty of murder is granted amnesty when a judge sentences him to life in prison instead of death, or when a juvenile charged with theft is not punished with incarceration but participates in a process of restorative justice that includes community service; (b) Generosity involves benevolent actions in which certain benefits are granted to vulnerable and marginalized people who do not directly earn those benefits but who, because they have little practical power of access to certain basic social and economic goods, are nevertheless granted them for the sake of their own and society's well-being. For example, programs of affirmative action may grant employment to a marginalized and oppressed minority in preference to equally or more qualified members of a majority population; or a policy may grant healthcare benefits to the vulnerable unemployed, who otherwise cannot afford it. Benevolence may entail, in other words, one of two kinds of actions: projects of amnesty that mercifully withhold burdens from wrongdoers and undeserving, and projects of generosity that mercifully grant benefits to the powerless and vulnerable. In either case, benevolence constitutes actions that situate themselves asymmetrically in relation to moral reason (justice) and accordingly include moral duties to which, as we shall see, no rights correlate. Finally, I do not intend to provide a comprehensive theological treatment of mercy; instead I intend to examine it only insofar as mercy manifests itself socially and politically in projects and policies of benevolence.

Throughout this book I use the phrase "sustainable livelihood" when speaking of mercy, benevolence, and egalitarian justice. By it I mean those basic necessities required to maintain over time the dignity of human life: including food, shelter, clothing, healthcare, education, training, gainful employment, and unemployment benefits. Of course, what constitutes "basic" and "necessities" is fluid, depending on the social and economic conditions of a particular country or region. In addition, by "community" I mean to refer to any self-indentified organization, religious or secular, whose mission and activities include moral and social dimensions. These organizations may be religious, including local churches and mosques, and international entities such as Bread for the World or Habitat for Humanity; or these organizations may be secular, including governments, non-governmental organizations (NGOs), and international entities such as the United Nations and the World Court.

The thesis for which I argue, then, is this: that merciful benevolence is an indispensable public as well as private virtue, for two inter-related reasons: first, because very often it alone possesses the moral power to "interrupt" and subvert destructive patterns of injustice that threaten the stability and harmony of societies. By "interrupt" I mean that capacity of benevolence both to "break" and to "breakthrough" projects and patterns of injustice. Merciful benevolence is indispensable, secondly, because very often it alone possesses the moral power that in the midst of injustice is able to establish and sustain in private and public life desirable patterns of justice. Under conditions of injustice, this is to say, justice itself is often not *sui generis*; under such conditions it often is not sufficiently powerful enough to establish and sustain itself but requires the moral power and practice of merciful benevolence. When injustice is present, practicing justice, ironically, cannot always guarantee a just outcome. If justice is to be established in the midst of injustice, then projects of merciful benevolence are often necessary. It follows, as I try to show, that because injustices are public and systemic as well as private and personal, benevolence must be practiced not merely as a private virtue, as some would have it, but necessarily also as a public virtue. If the ideal horizon of expectation for both humanist and religious traditions is a just, harmonious, and peaceable society, then, in an unjust world projects of public as well as private benevolence are necessary. If asked, many would say that to global problems of injustice justice is a solution and cure. In contrast, I argue that under conditions of injustice, merciful benevolence is the cure and remedy while justice is the result and reward. Just as medication interrupts a headache and restores the body to a health so merciful benevolence interrupts injustice and is alone able to restore justice.

Take affirmative action in college admissions as a case in point. In order to interrupt and break through embedded patterns of discrimination and centuries of inequalities, proactive policies of benevolence are required. Projects of justice by themselves only perpetuate unjust patterns already present. Those who oppose affirmative action generally treat such measures as "reverse discrimination" and "preferential treatment." They advocate instead standards of admission that are strictly and fairly and procedurally the same for all, as if such judgments are made behind "a veil of ignorance" regarding the applicants. "Behind a 'veil of ignorance'" means in this context "as if injustices do not exist." Not surprisingly, the outcomes of such judgments calcify even more patterns of injustice already present. Those advocating affirmative action, in contrast, argue that under extraordinary conditions of injustice extraordinary measures of affirmative action (benevolence) are required. Hence preferring qualified minorities contributes to subverting those patterns and to establishing and sustaining just outcomes. Such policies of benevolence are indeed merciful; but the mercy granted is toward both victim and vendor of injustice: to victim by granting the generosity of admission; and to vendor of injustice by granting unmerited amnesty from comparable centuries of retaliatory penalties that justice otherwise requires. In the midst of injustice it is often the case that justice results only if moral agents are willing to undertake private and public projects of benevolence, only if a society is willing to practice "a politics of mercy."

What, then, do I mean when I refer to "a politics of mercy"? I do not refer to a political system or ideology or theory or partisan agenda. I use it to refer to a people (*hoi poloi*) who gather themselves into a community (*koinoneia*) or a commonwealth for the sake of establishing social, moral, and civil order. To form a *polis* is "to recognize," as Stephen Toulmin puts it, "that its practices and organization had the overall coherence that qualified it—in both the ancient and modern sense of the term—as a 'political' unit."[3] A political unit is a community of people, of citizens, recognizing the need for social and moral order. There is also another order, of course; an order of nature, which the Greeks refer to as "cosmos," a natural order of things not entirely unrelated to the order of *polis;* for *cosmos* refers not just to nature but to a natural order discernable by reason, an order that includes physical laws but also certain natural laws that form the basis of moral and social order: hence, *cosmopolis*. So, by "a politics of mercy" I refer to a specific benevolent way a people organizes itself naturally, socially, and morally for the sake of maintaining order and safety. Political theories and systems and ideologies, accordingly, ought to conform and adapt to the aim and order of a benevolent *polis*, not vise versa.

From a Christian perspective in particular, and all religious/and humanist traditions in general, this aim and order enfranchises benevolence as well as justice; so that merciful benevolence, as Christianity's theological and spiritual core, is indispensable for establishing and sustaining the moral, civil order for which it is responsible. Fallen humanity, so the story goes, is redeemable, curable, not by justice alone but by merciful benevolence. But why? Theologically, why is mercy a prerequisite for establishing and sustaining justice? Why is it that without mercy's unmerited grace and benefits fallen humanity and society cannot be redeemed and justice established? For Christian communities to practice only a politics of justice in public life and not a politics of mercy compromises not only their gospel but often compounds moral and civil disorder. In a speech to the *Union pour la Verite* (Paris, 1935), Andre Gide articulated the failure of Christianity. "On account of its compromises Christianity," he argues, "is bankrupt." So as not to be an offense to secular societies, one of the fundamental compromises Christianity made, in separating itself from the state, is forfeiting mercy in political life in favor of justice. Not only by this compromise did Christianity eviscerate its gospel, according to Gide, but it forfeited its mission in the world. "If Christianity had really prevailed, and if it had really fulfilled the teaching of Christ, there would be today no question of communism—there would indeed be no social problem at all."[4] My aim in this book is to retrieve this "teaching of Christ," to retrieve in public and political life the merciful benevolence that is the core of the Christian gospel.

The author of the Epistle of James prioritizes mercy over justice: "So speak and so act as those who are to be judged under the law of liberty. For judgment (*krisis*) is without mercy (*aneleos*) to one who has shown no mercy (*eloes*); yet mercy (*eleos*) triumphs over judgment (*kriseos*)" (2: 12–13). *Krisis* refers to a judgment made regarding justice and injustice, right and wrong; it also refers to an act of condemning a person about whom a just judgment has been made. Such judgments, James is saying, are based on statutes that bind one to rational laws, like *lex talionis*, "an eye for an eye, a tooth for a tooth." Such judgments bind the moral agent steadfastly to a strict moral law of reason and preclude the freedom to act benevolently, mercifully, according to a law of liberty. As a moral value justice constrains; as a spiritual value mercy liberates. That "mercy triumphs over judgment" (i.e., justice) implies that the mercy of benevolence possesses a power absent from justice itself, that it possesses a capacity to redeem, restore, and reconcile in a way that in an unjust world justice itself cannot and cannot think of. In short, *merciful benevolence trumps justice;* it trumps justice, ironically, in order to establish and sustain justice. In poker a card trumped by another may very well still be a good and powerful card, even though it is superseded by one even more powerful. For citizens of a nation-state in which conditions of injustice persist, benevolence trumps justice in order that justice might thrive. For Christians at least, and indeed for devotees of many humanist and religious traditions, mercy supersedes justice, covenant supersedes social contract, faith's liberty supersedes rational law, grace supersedes merit, but always for the benefit of establishing justice, so that justice might flourish. This is gospel, and the business of this book is to advocate for a gospel in which for the sake of justice benevolent "mercy triumphs over justice" in public as well as private life.

I examine this thesis from two perspectives, philosophical and theological. I develop the idea of benevolence philosophically by interacting with the works of Hobbes, Locke, Smith, Hume, Mill, Rawls, and others. In so doing I trace a pattern of thought for those whose preference is secular and humanist. This philosophical approach provides a conceptual framework for a theological inquiry into the nature of mercy and benevolence.[5] My belief is that the argument I make here from a Christian perspective might very well be made from the perspective of most religious and humanist traditions.

In the remainder of this chapter I want to briefly map the way I intend to develop this thesis and argument. This map by itself may seem too rude and rough to do justice to the terrain it charts. Nevertheless, such a preliminary sketch is beneficial, I think, much as reading a map before a journey is helpful, not only in identifying one's destination but in tracing the route to be taken and in marking ahead of time points along the way that may be of special interest to the traveler. This sketch of the itinerary includes marking three fundamental distinctions. First, I distinguish three moral orders: the Created, Fallen, and Redeemed Orders; secondly, I distinguish moral symmetry, asymmetry, and supersymmetry as metaphorical ways of understanding moral virtues such as justice, mercy, and compassion; finally, I distinguish three evolutionary stages of moral consciousness: tribe as common law, justice as rational law, and merciful benevolence as spiritual law.

THREE MORAL ORDERS

From the biblical narrative and tradition scholars sometimes distinguish three moral/spiritual spheres or orders: the Created, the Fallen, and the Redeemed.[6] These orders represent three jurisdictions that overlap and interact in the life of a community of faith. All three have had an enormous impact on European political philosophy, its origin, shape, and development. Thinkers such as Hobbes, Locke, Smith, Hume, Kant, Rawls, among others, engage moral and political issues in terms of these orders or variations of them. By "Order" I refer to a distinct moral and spiritual jurisdiction and the relationship of that jurisdiction to God and faith communities. By "moral and spiritual" I refer to specific patterns of beliefs and values by which those who are stewards of a particular Order situate themselves in relationship to God and to each other. Different conceptions of peace help distinguish these three moral Orders; Jesus himself alludes to a couple of these orders when to his disciples he says, "Peace I leave with you; my peace I give to you; not as the world gives do I give to you" (John 14: 27). Although distinct, these three Orders are inseparable, simultaneous, and overlapping jurisdictions; they manifest themselves both religiously and secularly. Of each Order benevolent religious and secular communities alike are called to be good stewards. For each, I examine (1) its aim and (2) the moral/spiritual principle by which that aim is realized.

By the *Created Order* or *pax Dei* I refer to a moral/spiritual jurisdiction that in philosophy is referred to as "a state of nature." It is an Order established by God who is benevolent creator of all things good (Genesis 1 & 2). That all things are created good discloses both the benevolent character of the Creator and the quality of creation. *Pax Dei*, accordingly, refers to that original, harmonious state in which all things are as they should be and as God intended them to be. The *aim* of all things in the Created Order, then, is harmony with God and all creation; and the *means* whereby that harmony is sustained is obedience to God and God's laws, including the laws governing this original state of nature. The "good" characterizing this natural, Created Order is to be nurtured and cultivated by humans so that all live harmoniously with God and God's laws and altruistically with each other. This ancient, primitive vision of Eden as a natural place of benevolence, of harmony and innocence, as a place of peace and order, is deeply rooted in the collective psyche of the human race in general and of the Abrahamic traditions in particular. It originates the spiritual and moral vision that fires the magnificence of human imagination and creativity and prosperity. Like the ancient Hebrews, most cultural traditions similarly envision a primitive harmony and innocence, a moral/spiritual jurisdiction constituted by something approximating *pax Dei.* The philosophical version of the Created Order is often articulated in phrases like "state of nature" or "original position." Hobbes, Locke, Rousseau, and more recently Rawls, to name a few, find it helpful to ground moral and political analysis in some such hypothetical, "primitive" condition.

The moral/spiritual principle by which this original harmony constitutes itself has already been suggested. *Pax Dei* is achieved when each created thing, whether rose, cat, girl, or government, faithfully obeys and fulfills its purpose and potential. In so doing it honors, worships, and serves its Creator. Nature, accordingly, is teleological; each created thing encloses its own aim and purpose; by striving for and realizing the potential implicit in it (a blooming rose), each thing honors and serves its Creator and thereby lives wholly, harmoniously, and happily in itself and with each other. According to biblical narratives, humans created in the likeness and image of God occupy a unique place in the Created Order. Their obedience to God includes not only good stewardship of themselves *qua* human but also good stewardship of or "dominion over" the entire Created Order. Of the many ways "dominion" is interpreted, the core of it is that humans are authorized by God to care for the goodness of creation in the same way that the Creator cares for (or has dominion over) creation. This includes, first of all, stewardship of one's self, by submitting one's own will to the will of God, and secondly, stewardship of all life by protecting and preserving a proper harmony as originally intended. Human stewardship ought to emulate benevolent Divine stewardship, which aims at cultivating and preserving *pax Dei*, the goodness and harmony of creation. Hobbes and Locke sets forth philosophical versions of this argument. Locke insists, for example, that humans in the state of nature have a natural obligation not only to preserve themselves in their life, health, and property, but to preserve also the life, health, and property of others. Accordingly, it is fair to say that "obedience" to natural law is "perfect freedom," as Locke puts it, a harmony of creation's natural order. Or as Rawls more recently argues, from behind a "veil of ignorance" certain political and economic principles (e.g., of equal liberty and of difference) emerge from the natural innocence of an "original position."

By the *Fallen Order* or *pax Romana*[7] I refer to a moral and spiritual jurisdiction fabricated, according to the biblical narative, by Satan and humans; or inaugurated, according to political philosophy, by the self-interested exercise of executive power, as Locke puts it. In disobedience to their Creator, humans abuse their freedom and power by exercising it selfishly instead of altruistically, forsaking thereby their natural condition of benevolence and appointed role as good stewards of themselves and creation. Dysfunctional moral and spiritual chaos ensues undermining the harmony of *pax Dei.* Human responses to "fallenness" are various, but all commonly attempt to rescue from its chaos a kind of contractual, civil order. *Pax Romana* signifies one attempt to restore from the peril of chaos some measure of equilibrium; and it does so by exercising moral reason, by executing a just system of contracted benefits and burdens enforced by the sword. Just as Genesis depicts the Created Order as blessed so also it depicts the Fallen (Dis)Order as cursed, as one in which humans must suffer physical, moral, and spiritual consequences (e.g., wages of sin). Adam and Eve's expulsion from Eden powerfully symbolizes humanity's expulsion from *pax Dei*, from the presence and peace of an original state of nature, from the created order of things. It symbolizes humanity's fall into the moral and political chaos of injustice, a realm cursed with labor, travail, futility, discrimination, oppression, pain, retribution, retaliation, aimlessness, weeds, and wickedness the depth of which sometimes still startles. Stewardship of creatures and creation degenerates into exploitation, grace into greed, self-fulfillment into self-indulgence, selflessly shared property into selfishly hoarded property. The fallen, corrupted self's singular aim now is to satisfy its desires alone and to exploit the benefits of creation for the sake of indulging those desires. What results is a chaotic, oppressive sphere, a jurisdiction dis-ordered by injustice; a state that degenerates, as Hobbes and Locke both put it, into a state of chaos, disorder and war.

But in biblical narratives, the Fallen Order is a provisional state with a provisional aim. That aim, embodied in *pax Romana,* is to establish in the midst of chaos and conflict some semblance of a just civil order based on natural law and moral reason. Indeed, government is ordained by God, says the Apostle Paul (Romans 13), precisely for the purpose of combating the injustice of fallenness and of restoring the benevolence of creation; enforcing with the sword a just moral and civil order.

"Social contract" is the primary philosophical mechanism whereby governments are to practice *pax Romana.* I use "contract" here to refer to a liberal form of government whose moral authority is fundamentally legal and political, in distinction from "covenant" on the basis of which communities of faith exercise their moral and spiritual authority. These two terms are sometimes used interchangeably to refer to a consensual basis for political community. Hobbes in *Leviathan*, for example, uses them interchangeably in this way. But for my purposes, it is helpful to distinguish them. To insist that the Fallen Order is governed by a social contract is to say that those who govern and those who are governed mutually consent to be ruled by common, rational laws of justice.[8] Historically this principle of contractual justice establishes the liberal tradition; that is, it combines and protects *jus naturalis (rights)* and *lex naturale (liberties)* as a civil basis for the rule of law. Citizens ought rightly to "reap what they sow," so that if they sow justly they are fairly rewarded (compensatory justice), and if they sow unjustly they are fairly penalized (retributive justice). In so doing, the moral order of *pax Romana* establishes by means of rational law and consensual executive power a measure of civility amidst the chaotic injustices of the Fallen Order. That these laws of justice are "rational" indicates, it is supposed, that they are likewise universal and universally intelligible, and that the moral equilibrium of a just civil order is not random, arbitrary, and despotic. The aim of government and its social contract, then, is justice as fairness; to protect, preserve, and promote the rights and liberties of liberal, civilized life, and to do so by means of a fair, rational system of benefits and burdens enforced by the sword. Since by its very nature the jurisdiction of the Fallen Order *qua* fallen is devoid of God's redeeming grace, *pax Romana* is as much as can be morally and contractually expected of reason's just laws. As good stewards of the Fallen Order, faith and humanistic communities are obligated to help government promote and preserve a just, moral equilibrium according to laws of reason. But justice only protects humans from themselves and each other, only establishes civility among enemies. It possesses no power to redeem a fallen, unjust world; it cannot under its conditions of injustice themselves break the grip of injustice and restore the harmony of *pax Dei,* of the original, created state of nature. That takes something more; it takes a covenantal commitment to the "law of liberty," as James calls it, a law constituted by the grace of God's merciful benevolence. In a fallen, unjust world, merciful benevolence must supersede justice so, ironically, that selfsame justice might emerge and flourish.

The *Redeemed Order* or *pax Christi* refers to the initiative taken by God to rescue humans and all creation from the curse of the Fallen Order and to restore the harmony of *pax Dei.* All benevolent communities, religious and secular, create their own version of what Christians refer to as *pax Christi.* All benevolent communities, that is, not only aim at justice and peace but in their wisdom promote something like mercy as a means for achieving that aim. Transforming the Fallen Order into a Redeemed Order is articulated philosophically in terms of some ideal society or utopian vision. Plato, Augustine, More, Hume, Kant and Hegel, Marx and Mill, Rawls and Nielsen, are only a few who envision a way to bring into existence a just, harmonious society. For all their differences that "way" often includes practicing as a public as well as a private virtue something like benevolence. Whether religious or secular, these visions often enfranchise benevolence as a vital, indispensable power for redeeming, reconciling, and restoring the original vision of a just, peaceable civil order

For Christian communities *pax Christi*, of course, is central to shaping and sustaining their identity as Christian. Grace, love, repentance, forgiveness, meekness, suffering, self sacrifice, generosity, redemption, and reconciliation are at the core of what it means to be Christian and at the core of what it means to practice being Christian. A community can rightfully claim the identity of "Christian," then, only if theologically, morally, socially, economically, politically, and philosophically it actually practices these virtues that form the core of *pax Christi.* For a Christian community, then, to exempt public life, whether political or economic, from the practice of any of these virtues amounts to forfeiting that identity.

Benevolent communities co-habit all three of these overlapping Orders Created, Fallen, and Redeemed; hence, a few comments regarding their interrelationship. First, the Created Order establishes *pax Dei* and stands in relation to the other two Orders as a paradigm from which the Fallen Order deviates and toward which the Redeemed Order strives. Secondly, democratic governments and societies typically manage the Fallen Order via *pax Romana,* by promoting and enforcing just procedural policies whose aim is moral and civil order. Benevolent communities and governments manage the Redeemed Order via something like the merciful benevolence of *pax Christi.* Their primary aim is to restore the harmony and equilibrium of *pax Dei.* Such communities understand that in an unjust world a fully just and harmonious society is quite impossible without practicing merciful benevolence in public as well as private life. Benevolent communities are especially empowered to practice the kind of politics of mercy without which social and civil harmony is quite impossible.

Consider again the two parables with which this chapter begins. Suppose we imagine justice and not merciful benevolence as the supreme value; and suppose we employ it to interpret the two parables. How will the narrative and plot of these two parables alter? Now if the Hodja's intention is to preserve a simple moral order of just fairness then distributing the remaining three walnuts among the four children is a simple matter of mathematical precision, and truth be told what is needed is not wisdom from a Hodja but a calculator. Seventy-five percent of the remaining three walnuts will properly be distributed to each of the four children. The aim is a just moral order. No faith, no insight, no wisdom, no mercy or benevolence is required; only reason and calculation. It is what enlightened, rational moral law fairly demands. And what about the wages the householder distributes to the laborers, in Jesus's parable? Ignoring the reality of injustice, how will they be distributed to the various groups of laborers? Again, neither faith nor wisdom is needed from Jesus, only calculation: the hourly workers receive a fair percentage of what the day laborers receive. Such are the prosaic, rational demands of human justice, and rightly so. But does doing so thereby establish a moral and fair equilibrium in the midst of the chaos of an unjust world? Indeed, a liberal, social contract really has no story to tell at all, but only a calculation to make. And yet this "calculate" is not what the Hodja and Jesus, in their great wisdom, preach and practice. They practice a poetic sense of morality whose higher aim is not simply to distribute benefits and burdens equally, but to redeem and reconcile humans to God and to each other, to restore *pax Dei*. What is required for such restoration is the kind of politics of mercy that is the heart of *pax Christi*.

MORAL SYMMETRY, ASYMMETRY, AND SUPERSYMMETRY

I want now to bring more clearly into focus the central distinction I am making, between justice (*pax Romana*) and benevolence (*pax Christi*). Morally a distinction emerges between justice and benevolence (in philosophy) or mercy (in theology). Consider for a moment an analogy derived from particle physics and commonly applied in moral philosophy: the difference between justice and benevolence is analogous to the difference in physics between symmetry and asymmetry. In particle physics "reflection symmetry" establishes what physicists refer to as the "standard model," which entails the theory of fundamental particles and how they interact. It describes the strong, weak, and electromagnetic fundamental forces, as well as the fundamental particles of which all matter consists. Physicists use "standard model" both to describe the fundamental symmetries in the universe (matter) and to delineate the asymmetrical behavior of particles (antimatter) that deviate from and are incommensurable with that standard model. On the basis of the standard model's symmetry, physicists are able to make predictions that are relatively certain and reliable; they also are able to identify particles that deviate from the standard model, by noting the unpredictability of antimatter's asymmetrical behavior.[9] Analogously, I use "standard model" to refer to the "moral symmetry" of *pax Romana*'s social contract. It refers to a "moral law of reason," to "justice as fairness," to equal procedural liberty or what John Rawls refers to, in *A Theory of Justice,* when he refers to "moral symmetry" as "reflective equilibrium." The standard model, in other words, establishes civil order in terms of procedural justice, namely, that certain moral duties are correlated to certain human rights. This standard model of just fairness and equal liberty governs moral and civil life. It is comprehended by reason; its results and inferences are predictable and reliable. It is the moral anchor of a social contract's laws and policies and the core civil value for which government is responsible.

In contrast, I use "moral asymmetry" to refer to "the law of liberty" that situates itself asymmetrically in relation to the standard model's law of moral reason. It refers to a constellation of moral qualities that in philosophy is labeled "benevolence" and in religion "mercy," a constellation constituting the heart and soul of *pax Christi.* It is a law of liberty because merciful benevolence by its very nature freely deviates from the dictates of moral reason and the symmetry of the standard model (i.e., justice as fairness). Because benevolence deviates from the rationality and reflective equilibrium of this standard model, it is only by a certain kind of faith, secular or sacred, that a community apprehends and practices its asymmetrical duties. Benevolence, as we shall see, involves certain spiritual duties, but duties to which no rights correlate (e.g., turn the other cheek). It empowers humans to live economically as well as politically with a dignity and freedom commensurate with their species. Accordingly, benevolence entails a kind of "moral turbulence," for its duties deviate dramatically from moral reason's standard of just fairness and equal liberty; it empowers a community with the courage to grant unmerited benefits to some, including the vulnerable, undeserving, enemies, and even wrongdoers.[10] Not surprisingly, to those committed solely to the symmetries of justice, the asymmetrical duties of benevolence seem irrational, weak, unreliable, and unpredictable; they seem to be morally "turbulent." As the author of the Epistle to the Hebrews notes, that which is apprehended and practiced by faith, like mercifully benevolence, situates itself asymmetrical in relation to reason; Faith entails "the assurance of things hoped for," and "the conviction of things not seen" (11: 1), a kind of certainty that is incommensurable with reason for which "assurance" and "conviction" is properly the certainty of evidence, of things seen. But to act mercifully is to forsake the conviction of things seen, to forsake the predictability of moral reason and its inferences; it is to invite, from the perspective of the standard model, unpredictability and uncertainty. The "assurance" and "conviction" that belong to faith constitute mercy's promise and power to subvert injustice and to redeem, reconcile, and restore justice and freedom. Reason, in contrast, simply calculates the appropriate fair distribution of civil burdens and benefits that government adjudicates and enforces.

The question arises: At what point does the "turbulence" of mercy acquire the freedom to pass beyond the classical limits of justice? At what point does the asymmetry of faith's mercy justify liberating society from the symmetry of reason's justice? On what basis can mercy justifiably surpass the boundaries of justice? At what point does mercy become not only a moral possibility but a moral duty? I have already indicated the answer: when conditions of injustice are present for that population of humans whose social, political, and economic status is under consideration. I will have a great deal more to say about this throughout the remainder of the book. Suffice it to say here that the sole aim of mercy exceeding the boundaries of justice is for the sake of (re)establishing justice, for the sole aim of redeeming, reconciling, and restoring humans to the original peace and harmony God intended. The aim of the mercy, in the parables Jesus tells, is not to eradicate justice but to exceed it in order to establish it as a value central to his Kingdom. The discrepancy, in Jesus's parable, between the householder and laborers is precisely this difference between reason and faith, justice and mercy; the discrepancy between day laborers whose expectations are defined by the rational, moral symmetry of just fairness and the landlord whose expectations are informed by the moral turbulence and liberating asymmetry of mercy, so that justice may flourish.

Moral symmetry and asymmetry, however, do not quite exhaust the matter. Particle physicists also speak of supersymmetry. This too, by way of analogy, provides a method for interpreting Christian social ethics; for my analysis is incomplete if I neglect the relationship between justice and benevolence. Supersymmetry provides a paradigm for doing so.

Some physicists believe that underlying the symmetry and asymmetry of the universe is a more fundamental "final link" or "fifth dimension" or "SUSY" (supersymmetry).[11] SUSY supposes that there are as yet unknown, underlying "families of particles of fermions and bosons awaiting discovery." These unknown particles and the particles known "originally, at the start of time . . . were united" and are capable, at least on paper, of reconciling the universe's asymmetries in a "theory of everything."[12] Paul Davies argues that quantum physics introduces a "strong wholistic element" into the world "by blurring the distinction between subject and object, cause and effect."[13] How so? Certain experiments were conducted in which the experimenters themselves were involved in the construction of reality, in what actually occurs at the subatomic level. Imagine an electron that strikes an object and then careens off. It could careen either left or right. In fact, as a wave the electron produces ripples that travel both to the left and the right of the object and each set of ripples coexist in a kind of ghost-like hybrid unreality until an observer/experimenter actually "peeks," at which instant one of the ghostly unrealities vanishes while the other observed ripple solidifies into concrete reality. Davies concludes that "the electron keeps its options open until you [the experimenter] actually peek."[14] Supersymmetry refers both to the underlying unity of symmetrical and asymmetrical elements and to the active contribution experimenters make to constructing the reality of that unity.

I use supersymmetry metaphorically to represent compassion, a common human experience necessary for practicing benevolence. It operates as a catalyst for empowering the self to voluntarily suffer the demands and burdens of benevolence. By so doing compassion freely and intentionally contributes to constructing moral reality. Instead of defaulting to justice's law of reason, humans must exercise volition, identify compassionately with others, and act toward them benevolently. Practicing compassion, in other words, is the moral equivalent of an experimenter "peeking" and thereby contributing to the outcome of, in this case, moral reality. Compassion is a bridge between justice and benevolence, a sparkplug (to change metaphors) that ignites the moral engine to accelerate freely beyond the cold calculations of justice's law of reason and drive the human will to act asymmetrically, benevolently, mercifully. It is the fuel that powers communities to practice projects of benevolence and a politics of mercy, transforming the injustice of a fallen world into the just, harmonious patterns of a redeemed world. As in particle physics the experimenter participates in the direction the electron moves, so in moral life, the Righteous, benevolent agent participates in determining the direction moral reality moves, from justice to mercy and back. "For freedom Christ has set us free," declares the Apostle Paul; "Stand fast therefore, and do not submit again to the yoke of slavery" (Galatians 5: 1). The temptation for governments and communities, religious and secular, is in public life to yoke themselves exclusively to justice's law of reason and remand mercy's law of liberty to private life. Finally, compassion is the emotional and psychological force by which the faithful evolve morally from the rationality of justice into the joy, freedom, and turbulence of mercy's benevolence. Compassion is a moral energy that makes possible projects of benevolence and inspires hope for re-enfranchising the just harmony God originally intended.

EVOLUTION OF MORAL CONSCIOUSNESS

Mercy trumps justice. To fully heal the wounds of injustice and to nurture habits of justice, mercy is required. It emerges in biblical narratives as the culmination of an evolutionary process. Beginning most primitively with a kind of tribal, *common law*, I sketch moral consciousness as it develops into *justice as rational law* and as it further evolves and culminates in a *spiritual law* of mercy. This evolution of moral consciousness roughly parallels the more familiar evolution of the idea of g[G]od[s], an evolution from polytheism through henotheism to monotheism. Hebrew moral sensibility, in other words, is inseparably linked to the idea of Yahweh and evolves concomitantly with it: first as the moral orientation of a petulant, tribal God, then as a rational principle of justice manifesting the will of a national God supreme among gods, and finally as a universal principle of mercy whereby the one and only God is regarded as the universal, merciful Redeemer of all peoples. These three phases of moral consciousness and practice are not simply sequential; they are interactive, overlapping layers through which nevertheless higher forms should ultimately supersede lower.

Common Law. Although the final redactors of Hebrew Scriptures are monotheists, vestiges of polytheistic and henotheistic origins survive. Similarly, although these same narratives finally preach mercy and forgiveness as superior and supreme moral values, vestiges of tribalism (common law) and nationalism (justice) remain. Abraham is notable for saying "yes" to God's call and covenant (Genesis 12). His was a call not only to journey to a new land but to a new understanding of God; it was a call to forsake the polytheistic idolatry of his Sumerian tradition, a call to worship his God as one who is superior to the gods of other peoples (henotheism) and a God alone to be worshipped. This is one of Abraham's greatest legacies. His offspring seem to perpetuate his henotheism. When his grandsons Jacob and Laban take an oath it is in relation to two distinct gods, the God of Abraham and the God of Nahor (Gen 31: 51ff). Later, Jepthah acknowledges the authority of the god *Chemosh* for the tribe of Ammonites (Judges 11: 24).

Moses is popularly believed to be the first great monotheist of the Jewish tradition, but this claim is disputed by many scholars. The first of the Ten Commandments, "You shall have no other gods before me" (Exodus 20: 3; Deut. 5: 7), seems to indicate a henotheistic rather than a purely monotheistic conviction. This "commandment does not seek to repudiate the existence of other gods," insists Anthony Phillips, "but to prevent Israel from having anything to do with them."[15] Evidence of Hebrew henotheism is also found in texts such as Job and the Psalms (e.g., Psalms 82). The stories of Elijah often accent the struggle of allegiance to Yahweh over worship of other gods, such as Ba'al. The story of Elijah and the prophets of Ba'al on Mt. Carmel dramatizes the belief that Yahweh and not Ba'al is superior. Moreover, apostasy, or the tendency to worship the gods of other tribes, is explicitly forbidden and is one reason why, according to the Hebrew prophets, God punishes his people, destroys the Temple, and exiles Israel and Judah.

Concomitant with this evolving theology, from polytheism to henotheism, is a parallel progression of moral consciousness. Max Weber distinguishes the Hebrew word for common law or *chuk* from *mishpat* or justice,[16] a distinction useful for my purposes here. *Chuk* is interwoven with what anthropologists call "corporate personality," denoting collective responsibility as a mode of moral behavior. The will of the whole is prior to the will of the individual; the will of each is subsumed under the will of all, and the action of each is reckoned of all. Responsibility for the wickedness of an individual, accordingly, is divided equally among all members of his social group. If any member sins, the whole group is considered sinful, guilty, and liable to punishment. A vengeful, petulant, tribal God obligates the community to punish and utterly destroy a collective enemy. The sin of Achan is a case in point (Joshua 7). The Israelites loose a battle against the city of Ai, a battle Yahweh sanctioned. Joshua rends his clothes and calls upon the Lord. The Lord replies that "Israel has sinned; they have transgressed my covenant" (7: 11). In truth Achan sinned. He violates a common law that forbids anyone from profiting from the spoils of war. He has taken "a beautiful mantle from Shinar, and two hundred shekels of silver, and a bar of gold weighing fifty shekels" (7: 21). Congruent with the tribal notion of corporate personality, not only Achan but also all the spoils he has taken, his sons and daughter, his livestock and his tent and indeed all of his possessions are stoned to death and burned with fire (7: 25–26). Not only that, but we find that the entire nation of Israel is responsible and punished; it is subsequently defeated in battle. Many such violations of tribal common law are considered capital crimes (including murder, treason, prostitution, homosexual activity, kidnapping, and cattle stealing) that reap corporate consequences.

In ancient Hebrew tribal law, two chief forms of trial prevail, judgment by lot (*Unim* and *Thummim*; Ex. 28: 30; Lev. 8: 8) and judgment by ordeal, which entails a potent, deadly drink that only the innocent are thought to survive (Num. 5: 16–32). Both forms of trial are somewhat arbitrary from the perspective of more advanced forms of litigation, such as trial by judge and jury. But such is the nature of *chuk*, of common law: a tribal God exacts vengeance against a cooperate personality who is collectively responsible for the behavior of one of its members and whose guilt is determined by arbitrary means, by lot or ordeal. Clearly, the aim of common law is not what more advanced societies consider fairness, just reward or punishment; nor is its aim redemption, reconciliation, and restoration. Rather its aim is deterrence; to prevent social collapse and moral chaos and to preserve some semblance of cooperate civility. Achan's kin are not individually guilty and personally responsible for his disobedience; and yet, in order to deter other clans, other cooperate personalities like the nation as a whole, from exploiting for personal advantage the spoils of war, in order to forestall moral and social chaos, the entire corporate personality shares responsibility. Such was the character of tribal morality that co-existed with polytheistic and emerging henotheistic tendencies, during the time of the Patriarchs and Judges. But overlapping with the henotheism of the Mosaic period and emerging during the rise of nationalism (Judges and Kings) is a more advanced, rational form of social justice. In time, justice flourishes in Israel as the normative form of moral consciousness and practice.

Rational law. In the context of Hebrew henotheism there emerges from tribal common law a rational, moral orientation toward *mishpat* or justice. What distinguishes rational (*mishpat*) from common law (*chuk*) are two things, individualism and symmetry. First, although a strong sense of corporate and communal responsibility survives in Israel, Yahweh is viewed not as a God of cooperate vengeance (*chuk*) and superstitious means (trial by lot and ordeal), but as a God that fairly holds individuals responsible for their actions. Even as early as the Levitical code of Moses, individuals are held personally responsible for transgressions; "Whoever curses his God shall bear his sin" (Lev. 24: 15b); "he who kills is liable for his murder, and he who kills a neighbor's beast liable for doing so" (Lev. 24). Secondly, the moral core of this emerging tradition of just, rational law is a moral symmetry and equilibrium expressed most simply in *lex talionis*, "an eye for an eye, a tooth for a tooth" (Ex. 21: 24; Lev. 24: 20; Deut. 19: 21; Matthew 5: 38). Accordingly, "He who kills a man shall be put to death. He who kills a beast shall make it good, life for life" (Lev. 24: 17–18). There is a beauty and simple symmetry in this conception of justice; it is easily grasped by reason insofar as it strives to distribute benefits and burdens fairly. It presupposes that each individual member of the community (or in ancient times at least each free male) is of equal value and therefore entitled to his just due. Justice so conceived is rational insofar as it aims to treat each individual fairly and impartially, insofar as it aims at a moral equilibrium based on equal fairness, on the equal distribution of burdens and benefits. By so doing, justice curtails in a rational way the excesses of common law's "corporate personality" and the arbitrariness of judgment by lot and ordeal. For the agent of any given action no greater penalty or lesser reward is granted than what is fairly owed. It is this rational norm, this *mishpat* that functions as a civilizing force in Israel as well as other ancient societies. It is the moral symmetry of justice in a fallen, unjust world that is the heart and soul of *pax Romana* and even of civilized nation-states today. Indeed, *Mishpat's* symmetry constitutes itself in two ways: culturally as the "standard model" of moral and civil order, and philosophically as rational, "reflective equilibrium." It is "standard" in the sense that it is normative for social and civic behavior; and it is "equilibrium" in the sense that it entails a proportionality and balance of action and compensation, requiring an eye for an eye, reaping what is sown, distributing benefits and burdens, rewards and penalties fairly. When I refer to "standard model" and "rational symmetry" throughout this book, I am referring to justice's principle of moral equilibrium and civility.

But within Hebrew and Christian Scriptures themselves there develops a hermeneutic of suspicion regarding justice. Although justice is valuable for ordering social and civil life, and although it is a core political value of governments, it is limited in its moral and spiritual power. Indeed, there are at least two qualifications that need to be made. First, I have said that in a fallen, unjust world justice is not *sui generis,* it cannot originate or sustain itself by itself. This is true, but only partly true. We must distinguish two dimensions of justice: liberal, procedural justice and substantive, egalitarian justice.[17] *Pax Romana's* liberal, procedural justice is constituted by the social, legal, and political structures of justice that guarantee due process, *lex talionis*, equal access and equal opportunity to all. This procedural dimension of liberal justice establishes reason's moral law and comprises the core social contract that guarantees human and civil rights for all. It is sustaining this procedural dimension that is "liberal" and the business of government as well as faith communities. Furthermore, liberal justice is *sui generis*, it can via *pax Romana* establish and perpetuate itself. However, since it is procedural and not substantive, liberal justice often cannot of itself overcome injustice and establish the substantive, egalitarian economic outcomes that human dignity and social civility require. A politics of mercy is necessary in order to displace structures and habits of injustice and establish and sustain a dignified, sustainable livelihood all citizens.

Secondly, like the second law of thermodynamics, liberal, procedural justice left to itself, degenerates into a kind of moral entropy, into cycles of moral and social chaos and even violence. That is why both Hebrew and Christian Scriptures uniformly and consistently declare that the vengeance of *mishpat* always belongs to God and not to humans. God alone is the legitimate vindicator of justice and avenger of injustice (Deut. 32: 35; Nahum 1: 2; Psalm. 94: 23; Romans 12: 19; Hebrews 10: 30). No doubt this is because just as parents cannot and do not trust their children, when wronged, to take justice into their own hands and to fairly avenge each other, God does not trust fallen humans and nations to execute justice fairly? Throughout this book I discuss these two disabilities of liberal justice and show how a politics of mercy compensates for and triumphs over them. I show how in a fallen world merciful benevolence is necessary both to subvert injustice and to establish and sustain (against entropic tendencies) habits of substantive, egalitarian justice. In short, I show how mercy trumps justice, how the law of liberty trumps the law of reason, but always for the precise purpose of establishing and sustaining substantive justice.

Hebrew prophets, like Hosea and Jonah, demonstrate that and how mercy is required of covenantal communities if justice is to reign in the land. And Jesus famously subsidizes justice by advocating mercy, when he says, "You have heard that it was said, 'An eye for an eye and a tooth for a tooth.' But I say to you . . ." act mercifully by turning the other cheek (Matthew 5: 38ff). Many of the stories and parables in the Gospels similarly dramatize how in the Kingdom of God mercy trumps justice: the story of the woman caught in adultery (John 8: 1–11), for example, and the parable of the unforgiving servant (Matthew 18: 23–35). Never mind that it is the central plot of the Gospels, namely, the incarnation, ministry, passion, death, and resurrection in which the justice humans deserve is suffered by God and the unmerited grace of God's mercy and forgiveness granted to undeserving humans. In short, the biblical narrative's hermeneutic of suspicion regarding justice and its advocacy of mercy is a constant, continuous, and consistent refrain. Mercy (asymmetry) not justice (symmetry) is the evolved pinnacle of Christian moral consciousness, and compassion (supersymmetry) is the catalyst that drives the faithful community to cultivate public as well as private habits of mercy's benevolence.

Spiritual Law. Not only is justice not the highest, most evolved moral experience, neither is it the highest moral law of exilic and post-exilic Judaism. Although for Jews and Christians justice is a pivotal moral principle for orienting and organizing civil society, it is not the pinnacle of covenantal life. That place is reserved for a spiritual law of liberty, namely, the mercy embedded in God's benevolence toward humanity. Concomitant with the evolution of henotheism into monotheism, we find in both the Hebrew and Christian traditions an evolution of moral sensibility beyond mere justice toward the mercy of benevolence; beyond the parochialism of nationalism to the universalism of transnational redemption. The struggles of Jonah and the vision of Amos transcend the nationalism of the Judges and the Kings of Israel. Judgment and salvation, justice and mercy are for all nations, declares Amos. All are held to the same standard of justice, but at the same time there is in mercy's benevolence equally the hope of redemption for "all the nations who are called by my name, says the Lord . . ." (9: 12). Similarly, in the Great Commission (Matthew 28: 19–20), Jesus liberates his disciples from the nationalism of their Jewish heritage and commissions them to re-commit themselves single-mindedly to promoting and defending a transnational kingdom, the Kingdom of God. This evolution from local, nationalistic convictions to universal, transnational commitment is concomitant with an evolving moral sensibility; just retribution toward enemies is superseded by benevolence, by the forgiveness and reconciliation of all peoples. The Hebrew word most often translated "mercy" is *racham*, which is related to the word for womb (*rechem*) in which the foetus develops, is nurtured and cherished. It is translated variously as mercy, lovingkindness, and compassion. In Christian Scriptures, forms of the word *eleos* are most often translated as mercy, pity, sympathy, or compassion. In modern philosophy "benevolence" is the general virtue that embraces these values.

Mercy is the culminating spiritual orientation of Yahweh's covenant with Israel. Not only does Yahweh show mercy to his chosen people, but Yahweh expects those same people to show mercy to others. Throughout Hebrew Scriptures and especially in the prophetic literature, there emerges concomitantly with the universalism of monotheism a duty of Israel to practice toward all nations, including foreigners and enemies, the same mercy whereby God has graciously redeemed it. Many of the Psalms and Prophets call not only for justice but also for mercy, for repentance and forgiveness. The stories of Hosea and Jonah plot the tension between justice and mercy, culminating, in Jonah for example, in the triumph of mercy for the sake of redeeming, reconciling and restoring the Assyrian enemy. Similarly, in the Christian tradition mercy (*eleos*) is the heart of *pax Christi,* the heart of Christ's incarnation and atonement and the central focus of the apostles' teaching and practice. In both narratives, Hebrew and Christian, the duties of mercy are not for their own sake but for the sake of restoring God's just and peaceable Kingdom.

The spiritual law of liberty is this: theologically, to restore the peace and harmony from which humans have fallen requires the grace of God's mercy; the end, *pax Dei*, requires the means, *pax Christi*; philosophically, to establish egalitarian as well as liberal justice in an unjust world requires projects of benevolence; the end, liberal and egalitarian justice, requires the means, benevolence as public and private virtue. In an unjust world, mercy achieves its aim of justice by situating itself asymmetrically in relation to justice; mercy's moral asymmetry is under conditions of injustice a precondition for re-enfranchising the moral symmetry of justice. Whereas reason readily comprehends the symmetry of justice, faith is required to apprehend the asymmetry of mercy and its deviation from justice's standard model. Justice requires the asymmetrical, unmerited benefits of God's mercy; it requires benevolent faith communities to grant others, even enemies, the same unmerited goodness that they have received from God. In the midst of fallenness, acting justly will not do if the goal is to redeem and reconcile. For Jews, Torah is precondition for restoring Eden; for Christians Golgotha is pre-condition for a New Jerusalem. Although the discipline and suffering of mercy supersedes justice morally, it does not preempt it. It stands as a more highly evolved manifestation of moral consciousness and character that in a fallen world is necessary in order to subvert injustice in the first place and establish egalitarian justice in the long run.

Christian communities, then, have every reason to evolve beyond reason's law to mercy's liberty. But as often as not, they default, as did Jonah, to ancient habits of justice instead of to their ancient gospel of mercy. One contemporary example of the church's habit of defaulting to justice instead of mercy shows itself in an article by Scott McKnight in *Christianity Today* titled "The Mary We Never Knew."[18] McKnight quotes from Mary's Magnificat; "His [the Lord's] *mercy* extends to those who fear him, from generation to generation," after which Mary catalogues all the mighty and merciful things the Lord has done. These are "words of subversion," McKnight declares, and indeed they are. He goes on to explain that Mary's story, the meaning of which is encapsulated in her Magnificat, is "a dangerous story" because it "subverts injustice and establishes justice." But because McKnight's default mode is justice he neglects almost entirely the point of Mary's words and message, that it is "the *mercy* of the Lord" that is subversive, and not justice; it is faith and not reason; it is the courage of meekness and unmerited acts of mercy that "subvert injustice and establish justice." Herod the Great, who is the context for Mary's discourse on mercy, was a faithful vendor of *pax Romana*, the Roman version of justice. But Roman justice is justice without mercy; and as the Jews well knew, Roman justice does not subvert injustice and establish justice, but degenerates into vicious cycles of vengeance and retribution. Jewish revolutionaries, like the Zealots, advocated rebellion against Roman occupation and reaped Roman retribution. Not justice but *mercy*, Mary's Magnificat is insisting, is the key to overthrowing injustice and establishing justice. "[The Lord] has helped his servant Israel, remembering to be merciful to Abraham and his descendents forever, just as he promised our ancestors" (Luke 1: 50–55). Only benevolence, only a subversive politics of mercy, conquers injustice and establishes justice. But it is as if many Christians, both conservative and progressive, are myopic when it comes to seeing morally and politically; they lack the visual acuity to see three dimensionally, to see with depth perception politically; they are unable to see the moral depth that is before them in plain sight, namely, that under unjust conditions merciful benevolence is a pre-condition for establishing and sustaining a fully just society

One aim of this project is to acknowledge this fact and find ways to inspire Christian communities to see and be what they are called to see and be, to practice what they preach, to practice the same merciful benevolence they have received. Only then will "justice roll down like waters, and righteousness like an ever-flowing stream" (Amos 5: 24).

MORAL ENTROPY, MORAL INTEGRITY

Entropy, the Second Law of Thermodynamics, provides a metaphor and model for interpreting the (de)evolution of moral consciousness. This law states, first, that "*entropy is a measure of the amount of disorder in a physical system.*" "High entropy" means that a system is "highly disordered" so that any additional disordering is not readily recognizable; "low entropy" means that a system is "highly ordered" and any even minor disordering is readily recognized. Secondly, "in physical systems with many constituents . . . there is a natural evolution toward greater disorder, since disorder can be achieved in so many more ways than order." Accordingly, "*physical systems tend to evolve toward states of higher entropy,*" that is, toward greater disorder.[19] Since there are more ways for a system to have entropy than not, it is more likely that that system will de-evolve from a state of low entropy (higher order) into one with higher entropy (less order).[20] High entropy, then, is "the natural state of being" for physical systems; once in a state of high entropy a physical system tends to stay in it.[21] How does this entropic model of physical systems help us interpret moral systems?

Moral entropy measures the degree of order or disorder in a moral system. The assumption is that in *pax Dei,* in God's good Created Order, moral entropy is nil although possible. God creates all things good; the disobedience and chaos of the Fall triggers a process of relatively low moral entropy that, like physical systems, tends toward ever higher states of moral disorder, depicted in *Genesis,* for example, from Adam until the time of Noah. As in physical systems so also in moral systems, moral states always tend toward higher entropy (disorder). This is because there are more ways for humans to disobey, to sin, to act unjustly, to fabricate moral disorder, than there are ways to obey, to create moral order and low entropy. The fallen human's tendency is toward higher moral entropy. The energy and thrust of this tendency can be transformed and reversed only by the intentional exercise of will, only by carefully crafted actions of moral agents. Earlier, I traced how in the history of ancient Israel an evolving moral system endeavors through various phases to reverse the fallen human tendency toward high moral entropy. Israel's covenantal system establishes an intentional, evolving culture of spiritual and moral integrity toward ever lower states of moral entropy. First, by establishing tribal, common law and the notion of "corporate personality," secondly, by gradually evolving *lex talionis* and higher forms of justice wherein moral duties are correlated with certain rights; and finally, in the Hebrew prophets and in the teachings of Jesus, by evolving higher forms of moral integrity in which the relatively modest entropy of liberal justice is transformed into the relative low moral entropy of merciful benevolence and egalitarian justice.

Contemporary societies seem ill-equipped to pilot the turbulent moral waters from justice to benevolence and back. Although equipped with a keen sense of justice and moral symmetry, they have not cultivated for the most part a sense of mercy's power to "season justice." This is not surprising; the law of moral entropy predicts it; predicts that in laissez faire systems of modest entropy, like liberal democracy, the unjust conditions resulting from the self interest already present (Fallen Order) naturally progress and are only subverted and transformed by systems of higher moral integrity, systems like those powered by benevolence. Jesus seems to anticipate this principle of moral entropy. In his Sermon on the Mount he insists that justice's eye for an eye must be superseded by the benevolence of meekness and mercy; he knows that in a fallen world justice is susceptible to a progressive moral decay that is arrested and reversed only by radical asymmetry, by meekness (turn the other cheek), by mercy and the healing powers of *agape*. He knows just retribution in return for just retribution, insult in return for insult, degenerates into more of the same; he knows violence in return for violence, evil for evil multiplies moral chaos and that entropy is reversible only by practicing the awful, asymmetrical, turbulent benevolence of God's mercy.

One does not have to look far in personal, public, and political life to find examples of justice's natural entropy, how it devolves into inexorable cycles of retaliation. Famously, the Peloponnesian Wars between Athens and Sparta, a cycle of retaliatory battles between 430 and 404 BCE, demonstrate the entropic tendency of justifiable retaliation. Both city-states trumpet the justice of their cause; both refuse occasions for benevolence and for peace; both exhaust themselves, their human and material and moral resources, until both city-states are severely diminished. Although Sparta ultimately triumphs both Sparta and Athens are so exhausted materially, psychologically, and morally that they leave themselves mutually vulnerable, subdued, and soon conquered by Phillip II of Macedon and his son Alexander.

The treatment of Germany in the Treaty of Versailles (1919) is another case in point. Although considered fair and just by the Allies, its provisions nevertheless produced feelings of humiliation and anger instead of feelings of guilt and penance. Indeed, the harsh treatment of Germany and its allies by the Treaty generated a backlash of retaliatory justice by Germany that contributed to WWII.[22] Many of the Treaty's provisions were controversial, one of the most significant of which required Germany and its allies to accept full responsibility for causing the war and, under the terms of articles 231–248, disarm, make substantial territorial concessions, and pay reparations. The German response to such justice was immediate and unambiguous: anger, hostility, resentment; feelings of vulnerability and revenge. Germans did not feel that they were responsible for starting the war nor did they feel they had lost. The German people initially understood the negotiations at Versailles to constitute a peace conference not a treaty of surrender. Germans resented the burdens of the Treaty and almost immediately felt justified in violating its terms in the name of justice. In a world already unjust from the German perspective, the entropy of justice (absent benevolence) generated increasingly higher levels of moral disorder and incivility, culminating with time in the brutal efficiency of Nazism. Hitler and others nurtured German resentment, mythologizing it as ideology. From the perspective of reason's standard model of justice, this German ideology of resentment against Europe and especially European Jews warranted the retaliatory justice of WWII. Such is the entropy of justice and *pax Romana* left to their own devices. Absent mercy's benevolence, the cold calculus of justice executes with dreadful and savage precision "an eye for an eye, a tooth for a tooth." This entropic character of justice was acknowledged by the U.S. ambassador to Japan in the context of the Pacific campaign. In response to Japanese aggression, Roosevelt allowed Dean Acheson's decision to freeze all Japanese funds and cut off all trade. U.S. Ambassador Grew wrote, "The vicious cycle of reprisals and counter reprisals is on. *Facilis descensus Averni est* [The descent into Hell is easy]. Unless radical surprises occur, it is difficult to see how the momentum of the down-grade movement can be arrested, or how far it will go. The obvious conclusion is eventual war."[23]

The entropy of justice can clearly be seen in the stalemated Israeli-Hamas conflict (2012) over the Gaza Strip. Through mutual projects of retaliation each side spirals into an ever more inexorable cycle of justice, each side providing cogent reasons for their actions. But this is only a compelling contemporary example that belongs to a larger picture of justice's moral entropy, namely, the ongoing seemingly interminable Israeli-Palestinian conflict. Insofar as each government defaults to *pax Romana*, the conflict devolves into cycles of retaliatory violence, each side executing with great fidelity the demands justice makes on it. The First Intifada (1987–1993) and the *al-Aqsa* Intifada (2000) are prime examples of justice's moral entropy, of increasingly higher levels of moral disorder and violence. The First Intifada ended with the promise and hope of the Oslo Accords (1993). Although many deem these Accords a failure, it nevertheless represents a moment for the power of mercy's moral integrity; a moment that halted, at least temporarily, the entropy of justice. Prior to the Oslo Accords both sides appealed to the standard model of moral reason to justify their positions. For the Palestinians, on the one hand, the retaliatory violence of the Intifada was justified; Arafat and the PLO originally held the view that justice for the Palestinian people required the destruction of Israel. On the other hand, Israel held that its occupation of Gaza and the West Bank was entirely justified as a fair re-habitation of part of its ancient homeland. In the Accords both sides managed a measure of moral integrity by showing mercy: Arafat and the PLO, by acknowledging the right of the state of Israel to exist; Rabin and Israel, by promising to withdraw forces from Gaza and the West Bank. Both "concessions" included acts of benevolence that required mutual faith; each act of faith deviated from the standard model of moral reason that previously had sucked both governments into a vortex of just retaliatory violence. Indeed, it was because of such acts of faith and mercy, that justice as mutual fairness and respect amongst enemies was possible and sustainable.[24]

It is not that justice is a vice; it is indeed a virtue. But just as in poker a Queen, a very good card, is trumped by an Ace; the Ace does not diminish the power of the Queen, it only supersedes it. The benevolence of mercy does not diminish justice, but supersedes it in order to establish and sustain it. Mercy's benevolence "seasons justice" so that injustice is subverted and the egalitarian harmony of *pax Dei* secured.

PLAN OF THE BOOK

All of these "points of interest—" the three moral orders, symmetry and asymmetry, the evolution of morality from justice to mercy along with the demands of moral integrity—weave together throughout the argument of this book. The first section, "Philosophical Inquiry," addresses the question: "On what historical and intellectual basis was benevolence disenfranchised from American public and political life and on what basis might it be re-enfranchised?" I begin by focusing on benevolence as a private virtue, drawing especially on the work of John Locke and Adam Smith and tracing their influence on founders like James Madison and Thomas Jefferson (chapter 2). I then analyze benevolence as a public virtue, sketching its development from Locke to Hume and Mill and eventually in the United States to Alexander Hamilton and a variety of societies and organizations that constituted a "benevolent empire" (chapter 3). In the second section, "Theological Inquiry," I establish a theological foundation for an ethics of benevolence and a politics of mercy. Chapter 4 examines the relationship between benevolence and justice, chapter 5 the relationship between benevolence and mercy. Chapter 6 examines compassion as a moral bridge between justice and mercy. I argue that compassion is the moral, psychological, and spiritual catalyst whereby a community evolves in public as well as private life from mere justice as its primary occupation to projects of merciful benevolence. Finally, in section three, "Moral Integrity," I examine certain historical figures (Gandhi and King) who put into practice the power of mercy for establishing justice and freedom; and in the final chapter the social and political implications for practicing with integrity merciful benevolence in contemporary societies.

NOTES

1. A Turkish tale, adapted from a retelling by Paul Jordan-Smith, "Man's Justice and God's Justice," *Parabola* 16, 4 (1991), 71–72.

2. This and all other biblical references and quotes are from the "Revised Standard Version" of the *Holy Bible*, unless otherwise noted.

3. Stephen Toulmin, *Cosmopolis* (Chicago, IL: University of Chicago Press, 1992), 67.

4. From Gide's autobiographical essay in Richard Crossman's edited collection, *The God That Failed* (Chicago, IL: Regnery Gateway, 1949, 1983), 169.

5. Theologians, especially Christian ones, customarily gravitate toward Continental thinkers for moral, ethical, and political sustenance, John Locke, perhaps, excepted. Kant and Hegel, Kierkegaard and Nietzsche, Barth and Boenffer are among the favorites. My orientation in this book is toward the British philosophical, moral tradition; not, of course, to supplant the other, but to supplement it.

6. By referring to these "orders" or "jurisdictions" I do not intend to favor any particular historical, theological tradition(s). By referring to the Fallen Order, for example, I do not intend one classical interpretation of sin or evil over another; or by the Redeemed Order any theology of redemption instead of another.

7. Historically, *pax Romana* refers to the infamous way in which the Roman Emperors tended to maintain peace and order in their vast empire, namely, by using superior military might. They use intimidation, fear, coercion, and violence to execute justice according to Roman law and to maintain order. My use of "*pax Romana*" includes this historical reference and much more.

8. This phrase, of course, has been popularized by John Rawls's *Theory of Justice* (Cambridge, MA: Belknap Press of Harvard University Press, 1970). See my discussion in chapter 3.

9. "The standard model" is a label used to refer to the results of research into particle physics in the 1970s. It incorporated all that was known at the time regarding the behavior of particles and it has been used to successfully predict the outcome of how particles behave in a wide variety of experiments. Today it is considered to be well established, although not entirely complete. Research establishing the standard model is ongoing: for example a collaboration of several teams of scientists in the Belle Experiment as the Japanese National Laboratory for High Energy Physics (KEK); also, researchers at the Stanford Linear Accelerator Center, as well as findings of the Hyper CP Experiment and CKM sponsored by the High Energy Physics group at the University of Virginia. See K. Abe, et al. (Belle Collaboration), "Observation of Large *CP* Violation in the Neutral *B* Meson System," *Physical Review Letters* 87, 091802, Issue 9-27, 14 August 2001; B. Aubert, et al. (BARBAR Collaboration), "Observation of *CP* Violation in the *B* 0 Meson System," *Physical Review Letters*, 87, 091801, Issue 9–27, 14 August 2001.

10. Granting unmerited benefits to wrongdoers obviously entails works of mercy; likewise with the undeserving, such as the lazy and slothful. It is not so obvious that those who are vulnerable are recipients of mercy when they receive benefits to which they have a right. By vulnerable I refer to people who are disabled in ways that prevent them from participating in social and economic activities/institutions so that they reap for themselves the basic necessities of life: adequate food, clothes, shelter, healthcare and so on. I mean them to be recipients of mercy and not merely justice, when they receive such benefits, because strictly speaking,

according to the laws of distributive justice and free market economies, they should earn and merit these benefits by voluntary participation in and contribution to production and exchange.

11. Frank Close, *Lucifer's Legacy: The Meaning of Asymmetry* (London: Oxford University Press, 2000), 248.

12. *Ibid.*, 249–250.

13. Paul Davies, *God and the New Physics* (New York: Touchstone Books, Simon & Schuster, 1984), 111.

14. *Ibid.*, 112–113.

15. Anthony Phillips, *Deuteronomy: The Cambridge Bible Commentary* (Cambridge, UK: Cambridge University Press, 1973), 219.

16. Max Weber, *Ancient Judaism* (New York: The Free Press, 1952), especially chapter 2.

17. I examine this crucial distinction more fully in chapter 3.

18. Scott McKnight, "The Mary We Never Knew," in *Christianity Today*, December 2006, Celebrating 50 Years.

19. Brian Greene, *The Fabric of the Cosmos: Space, Time, and the Texture of Reality* (New York: Vintage Books, Random House, Inc., 2005), 154–155.

20. *Ibid.*, 156.

21. *Ibid.*, 164.

22. Donald Shriver Jr., in chapter 4 ("Vengeance and Forbearance: Germans and Americans") in *An Ethic for Enemies: Forgiveness in Politics*, writes of the damage done by the just vengeance of the Treaty of Versailles to Germany and how justice so conceived devolved into the atrocities of Nazism and the Holocaust.

23. Quoted in *FDR* by Jean Edward Smith (New York: Random House, 2007), 518.

24. Because they acted in good faith Arafat and Rabin, along with Shimon Peres, jointly received the Nobel Peace Prize, 1994. A similar analysis could be applied to the earlier and continuing success of the Camp David Accords (1978) signed by Egyptian President Anwar Al Sadat and Israeli Prime Minister Menachem Begin and negotiated by President Jimmy Carter.

Part One

Philosophical Inquiry

. . . for I knew
that thou art a gracious God, and merciful,
slow to anger, and of great kindness,
and repentest thee of the evil.
(Jonah 4: 2, KJV)

Chapter Two

Benevolence as Private Virtue

"Render to Caesar the things that are Caesars, and to God the things that are Gods" (Luke 20: 25) is one of the more celebrated and provocative precepts in Western political tradition. Its ambiguity discloses just how perplexing and precarious the relationship really is between politics and religion. The fact that it has been subjected to a wide variety of sometimes conflicting interpretations substantiates the point. From theocracy to anarchy, from liberalism to communalism, from establishment to disestablishment, philosophers, theologians, and politicians impose on this precept their political preferences. How one faithfully renders to Caesar and to God in first-century Jerusalem or thirteenth-century Rome differs considerably from how one faithfully does so in twenty-first-century Washington, DC. Even though in the modern West "Render to Caesar and render to God" is interpreted variously, a broad consensus has evolved on at least one issue, namely, the "disestablishment" of religion. What is not so widely acknowledged, however, is that along with the disestablishment of religion there evolved concomitantly, at least in the United States, the disestablishment of benevolence,[1] which historically and logically rooted and flourished in the soil of religion. The impact of this parallel disestablishment (along with economics) has been enormous for the practice of politics in the United States. The recent and ongoing economic recession of 2007; the global financial crisis; the decline in housing values and construction, the rise in oil and food prices, the increase in foreclosures and personal bankruptcies, banking mismanagement and corporate greed, outsourcing of jobs and rising unemployment, reductions in labor's bargaining power, wages and benefits, all of this and much more produced worldwide economic unrest. In this chapter I intend to examine how and why this disestablishment of benevolence occurred and in the next to what extent its re-establishment might be beneficial politically and economically and morally.

What is now needed is a critique of existing moral, political, and economic values; values like laissez faire, free enterprise, justice, equality, self-interest, and benevolence as currently practiced. The current worth and practice of these values must be called into question. To this end we need to know the conditions from which these values have sprung and how they have developed and changed. Hitherto, especially among Christians, such knowledge has neither been forthcoming nor solicited. The intrinsic nature and worth of these values was and is taken for granted as a fact of modern life, beyond question. Few in the United States up to now have doubted that "limited government" represents a higher value than "bloated government," especially in terms of promoting and benefiting citizens generally. But what if "limited government" represents not merely a retrogression and moral neglect but a danger, a temptation, a narcotic enabling the present to live at the expense of the future, the wealthy at the expense of the poor, bankers at the expense of investors, majorities at the expense of minorities, even minorities at the expense of majorities, and bureaucrats at the expense of laborers? What if limited government should turn out to be for most citizens the danger of dangers to freedom and fairness? When we have the courage to analyze and ask questions of all of this, might we not be persuaded of a new claim, a new understanding of these values, a new way of seeing and living as citizens. So, under what historical and philosophical conditions did the current understanding and practice of freedom and justice and benevolence come to be? Why and how is it that benevolence, and related public virtues, came to be progressively alienated in modern America from politics and economics? What fears and forces disestablished benevolence and how? Why and how did freedom and justice, largely to the exclusion of benevolence, come to dominate politics and economics? What liabilities to politics and economics resulted from this disenfranchisement, and what benefits?

These and related questions are addressed in this chapter. In chapter 3 I sketch in outline an argument (which in the remainder of the book I develop and defend) in support of re-establishing in political and economic life certain public virtues that are encapsulated historically and philosophically by "benevolence" and religiously and theologically by "mercy." I maintain that "merciful benevolence" is comprised of certain compelling public virtues without which any modern society cannot categorically claim for itself the title of "civil."

Recall, first of all, the historical and theological background from which modern democracy and economics emerged. What is the general nature of medieval thought (moral, political, and economic) out of and against which Enlightenment thinkers began inventing what we know as modern European civilization. More particularly, what was the status of liberty, justice, and benevolence in public life? What was the Medieval Catholic vision of moral and political life? Thomas Aquinas, of course, most fully embodies the best of medieval scholasticism. In *Summa Theologica* he famously outlines three interdependent systems of law that constitute moral and political life. Divine, eternal law most fundamentally establishes the possibility of the other systems; it is the manifestation of God's very nature and being. Secondly, natural law reflects God's eternal law; it is embedded in the structures of the physical and moral character of creation. It is "natural" in that it is discoverable by rational deliberation. It is "law" in that it embodies a "final cause" in terms of which each thing fulfills its divinely crafted purpose. Finally, civil law properly and faithfully extends natural and divine laws to the social, political, and economic systems.

Consider poverty, as does Aquinas, as an example. He argues that there are compelling reasons for private property and for civil laws protecting private property. Aquinas, following Aristotle, suggests at least two benefits; one, people are more likely to be good stewards of property they privately appropriate than property held in common; and, two, peace is more easily secured and sustained. Along with justifiable reasons for private property, however, come moral responsibilities, argues Aquinas, duties of civil law that codify divine and natural law. Property owners cannot use their property simply as they wish, capriciously, selfishly. Property must be in service to that purpose for which God created material goods, namely, to sustain decent and dignified human life. Pemberton and Finn put Aquinas' argument this way: "Since material goods were created by God for the very purpose of meeting human needs, the possessor of goods has the obligation to use them in accordance with their nature—to meet needs." There is a divinely ordained correlation of right and duty; the poor can claim a right to private property sufficient to a sustainable livelihood, and society has a correlative duty of benevolence to guarantee and satisfy that right. From their surplus, accordingly, the rich are obligated to practice benevolence, to share with the poor from their superabundance. Even more boldly, Aquinas argues that "the poor man is justified in taking those goods if the rich man will not give them to him."[2] The poor are justified because what humans have a right to is simply a reflection and mandate of natural and Divine law. Since non human nature is ordained by God for sustaining all human life, those possessing wealth or superabundance have a moral obligation to act benevolently and help the poor. If they do not do so willingly, then, Thomas argues, the poor have a divine and natural right to it, even to steal it. The wealthy in their superabundance, in other words, possess what they have no right to, namely wealth, as long as there are poor; either they voluntarily practice benevolence or at least suffer the poor's right to a portion of it. Indeed, since a poor man has a divine and natural right to a sustainable life and since he is thereby entitled to a portion of the other's superabundance, he is justified in taking it either openly or secretly.[3] Given Aquinas' way of envisioning creation and those laws governing it, it is easy to see why he might favor a theocratic model of government. All creation falls necessarily and normatively within God's jurisdiction and sovereignty; nothing is properly conceived independent of its divine cause and *raison d'etre.* "Nature" and "natural," in this Scholastic sense, refer to the alignment of creation with the will of God and God's laws. "Natural rights" refer to that to which a person is entitled in concert with the normative demands of God's will; these are refracted through natural and civil laws crafted to preserve God's will that all humans have provisions necessary for a sustainable livelihood. Not all Mediaeval theologians subscribed to Aquinas' argument and conclusion,[4] of course, but his vision of divine and natural law came to dominate medieval Christian thinking, until it was challenged by the emerging "enlightenments"[5] that came to shape the character of modern European civilization.

Even in the early centuries of an emerging modern civilization, economics, religion, and benevolence remained established. British Imperial benevolence, for example, was thoroughly and officially institutionalized in the colonial period of the seventeenth and eighteenth centuries. As noted in the compelling research of *Burden or Benefit? Imperial Benevolence and Its Legacies*,[6] the rhetoric and practice of Imperial benevolence was largely paternalistic and patronizing, subjugating indigenous peoples to "the magnanimity" of the British and other colonial powers. This degrading, imperial, colonizing exploitation of benevolence, its extension through the auspices of missionaries and humanitarians, rendered its value doubtful. Indeed, as suggested by the book's primary proposition: "benevolence has been a rather expansive and even ambiguous concept over centuries, as benevolent practices and principles have been adapted to respond to particular cultural, political, social, religious, and economic imperatives."[7] Gradually, eventually, the idea of benevolence evolved from its form as institutionalized paternalism to a form of collective responsibility for others, including the vulnerable and marginalized. Although some still think of benevolence as a form of paternalism, its more contemporary meaning, as collective responsibility for the marginalized, was developed by philosophers of the Scottish Enlightenment, especially David Hume, Francis Hutcheson, and Adam Smith. The trajectory of their thought included the belief that democracy and free enterprise would not likely succeed without the rhetoric and practice of benevolence, including economic benevolence. They differed, however, over whether benevolence should be practiced strictly as a private virtue of individual philanthropy and charity or also as a public virtue of collective responsibility and public policy. Early in the American tradition the Founders themselves were divided on this issue. Some (Madison) favored benevolence only as a private virtue, while others (Hamilton) favored it as a public virtue as well, with the former view largely prevailing.

How did this transition come about? How is it that the medieval and early modern versions of benevolence get progressively undermined? Why was it virtually impossible in Western societies not to believe in benevolence as a political ideal in 1500 while in 2014 many in the United States find it equally impossible to support benevolence as a public, political virtue? How is it that the correlation of the individual's right to a sustainable livelihood (egalitarian justice) with the duty to sustain the life of all humans (benevolence) was historically and logically eroded in much of modern thought and practice? The answer to these questions is important for sustaining the promise of this book, namely, to show how and why benevolence can and should be re-established as a public virtue without at the same time re-establishing religion. My sense is that doing so is urgent if modern Western civilization in general and the United States in particular are to avoid sinking into the mire of plutocratic oligarchy disguised by a fragile, hollow shell of democracy.

The philosophical trick is to re-enfranchise into political and economic life the virtues anchored in benevolence without re-enfranchising religion. This is a path that some will insist is too precarious to travel; it is one that I think not only worth the risk but incumbent on societies if they are to thrive as civilized democracies and not merely as plutocratic oligarchies. In this chapter I trace highlights of how benevolence along with religion gets disestablished from public life. This is a process to which John Locke and Adam Smith both contribute, impacting the likes of James Madison, Thomas Jefferson, et al. In the next chapter I sketch briefly a model for re-establishing benevolence without re-establishing religion.

DISESTABLISHING BENEVOLENCE: LOCKE AND SMITH

What, then, are the historical and philosophical conditions that disenfranchised benevolence from public and political life? How is it that benevolence, which in seventeenth century Imperial Britain was still a public virtue, became progressively disestablished? An answer lies in the fact that in the seventeenth and eighteenth centuries, religion, benevolence, and economics were interdependent, blended, established enterprises; so that when forces emerged disestablishing religion, benevolence and economics were concomitantly disestablished. This interdependence is evident, as Chris Toffin argues, in periodicals like the *Edinburgh Review* and *Quarterly Review,* which promoted anti-slavery and benevolent sentiments; and the rhetoric they used for such promotion was religious and ethical as well as economic: "Fundamentally in agreement about the abstract injustice of the slavery itself, their discussion of right remedies shows a fascinating range of skillful polemic and ingenious compromise"[8] that includes religious, moral, and economic language. Similarly, Leigh Dale notes that Frederick Weld, who partly designed British Imperial policy, thought of colonization as a benevolent project grounded in the soil not only of politics and economics but also of religion. Such projects are undertaken at the "invitation not merely from ruler of Empire, but from God, whose creative powers have been co-opted to the provision of pastoral resources. Colonization, naturalized as pastoralism, comes to constitute a benevolent and beneficent project."[9] The patronizing paternalism of British Imperial benevolence was in colonial times so interconnected with established religion and economics that in disestablishing economics and religion benevolence as a public virtue was likewise disestablished. In Britain, for example, taxes were used not only to pay clergy but used by the established church on behalf of the state to assist the poor.

John Locke's contribution to disestablishing benevolence is partial and perhaps inadvertent; it results from his insistence that the political and the religious are distinct jurisdictions and that each should have no authority over the other. In *A Letter Concerning Toleration* (1689) Locke recapitulates the kind of progressive thinking about the separation of church and state occurring toward the end of the seventeenth century, although he represents only one of several approaches.[10] Although his argument does not disestablish values of benevolence entirely, it represents an intermediate step toward doing so. He was not the first to pursue the trajectory of religious disestablishment, of course; many contributed, including Dante, Machiavelli, Luther, Calvin, Hobbes, Grotius, Marsiglio of Padua to name a few. The Reformers' protestations against the Medieval Catholic tradition, for example, contribute greatly to the increasing marginalization of religion form the secularity of culture, not only among the elite but among ordinary practicing Christians.[11] For early Protestants, Charles Taylor shows, the devotion expected of the renunciatory vocations (monasticism, priesthood) alone soon become qualities expected of all Christians, of all citizens. The Protestant sense of the sacred is progressively absorbed into ordinary, profane life. Now, all Christians at all times were to be somewhat like "monks," totally dedicated to Christ.[12] The Reformer's expectation was that even the ordinary affairs of ordinary life would be infused with the sacred. But what actually occurs, ironically, is that the sacred increasingly begins to reshape itself to the contours of profane life until finally, in Western society, it becomes indistinguishable from the profane. Religion eventually survives only insofar as it casts itself off from secular cultural and political life.

Locke inherits the momentum of these powerful forces and focuses them into a pattern of thought that contributes not only to the disestablishment of religion from politics but also momentum toward the disestablishment of benevolence. His purpose in writing the *Letter* and his constant plea is for "mutual toleration" among religious sects. The possibility of such toleration is contingent on the intentional and official separation of authorities and jurisdictions, of priest from magistrate, of church from state, to the benefit of both. In making his argument, we find Locke insisting on a concomitant separation of values; especially the separation of what he refers to as temporal from eternal values. So, these separate spheres of values, temporal and eternal, contribute to the separation of church and state that eventually alienates benevolence, an eternal virtue, from justice, a temporal virtue, with the former eventually remanded to the private sphere. What, then, is the nature of Locke's argument for mutual religious toleration and for the separation of eternal and temporal values? And how does it lay the foundation for the disestablishment of benevolence?

First and simply, the aim of Locke's *Letter* is to promote and advance the virtue of "mutual toleration" and peace between religious sects. The state should not favor any particular religious tradition; it should permit all sects to practice their version of faith as they wish. Mutual toleration between religious sects requires a "distance" between religion and state so that toleration is a public and not just a private reality. In Locke's day, of course, religion and state were inextricably intertwined, so that it was difficult even to distinguish their roles theoretically let alone practice them separately. Predecessors like Dante and Luther had argued for some such separation. Certain historical conditions, such as the hostilities between Catholics and Anglicans and Puritans in Britain, between Catholics and Protestants on the continent, and internecine conflicts between Protestant sects triggered various attempts to find common cause for resolving religious hostilities. The Peace of Westphalia, for example, was a series of treaties signed between May and October 1648 that established a new system of political order in central Europe. This order entailed the idea of a state governed by a sovereign whose preference officially established religion within his jurisdiction. However, communal worship by minority faiths in "clandestine" churches was tolerated.[13] In his *Letter*, Locke elevates this "clandestine" toleration to a public and universal value extending equally to all religions. He insists that "toleration be the chief characteristic mark of the true church";[14] and argues that such internecine toleration is possible only if governments mind their own civil business and not the business of religion.[15]

Secondly, this aim of peaceful coexistence between religion and politics is possible, according to Locke, when their respective authority and jurisdictions are acknowledged and maintained. In making this case, Locke typically anchors his views in scripture, referring to the episode in Luke's gospel (22: 25), for example, where Jesus instructs his disciples not to be like the Gentiles who "exercise lordship over [their subjects]," but to be like servants who minister to each other's souls. In other words, there are two kinds of legitimate authorities and jurisdictions, public and private. The business of secular, political authority (the Gentiles) is "dominion," the use of "compulsive force" regarding the execution of values related to justice. The business of ecclesiastical authority is "the regulating of men's lives, according to the rules of virtue and piety." To the extent that benevolence is a function of religious "virtue and piety" Locke relegates it to the private jurisdiction of religious authority. For Locke, then, the "compulsive force" exercised by political authority correlates with justice and compels citizens externally to abide by just laws. In contrast, true religion does not compel at all but persuades people internally to qualities belonging to benevolence and mercy, to "holiness of life, purity of manners, benignity and meekness of spirit."[16] Throughout the *Letter* Locke typically contrasts these jurisdictions by insisting that religion's business is internal and private, the "salvation" or "edification" or "care of souls"; and that politics' business is external and public, "the care of the commonwealth."[17]

"Care of souls," insists Locke, means that true Christians "would sincerely [desire] the good of souls, [and] they would tread in the steps and follow the perfect example of that Prince of Peace, who sent out His soldiers to the subduing of nations, and gathering them into His church, not with the sword or other instruments of force, but . . . with the Gospel of peace and with the exemplary holiness of their conversation."[18] In other words, religion properly and privately fosters "the care of souls" by persuasion and attraction, by exemplary lives of righteousness and peacemaking and not by political coercion, not by compelling religious worship or articles of belief.[19] In contrast, "the care of the commonwealth" entails universal values of public interest, like justice, retribution, and the welfare of a citizen's "life, liberty, health, and the indolency of body; and the possessions of outward things, such as money, houses, furniture, and the like." Guaranteeing justice and related civil interests requires a kind of external compulsion and force. Indeed, "the magistrate [is] armed with the force and strength of all his subjects, in order to the punishment of those that violate any other man's rights."[20] Whereas the religious "care of souls" is private and aims at "salvation" through the persuasive powers of righteousness; the political "care of the commonwealth" aims at "protection of rights and liberties" through coercion. Since these two human enterprises are so fundamentally different in aims and interests, their respective authority and jurisdictions should be sustained separately. In short, care of the commonwealth and its temporal values cannot belong to ecclesiastical magistrates; and care of the souls and its eternal values cannot belong to civil magistrates.

Finally, the consequences of separating church and state, religion and politics, in this way laid the groundwork for a concomitant separation from political life of values belonging to benevolence, although in Locke this disestablishment is only suggested and not consummated. Nevertheless, certain qualities of mercy rooted in religion are remanded to the private sphere. It was only a matter of time and further analysis that public virtues related to benevolence, which historically and philosophically are anchored to and in religion, would likewise be fully disestablished as they are, for example, in

Smith. It was only a matter of time that values such as charity and meekness would be relegated, along with piety, to the private domain of religion. The foundation for this estrangement of values is delineated by Locke in his *Letter* as well as in his *Second Treatise on Government.* As with Enlightenment thinking generally, Locke discovers a secular basis for morality and values in reason and natural law, even though he also acknowledged the worth of morality's religious foundations. Nevertheless, the secular state's aim is justice, protecting and preserving property individuals naturally have in the rights and liberties of their own person; its purpose is "procuring, protecting, and advancing . . . civil interests." What is required for protecting rights and liberties, he argues in his *Letter*, is justice, just laws and penalties:

> It is the duty of the civil magistrate, by the impartial execution of equal laws, to secure unto all people in general, and to every one of his subjects in particular, the just possession of these things belonging to this life. If any one presume to violate the laws of public justice and equity, established for the preservation of those things, his presumption is to be checked by fear of punishment consisting of the deprivation or diminution of those civil interests or goods which otherwise he might and ought to obey. . . . [T]he magistrate [is] armed with the force and strength of all his subjects, in order to the punishment of those that violate any other man's rights.[21]

The civil magistrate's business is justice and equity and he is armed with the state's coercive executive power to guarantee "the temporal good and outward prosperity of the society. . . ." These temporal values, according to Locke, are well suited to civil society's temporal mission: namely, that "by mutual assistance and joint force [the civil magistrates] may secure unto each other their properties, in the things that contribute to the comfort and happiness of this life, . . . for the defense of their temporal goods."[22]

Part of Locke's point is that guaranteeing justice and equity, as temporal, public values, is not the business of religion, for which "all force and compulsion are to be foreborne."[23] Instead, eternal, private values belong to religion whose business it is to inspire and persuade by the magnetism of righteous virtues like charity and mercy and peacemaking. Since every human "has an immortal soul" it is incumbent on humans to believe eternal truths and practice immortal values as "the highest obligation that lies upon mankind, and, that our utmost care, application, and diligence ought to be exercised in the search and performance of them; because there is nothing in this that is of any consideration in the comparison with eternity."[24] The promotion and protection of these eternal values are in trust and charge to religion, not politics. Locke sums up these virtues of benevolence succinctly in his *Letter*. The religious "ought to industriously exhort all men, whether private persons or magistrates . . . , to charity, meekness, and toleration. . . . [H]ow happy and how great would be the fruit, both in church and state, if the pulpits everywhere sounded with this doctrine of peace and toleration."[25] This constellation of piety's private, eternal values (charity, meekness, mercy) are for "the care of each man's salvation" and "belongs only to himself" (46) and to his religion. They are voluntary and encouraged of persons only with persuasion not coercion, with the mercy of meekness not with the retaliation of vengeance, with tolerance and not bigotry, with peace and not violence.

Locke's conclusion regarding the separation of church and state and the virtue of "mutual toleration" at times perhaps seems overly optimistic. "[I]f each of them would contain itself within its own bounds—the one attending to the worldly welfare of the commonwealth, the other to the salvation of souls—it is impossible that any discord should ever have happened [or will happen] between them."[26] Theoretically, perhaps, but he seems at the same time to sabotage the possibility of such happy co-existence. For both religion and state contribute to the same end, "the good life," a life presupposing that "Moral actions belong therefore to the jurisdiction both of the outward and the inward court, . . . both of the magistrate and conscience." Locke does at times recognize the "great danger, lest one of these jurisdictions entrench upon the other and discord arise between the keeper of the public peace and the overseers of souls." But if religion and state practice boundaries, "[they] will easily remove all difficulty in this matter."[27] This separation of jurisdictions into public and private is all the more likely to succeed, as Locke well recognizes, if each jurisdiction remains quite separate from the other and minds its own moral business. What distinguishes political and public from religious and private values for Locke is articulated in terms of the difference between equity of justice and the benevolence of charity; the former are public matters of commonwealth, the latter private matters of conscience; the former are subject to coercion and force, even violence, and the latter subject to influence and persuasion, in expectation that such a separation will secure the ultimate aim of civil societies, namely, mutual toleration and peace. This marginalization of charity and benevolence from public life is in Locke only partial and perhaps somewhat inadvertent; as eternal verities they are privatized as auxiliaries to the disestablishment of religion.

Locke, then, takes an intermediate step in the historical and philosophical trajectory that eventually results in the disestablishment of benevolence. By the time of Adam Smith, a century on, the argument for expanding the liberal reach of the Enlightenment's pursuit of liberty disestablishes deliberately and intentionally not only religion and economics but benevolence as well. Indeed, for Smith the disenfranchisement of benevolence is calculated, systematic, and complete. Given the resurgent interest in all things Scottish, it is somewhat puzzling that Smith's influence on liberalism's project of disestablishing religion and benevolence is little known, even though disestablishing them parallels his celebrated disestablishment of economics.[28] Indeed, his impact rippled as far as Madison and Jefferson and other Founders who were in the process of crafting the United States of America.[29]

By all accounts a friendly dispute between David Hume and Smith developed regarding the (dis)establishment of religion. What is common to both arguments is the belief of each that society will benefit socially, politically and morally. Hume argues that enlightened thinking and moral progress is more likely with church and clergy established. The danger of disestablishment is that clergy will likely inspire in followers "the most violent abhorrence of all sects. . . . No regard will be paid to truth, morals, or decency. . . . Every tenet will be adopted that best suits the disorderly affections of the human frame." In contrast, "[T]he most decent and advantageous composition [the civil magistrate] can make with the spiritual guides, is to bribe their indolence, by assigning stated salaries to their profession, and rendering superfluous for them to be further active. . . . [I]n this manner ecclesiastical establishments prove in the end advantageous to the political interests of society."[30] Established religion, Hume concludes, is likely do less damage to enlightened thinking and liberal progress, on the one hand, and may even benefit political interests, on the other.

Curiously, Smith includes in its entirety this passage from Hume's *The History of England,* but he does so in order to lodge a complaint by respectfully disagreeing with Hume regarding religion's establishment.[31] His reasons for disestablishment are similar to Hume's for establishment: that society is likely to benefit intellectually and morally from disestablishment. The clergy's "exertion, their zeal and industry, are likely to be much greater in the former [disestablishment] situation than in the latter [establishment]."[32] Indeed, the benefits of religious disestablishment, of a competitive, religious market place are for Smith analogous to the benefits of laissez-faire, economic disestablishment. Smith argues, for example, that clergy in established systems "neglect to keep up the fervour of faith and devotion in the great body of the people; and having given themselves up to indolence, were become altogether incapable of making any vigorous exertion in defense even of their establishment. . . . [T]hey are apt gradually to lose the qualities, both good and bad, which gave them authority and influence with the inferior ranks of people, and which perhaps had been the original causes of the success and establishment of their religion."[33] Similar to economics, the disestablishment and free exercise of religion for Smith is vital for the formation of political character; government establishment and control of it dilutes its power to bring about creative social and moral progress.[34] Although Hume and Smith disagree over the establishment of religion, the rationale for their views is similar; both conclude that state and religion benefit.

But along with religious and economic disestablishment comes a concomitant disestablishment of benevolence; and without benevolence, Smith soon discovers, unbridled self-interest produces economic injustice and deprivation. Indeed, he came to see the disenfranchisement of benevolence as somewhat detrimental to distributing economic goods and sought to address it, but not by re-establishing it.

Early on in *The Theory of Moral Sentiments* as well as in *The Wealth of Nations* Smith argues that self-interest and sympathy are fundamental to human behavior in general and to *homo economicus* in particular; both are natural and dialectically related to each other. "How selfish soever man may be supposed, there are evidently some principles in his nature, which interest him in the fortune of others, and render their happiness necessary, though he derives nothing from it except the pleasure of seeing it."[35] Both sentiments are powerful and operate as guides to human conduct, including conduct in political economy. Self-interest as a motive is complemented by a countervailing natural motive, sympathy. It is the power of this latter motive that inspires humans to undertake altruistic projects of benevolence. Self-interest guarantees survival; mutual sympathy "guarantees both the morality of human actions, together with social order and cohesion,"[36] in society generally and in political economy especially. Smith seems to have calculated that these two natural sentiments, self-interest and sympathy, left to their own devises, independent of political coercion, will generate economic equity. Indeed he suggests at times that not only benevolence but self-interest itself will promote the public interest. Every individual in laboring "neither intends to promote the publick interest, nor knows how much he is promoting it. . . . [H]e intends only his own security; and by directing that industry in such a manner as its produce may be of the greatest value, he intends only his own gain, and he is in this, as in many other cases, led by an invisible hand to promote an end which was no part of his intention."[37]

This expectation, that self-interest entails a law of unintended consequences, that it will somehow unintentionally promote the public good, it turns out, was a miscalculation, as even Smith eventually admits. Not long before his death in 1790 he famously revised (Sixth Edition) his *The Theory of Moral Sentiments* with an eye to retrieving the virtues of altruistic benevolence in economics, but without at the same time re-establishing it. He continues to hold that economics itself is primarily if not exclusively a matter of science and social analysis (division of labor, reciprocal self-interest, competition, free markets and exchange, government deregulation of mercantilism), in hope that the natural, private motive of sympathy and the unintended benevolence from self-interest would counterbalance emerging economic inequalities and deprivations. Most scholars now agree[38] that Smith did not envision laissez-faire economics as the sort of raw, untamed, amoral beast the tradition he helped originate tends toward; nevertheless the reciprocal self-interest, upon which his commercial society depends, denies that it is:

> from the benevolence of the butcher, the brewer, or the baker, that we expect our dinner, but from their regard to their own interest. We address ourselves, not to their humanity but to their self-love, and never talk to them of our own necessities but their advantages. Nobody but a beggar chuses to depend chiefly upon the benevolence of his fellow-citizens.[39]

Disciples often traduce the message of the master; and the Capitalist heirs of Smith are no exception. They paid precious little attention to the fact that in this early section of *The Wealth of Nations* Smith is addressing the production and exchange of goods (commutative justice) and not their egalitarian distribution (distributive justice). This contrast is one Smith makes in *The Theory of Moral Sentiments*,[40] where commutative justice belongs to a science of social analysis and distributive justice (benevolence) belongs to "the domain of private virtue."[41] In other words, just as religion disestablished is a matter of private virtue so too, Smith argues, benevolence (distributive justice) disestablished should be private and personal, and yet it should still be.

There are a variety of scholarly interpretations of this distinction, but the point to which I want to draw attention is Smith's tendency to assign different jurisdictions: public and political for the one (commutative, liberal justice) and personal and private for the other (distributive justice, benevolence). Allocating values among public and private spheres in this way is really a function of his argument for the disestablishment of religion, which implies the disestablishment of those virtues distinctively belonging to religion, namely, benevolence, charity, generosity and the like. With Verburg, I agree that the status of benevolence as distributive justice, both in *The Theory of Moral Sentiments* and *The Wealth of Nations,* is finally something more than a mere "ornament which embellishes," although this is how Smith refers to it in the former work.[42] He does insist that benevolence is "less essential to the existence of society than justice. Society may subsist, though not in the most comfortable state, without beneficence; but the prevalence of injustice must utterly destroy it." Hence, "though nature exhorts mankind to acts of beneficence, . . . it is . . . not the foundation which supports the building, and which it was, therefore, sufficient to recommend, but by no means necessary to impose."[43] Smith assumes, furthermore, the interdependence of benevolence and religion, in *The Wealth of Nations*, and concludes that concomitant with the disestablishment of religion benevolence is rightfully disestablished, along with all the arts. Quoting Hume, Smith argues that religion and benevolence, like "the arts and professions in a state . . . are of such a nature, that, while they promote the interests of the society, they are also useful or agreeable to some individuals; and in that case, the constant rule of the magistrate . . . is to leave the profession to itself, and to trust its encouragement to the individuals who reap the benefit of it."[44] Benevolence and distributive justice, like art and religion, should not be publicly imposed like matters of commutative justice; instead, the great benefits to society of both religion and benevolence manifest themselves best when left to those private individuals and communities who find them agreeable. This is not to infer, as some are wont to do, that for Smith religion and benevolence are unimportant to politics and economics, but that the practice of them and their benefits to society are likely to be much greater if they are disestablished and free of political coercion. But after several centuries of disestablishment, it is clear that sympathy and benevolence, although natural human capacities, are not necessarily automatic human responses to human need, and that in disestablishing benevolence politics and economics naturally default to gross self-interest and greed and not to the fair and equal distribution of goods.

Nevertheless, not only did Smith consider self-interest a natural motive of production benefiting the public good, he also considered sympathy a natural capacity and sentiment that if disestablished would inevitably freely distribute social and economic goods. Both forces, self-interest and benevolence, should always be "free"; neither can nor should be "extorted by force," by government.[45] Here again we see from Smith the alienation of justice and beneficence in a way that parallels the alienation of state and religion. Justice (commutative), Smith argues, is a virtue that should not be "left to the freedom of our own wills" but should be "extorted by force, and of which the violation exposes to resentment, and consequently to punishment." Why justice? Why should justice be fairly "extorted" by governments and not benevolence? Justice, because "the violation of justice is injury; it does real and positive hurt. . . . It is, therefore, the proper object of resentment, and of punishment. . . ." In contrast, Smith insists that benevolence (distributive justice) should not be "extorted by force" because "the mere want of it exposes to no [resentment or] punishment; because the mere want of beneficence tends to do no real positive evil. It may disappoint of the good which might reasonably have been expected, and upon account it may justly excite dislike and disapprobation: it cannot, however, provoke any resentment which mankind will go along with."[46] Although Smith "did not teach the ubiquity of self-interest,"[47] and although he dissents vigorously from Hume's indifference to distributive justice,[48] and although he increasingly emphasizes the importance of benevolence for distributive concerns, especially in his revisions to *The Theory of Moral Sentiments*; and although, as Verburg notes, Smith "claimed distributional outcomes of the market process bear upon the moral and economic validity of commercial society,"[49] still, I take issue with Smith's analysis of and reasons for the disestablishment of benevolence, namely, that "want of it" does no direct and immediate harm and "exposes to no punishment," and "tends to do no real positive evil."

Counterexamples are not hard to come by. In his own lifetime Smith was aware of and tried to revise his work in light of them. In our own day counterexamples are glaring and disturbing; the disestablishment of benevolence does do "real and positive" harm and elicits resentment. The 99 percent movement in the United States (in 2011–2013) is a collective sigh of persons economically oppressed and marginalized by the wealthy 1 percent of the population. The U.S. Census Bureau declared that in 2010, 15.1 percent of the general population lives in poverty: 9.9 percent of all non-Hispanic white persons; 12.1 percent of all Asian persons; 26.6 percent of all Hispanic persons; and 27.4 percent of all black persons, and this in the wealthiest Capitalist country in the world. So, although wealth may be generated by free enterprise, at the same time, when it is alienated from benevolence as a public virtue, it is not justly distributed by forces of self-interest and invisible hand, and indeed it does real, positive evil and harm to people.

DISESTABLISHING BENEVOLENCE: JEFFERSON AND MADISON

In much of colonial America, as in Imperial Britain, benevolence and economics were established along with religion. In Virginia, for example, the Church of England was established, as was its benevolence and economics. This meant that local taxes were collected and filtered through local parish vestries for the purpose of meeting the needs of local governments. Not only were they used to pay the salary of the parish priest but, as in England, they were used to build roads and provide relief to the poor. Jefferson and Madison both were critical of this establishment model and were accordingly receptive to ideas critiquing it, including the writings of Locke and Smith, whose impact on them, as it turns out, was considerable.

The widely acknowledged weight of Locke's views is reflected, for example, in founding documents. Madison's "Memory and Remonstrance," for example, and Jefferson's "Act for Establishing Religious Freedom" shaped why and how religion was disestablished in the United States. My purpose here is not to trace their familiar arguments for disestablishment, for religious freedom and tolerance; they parallel quite closely Locke and Smith's ways of arguing. Instead, I want to show from these documents the concomitant disestablishment of virtues like benevolence.

Locke's influence on Madison and Jefferson was substantial.[50] The occasion for Madison's "Remonstrance" (1785) is a rejoinder to a Bill introduced into the Virginia House of Delegates providing for the legal and civil support of Teachers of the Christian Religion (1784–1785). Although Madison's primary concern is separating state from religion, he does address incidentally the different virtues belonging to each in a way that parallels Locke. The state is concerned with commutative justice, with "the liberties, the prosperity, and the happiness of the Commonwealth" and is armed with the "force of law." To religion, on the other hand, belongs benevolence, such things as "forbearance, love, and charity," which are subject to "the dictates of conscience" as private judgments and not "as an engine of civil policy." In other words, Madison allocates public, civic values (justice) to the jurisdiction of politics, which accordingly are subject to the "force of law"; and he allocates personal, private virtues (benevolence, charity, love, distributive justice) to a private jurisdiction which along with religion, now disestablished, are not subject to the "force of law."

This public/private allocation of values not only reflects Locke's vision but also impacts Jefferson's "Act for Establishing Religious Freedom" (1779, 1786).[51] The famous Prologue to Jefferson's "Act" insists that since God has created the mind of humans free and since religion is a function of mind it is properly "exalt[ed]" and influenced by "reason alone" and not by "temporal punishments, or burthens, or by civil incapacitations," so that no human or authority is permitted to "propagate [religion] by coercions on either [body and mind]. . . ." One example Jefferson offers of tyrannical authority in regards to religion is the practice of "compel[ling] a man to furnish contributions of money for the propagation of opinions which he disbelieves and abhors. . . ." A familiar refrain: that the beliefs and values of religion, and by implication the virtues of benevolence prompted by religion and clergy, are matters of mind and conscience, and should be disestablished; as such they are properly susceptible only to persuasive and not to coercive forces, and therefore properly independent of politics and public life. Indeed, toward the end of his "Act for Establishing Religious Freedom," Jefferson insists that the persuasive power of Truth and not political coercion is a better defense against error and corruption; so that the beliefs and values of religion, insofar as they are true, will inevitably prevail if disestablished and left to the free range of thought.

Less well-known is Smith's influence on the American Founders. "Despite all the recent scholarship on the impact of Scottish thought on the American founding," says Samuel Fleischacker, "curiously little attention has been paid to the influence of Adam Smith." Scholars have argued, if sometimes spaciously, for the influence of Hutcheson on Jefferson, Hume on Madison, and Reid on James Wilson. "Yet, it is well-known that Smith was extremely interested in America, and there is good evidence that many of the Founders, including Jefferson, Madison, and Wilson [among others], were reading his work . . . [and] indeed . . . were among the earliest readers of Smith's *Wealth of Nations*." Consider, for example, that "a specific connection between Smith and *Federalist* No. 10, clarifies the role Madison saw for society, as opposed to government, in shaping individual behavior. There are also a number of other resonances between Smith's views on virtue and how to foster it and the views of his American readers."[52] Like Smith (as noted in passages above from *The Wealth of Nations*), Madison argues (in *Federalist* No. 10) that a disestablished, competitive religious and sectarian marketplace, independent of governmental coercion, is most beneficial for inhibiting the tendencies of factions and religious sects to do violence and injustice toward others and other factions. If a nation embraces "a greater variety of parties and interests; you make it less probable that a majority of the whole will have a common motive to invade the rights of other citizens. . . . A religious sect may degenerate into a political faction in a part of the Confederacy; but the variety of sects dispersed over the entire face of it must secure the national councils against any danger from that source."[53] Madison is echoing Smith, who argues that "The interested and active zeal of religious teachers can be dangerous or troublesome only when there is, either but one sect tolerated in that society, or where the whole of a large society is divided into two or three great sects; . . . But that zeal must be altogether innocent where the society is divided into two or three hundred, or perhaps into as many as a thousand small sects, of which no *one* could be considerable enough to disturb the public tranquility." The beneficial social effects produced by this open marketplace of religious sects is toleration or, as Smith puts it, the virtues of "candour and moderation," "respect" for other sects, and mutual "concessions" with one another.[54]

The point I want to make is that for both Smith and Madison a disestablishment of certain benevolent virtues is concomitant with the disestablishment of religion; and it is no business of government to "extort by force" the common good produced by practicing virtues of prudence, tolerance, and mutual respect. Indeed, the disestablishment of benevolence is an occasion for spontaneous "natural sympathy" and "good temper,"[55] Smith would say, so that what is withdrawn as a public project is retrieved as a private one. Madison seems especially to agree. He opposes benevolence as a public virtue, as a power enumerated and granted to the federal government. A question arose in 1794, at the time of the Haitian revolution, regarding government funds for supporting French refugees. Madison famously replies that "I cannot undertake to lay my finger on that article of the Constitution which granted a right to Congress of expending, on objects of benevolence, the money of their constituents."[56] Although Madison might concede such powers of benevolence to the states, he is clear that they are not enumerated and as such no business of the federal government. So, along with the disestablishment of religion there is, among some founders at least, a tendency toward disestablishing benevolence as well.

Modern philosophers in Europe and American were generally successful in arguing for disestablishing religion and along with it disestablishing economics and benevolence. The impact of philosopher's like Locke and Smith, Madison and Jefferson, at least partially accounts for the fact that in 1500 in Western societies it was virtually impossible not to believe in benevolence as a public and political virtue, while in 2014, at least in America, it is difficult for many to believe in its (re)establishment.

RE-ESTABLISHING BENEVOLENCE

It is of some urgency that we find ways of re-establishing officially into public and political life policies and practices of benevolence and egalitarian justice, and this without forsaking a constitutional commitment to disestablishing religion. However, given the treacherous history of politics and religion, some will find such a proposal dangerous if not highly improbable. Others are so far enticed by dogmatic, laissez-faire ideology that any modification, including re-establishing benevolence, is simple betrayal. My sense, however, is that if civility in society is to triumph over barbarity, justice over injustice, and sympathy over self-interest, then re-enfranchising benevolence into political and economic life is of some urgency. What I sketch here is an outline of an argument that in the remaining chapters I develop and defend in greater detail. What I hope finally to show is that disestablishing benevolence from politics and economics, is ill conceived and its impact positively harmful; and that benevolence, especially in its form as egalitarian economic justice, is essential to extinguishing injustice and oppression and to sustaining civil society.

Benevolence as a public virtue is essential, then, for sustaining a just world, a world in which humans are valued enough to grant and guarantee all with a sustainable livelihood. Many today, whether religious or not, uncritically assume that the disestablishment of benevolence from liberal politics and economics constitutes "the best of all possible worlds," or at least the most efficient. The ubiquity of this assumption in the United States is a tribute to the persuasive power of Locke, Smith, Madison, and others who helped shape modern democracy and free market economics. That benevolence was disestablished concomitantly with religion and economics makes its re-establishment more formidable. The fact that especially religion and benevolence have been intricately linked historically and logically, makes it difficult to envision re-establishing the one (benevolence) without establishing the other (religion). In succeeding chapters I intend to show that and how this is nevertheless possible and on what basis. Indeed, I show that and how the private practice of religion is crucial to the public re-establishment and practice of benevolence. But for now I first critique Locke and Smith in order to clear space for making such an argument, and secondly, in chapter 3, outline the general nature of my argument by drawing on suggestions made by Hume and Mill that provide philosophical and moral footing for re-enfranchising benevolence in public life.

John Locke's treatment of political and economic matters is mixed in terms of benevolence. He seems at times favorable to establishing benevolence. In his *Second Treatise* he identifies a law of nature that is binding on humans not only in the state of nature but in political society: "Every one, as he is bound to preserve himself and not to quit his station willfully, so by the like reason, when his own preservation comes not in competition, ought he, as much as he can, to preserve the rest of mankind, and may not, unless it be to do justice to an offender, take away or impair the life, or what tends to the preservation of life: the liberty, health, limb, or goods of another."[57] Locke here seems to advocate not only a duty not to injure or "harm" others in securing for themselves a sustainable livelihood, but also the positive good of benevolence, of helping others preserve a sustainable livelihood for themselves. Similarly, when speaking of "property" Locke seems to draw, at least in the context of an agrarian economy, a boundary to self-interested appropriation, arguing that a human has a right to whatever he "mixes" his labor with, "but not a right to more than he needs to sustain his life, with the remainder left in common for others."[58] In other words, one can appropriate "as much as any one can make use of to any advantage of life before it spoils, so much as he may by his labor fix a property in; whatever is beyond this is more than his share, and belongs to others."[59] For Locke self-interested and unlimited accumulation of property violates both the natural boundary of a person's own entitlement as well as infringes the entitlement of others to that property, insofar as others have need for a sustainable livelihood. Hence, in the context of an agrarian commerce, Locke insists on benevolence, both by limiting the appropriation of material goods to what is needed to preserve life, and by helping others in preserving and sustaining a livelihood for themselves.

But what Locke gives with one hand he takes with the other. The "moderate proportion" that agrarian humans have a right to appropriate no longer holds for modern, industrial humans, who with the invention of money are liberated from "moderate proportion" and "by consent" are permitted "larger possessions and a right to them."[60] Indeed, modern persons, although politically constrained by the rights of others, are no longer economically constrained by the needs of others; they have a right to as much money and wealth as they can appropriate, according to Locke, because it violates neither the natural economic limit of "spoilage" nor the political limit of "the rights of others"; for money may be "hoarded up without injury to anyone, these metals [gold and silver] not spoiling or decaying in the hands of the possessor."[61] Since appropriating vast wealth in money does not harm others, humans have a right to it. In short, although Locke at first seems to make a place for benevolence in agrarian life, in the end he seems to forfeit it in modern life to a kind of "possessive individualism"[62] that foreshadows Smith's unrestrained, self-interested motive and matrix for liberal economics.

Adam Smith, of course, did not advocate "the ubiquity of self-interest," as many today seem to believe, to the exclusion of virtue. Nor did he believe that benevolence and distributive justice and charity were unimportant in political and economic life. His final edition to *The Theory of Moral Sentiments* (1790), as already noted, shows his increasing concern for the role of benevolence and distributive justice in economic life.[63] He did acknowledge, as Verburg puts it, that "the folly and vice involved in the pursuit of wealth and greatness stand counterpoised to man's moral sentiments, whereby man is induced to restrain his selfish impulses. . . ."[64] And yet Smith, and certainly the trajectory of the free market tradition he helped foster, never acclimates itself to the notion of benevolence and distributive justice as an official, compelling obligation of public life. He regularly attacks "the ideal of civic virtue" and recommends its disestablishment to the "private" sphere. Consistently suspicious of those advocating public virtue and benevolence, he asserts, in a familiar albeit anecdotal way that "I have never known much good done by those who affected trade for the publick good."[65]

Granting Smith's concern for benevolence and distributive justice, including his concern for addressing the needs of the poor, and granting his argument for their disestablishment as matters best regulated naturally, by "mutual sympathy" and "invisible hand," I would like to take Smith to task over three issues: the notion of "natural sympathy," the nature of benevolence as a private not public virtue, and his view that the absence of benevolence from public life does no positive harm. Doing so is necessary in order to clear ground for re-establishing benevolence.

1. "Natural sympathy" and "mutual sympathy" are crucial to Smith's thought in both *The Theory of Moral Sentiments* and in *The Wealth of Nations*. Part I of *Moral Sentiments* begins with sympathy as "natural" and "mutual," as a primary social sentiment that helps civilize society. It is the primary "natural" constraint and countervailing force to self-love and self-interest. Smith's notion of natural sympathy, of course, is something quite other than the ubiquitous "invisible hand,"[66] which is a force that he surmises promotes an end and common good unintended by self-interest. At least two difficulties plague Smith's notion of natural sympathy.

First, Smith's tendency to conflate the words "natural" and "sympathy"[67] renders the phrase "natural sympathy" ambiguous and misleading. He insists that an "invisible hand" will necessarily and sufficiently distribute goods and wealth; that even self-interested humans will automatically, naturally, and mutually show concern for the welfare of others. He assumes that "sympathy" as "natural" is an automatic human reflex, as involuntary and inevitable as any other instinct, such as blinking. Indeed, *The Theory of Moral Sentiments* begins: "How selfish soever man may be supposed, there are evidently some principles in his nature, which interests him in the fortunes of others. . . ." Yet, Smith fails to distinguish the "capacity" for sympathy as "natural" from the sympathetic sentiments that move people to actually practice it. What is natural to humans is the capacity for sympathy; what is not natural, or at least not inevitable, are sympathetic sentiments and actions. The practice of sympathy is an intentional, volitional activity, and Smith's failure to attend to this distinction between capacity and praxis, faculty and volition, precipitates a profligate estimation of human and social progress. This failure, common to Enlightenment thinkers, results not only from an overestimation of the power of natural reason and sympathy to order social relations morally, but also from insufficient attention to human will and especially its power to suppress and nullify a natural capacity and succumb to a fallen, selfish indifference to others. Besides reason and sentiments, human will is a powerful variable in social analysis; it allows fallen humanity, individually or collectively, to preempt or nullify or counteract occasions for sympathy, even though the capacity to do so may be natural.

True, Smith is not without a significant view of the capacity of humans for corruption. He examines, for example, at least two causes of corruption, one external and the other internal: "Not only the prejudices of the publick," are corrupt, "but what is more unconquerable, the private interests of many individuals, irresistibly opposed to [justice, natural liberty, and sympathy]."[68] Human corruption arises externally from public prejudices as manifestations of class distinctions and preferences; it arises internally from the private self-interests of individuals whose capacity for altruistic interest is severely limited, as illustrated famously by Smith's China tragedy.[69] But as keen and compelling as Smith's analysis of human nature and society sometimes is, he nevertheless subscribes to Enlightenment beliefs that more than two centuries later seem naïvely optimistic if not simply superstitious.[70] He tends to subscribe, for example, to a benign view of human nature, common among his peers (including Hume and Rousseau) that altruism and morality generally (e.g., "natural liberty and sympathy") will manifest itself so long as people are permitted to be natural, that is, so long as religion or society or political authority does not interfere and corrupt with intolerance and persecution: "All systems either of preference or of restraint . . . being thus completely taken away, the obvious and simple system of natural liberty establishes itself on its own accord."[71]

Smith's keen analysis of excessive self-interest as a force for corruption correlates to the religious notion of pride; but his valuation of prideful self-interest diverges sharply from religious valuations. This casts suspicion on Smith and his law of unintended consequences and makes it susceptible to the *fallacy of self-interest*. There is no reason to believe, and Smith gives no supporting empirical or statistical evidence, that the human instinct to always act out of self-interest results, as he insists, in some reflexive "interest in the fortune of others." Because there is no available empirical link or inference between the two, between egoism and altruism, Smith concocts the alchemy of an "invisible hand" that conjures, he surmises, altruism out of selfish interest.[72] This is not to say a person cannot be both simultaneously self-interested and altruistic; only that there is no evidence that the former somehow engenders, whether inadvertently or intentionally or "invisibly," the latter. Beneficent altruism is a conscious, intentional volition on the part of agents, not an incidental, "invisible" by-product of excessive self-interestedness. But since Smith pays little attention to the "Fallen Order," human volition and the corruption of human will and nature, he uncharacteristically succumbs to a "superstitious" belief in an "invisible hand," a belief that conveniently fills the gap between self-interest and benevolence, between my own fortune and the fortunes of others. The actual historical development of laissez faire economics, it seems to me, is itself evidence to the contrary.

A view more consistent with empirical reality and biblical narratives must take more seriously than does Smith the fallenness of human nature and the damaging reach of its corruption. Self-love and self-interest, about which Smith speaks a great deal, result from pride. Left to its own devices moral entropy predicts that the self-interestedness of pride will inevitably reproduce itself in kind and its momentum energize not benevolence, as Smith insists, but progressively acute and expansive forms of self-interest and moral decay. The power of pride's moral entropy is subverted and reversed only by the power of moral integrity, only by the superior power of will that intentionally undertakes in private and public life projects of benevolence and good will. A more apt image than "invisible hand" for Smith's self-interested, free market economics is of a black hole from whose centripetal egoistic force of pride little escapes that promotes public interest and common good. The moral and social order, if there is to be any at all, does not and can not arise not from unintentional and inadvertent acts of selfishness; unrestrained self-interestedness creates the problem, creates moral and social disorder; it does not and cannot contribute to its solution. Indeed, the entropy of self-interested moral decay is arrested and reversed, I shall argue, only by the radical, asymmetrical, intentional power of merciful benevolence. Hence, neither the capacity for natural sympathy nor the centripetal force of self-interest can fairly distribute, as Smith hopes, social and economic goods.

2. Little doubt among scholars remains, however, of Smith's growing attention throughout his life to benevolence and distributive justice as crucial for countering passions of self-interest and for establishing moral order. The revisions he made in the sixth edition of *The Theory of Moral Sentiments* demonstrate this,[73] and indicate a trajectory in Smith's thinking that finds its most satisfactory fulfillment not in his own political economy but in that of philosophers like J. S. Mill. Yet, for all his willingness to amend his views, Smith always insisted on benevolence as a strictly private and personal virtue and not a public, political one. Smith's argument for disestablishing benevolence, along with religion, is less than persuasive. Smith is correct in arguing that benevolence is a virtue necessary to counteract the impulses of self-interest and fulfill a social need. But for him the human capacity for mutual sympathy, distributive justice and benevolence is limited primarily to personal, private relations. "Distance," proximity or remoteness, is crucial to the human capacity to sympathize with and show benevolence to others. As

Smith shows in his "China tragedy," the death of thousands in distant China would not affect him with the same power and intensity as "The most frivolous disaster which could befall himself . . . if he was to lose his little finger tomorrow. . . ."[74] The value of sympathy and benevolence is local; they are virtues, as Fleischacker puts it, "that encouraged individuals to care about the good of others whom they knew and sympathized with. . . . [S]ympathy worked primarily in relation to particular individuals, whose situations were known intimately." Sympathy and benevolence cannot and should not be politically coerced virtues, in other words, since "nature had not equipped [individuals] to understand or feel strongly about the good of anonymous others." Benevolence is properly, then, a free and not a coerced public virtue, since it is "directed pragmatically toward friends, relatives, and close neighbors."[75] Indeed, Smith argues that it is more likely that a person will "prevail" and get what they want from others, from society, not so much by soliciting their benevolence but by soliciting "their self-love in his favour, and shew[ing] them that it is for their own advantage to do for him what he requires of them."[76] The free, invisible hand resulting from self-interest, in other words, is more likely to distribute social and economic goods fairly than any benevolent public and political policies. In opposition, I argue that sympathy (compassion) and benevolence (distributive justice) are indispensable to establishing a morally just and fair society and that, accordingly, they should be established politically as a matter of public policy. The human capacity and practice of sympathy and benevolence from a distance is far greater, I believe, than Smith gives credit; perhaps because of technology the "distance" between people today is far less than Smith could ever imagine is his day. Even though practicing sympathy and benevolence is not inevitable, the power of philosophies and religions to persuade communities and nations to solicit benevolence from citizens and distribute goods to remote anonymous others is substantial and, I will argue, should be practiced as public policy.

3. Finally, I take issue with Smith's view that since the absence of benevolence does no "positive" harm or injury, it should not be coerced as a public virtue. I have noted already his view: "Beneficence is always free, it cannot be extorted by force, the mere want of it exposes to no punishment; because the mere want of beneficence tends to no real positive evil." The person who refuses to show beneficence "does no positive hurt to any body."[77] American common law especially views Smith's argument favorably; it advocates a similar "no duty to act" tradition, an issue which I address in the next chapter. But there are at least two bases for objecting to Smith's view—empirical and moral.

Empirically, if we take "positive evil" or "hurt" to mean direct, real, and actual harm or injury to one's person and livelihood, then the disestablishment of benevolence more than qualifies; the inevitable result is direct and positive harm. When absence of benevolence results in hunger, homelessness, poverty, illness, depression, crime, and so on, that harm is direct, substantive, and personal; and permitting them when resources are available constitutes real positive evil. For example, when benevolence could provide the medical care a mother needs to sustain a healthy pregnancy and infant, and when the absence of public policy fails to provide that care and undermines the health and/or life of that mother and infant, then direct and actual positive harm is done to the mother and infant. The poverty rate in the United States (15.1 percent as noted earlier), let alone poverty rates in the global economy, indicates that real harm and positive evil results from economies spurred primarily by self-interest and not by policies of benevolence. Secondly, there is a moral objection to Smith's view, especially if we take him at his word when he insists that humans have a right to a sustainable livelihood: "A man must always live by his work, and his wages must at least be sufficient to maintain him. They must even upon most occasions be somewhat more; otherwise it would be impossible for him to bring up a family."[78] Thus, when a person's labor or lack of labor is insufficient to provide a sustainable livelihood, benevolent public policy is morally obligated to do so. Any society that does not do so forsakes its aim of preserving social and moral order and forfeits its moral integrity to the vicissitudes of self-interest. Indeed, that society has yet to evolve in consciousness and character from preoccupation with liberal justice to patterns and policies of benevolence without which moral and social order is impossible. When a person's free exercise of religion is infringed it can be "extorted by force," as Smith puts it. Indeed, sustainable livelihood, survival, is the most fundamental condition of being human, and to collectively and publically neglect it is morally reprehensible.

In opposition to Smith and the vendors of free-market economics, I will argue: 1) that in a fallen world sympathy (compassion) is not an inevitable, natural human reflex to the self-interestedness of the free-market; nor is there an invisible hand that somehow from the power of self-interest promotes inadvertently the public interest. Instead the moral integrity and intention of benevolence as a public virtue is required; 2) that "distance" from anonymous, suffering others is for sympathetic benevolence not the obstacle Smith alleges; that sympathy can and should be as much an intentional public, political virtue as it is a private, personal one; and 3) that the absence of benevolence causes as much direct and positive evil as Smith insists the absence of justice (injustice) does, and that therefore benevolence is an indispensable political virtue that should be "extorted by force" and made a matter of public policy.

In this chapter I have tried to critique certain moral, political, and economic values that helped shape and re-shape a world that we now call modern. These values arose historically in order to address emerging political and economic conditions that for the most part no longer exist. How successful this liberal, free market project has been is a matter of continuing debate. What is certain, however, is that these liberal values, as originally conceived and practiced at least, are largely bankrupt, powerless to invest the kind of moral capital needed to meet global political and economic needs. In chapter 3 I show how practicing benevolence as a public virtue begins to address some of these demands.

NOTES

1. "Beneficence" and "benevolence" are terms customarily used in the seventeenth and eighteenth centuries to refer to a constellation of public virtues, including charity, love, sympathy, compassion, mercy, that were desirable and beneficial to society but not officially and legally mandated. These virtues were typically distinguished from "justice," a political virtue that governments mandated in order to secure political and social order. Especially British thinkers like Locke, Hutchinson, Hume, and Smith were fond of these terms and this distinction.

2. Prentiss L. Pemberton and Daniel R. Finn, *Toward a Christian Economic Ethic: Stewardship and Social Power* (Minneapolis, MN: Winston Press, Inc., 1985), 39.

3. See Thomas Aquinas, *Summa Theologica*, II–II, Q. 66; aa. 1–7. Aquinas distinguishes between "theft" (secretly taken), "robbery" (violently taken), and "stealing" (rightfully taken, out of need). See especially a. 7.

4. In this section of the *Summa Theologica*, Aquinas discusses and replies to Objections from the likes of Aristotle, Ambrose, Basil, and Augustine, and draws liberally on Scripture to support his case.

5. I am in agreement with Gertrude Himmelfarb and others who argue that there was no such monolithic thing as "the Enlightenment," but rather overlapping and variable "enlightenments." In *The Roads to Modernity: The British, the French, and the American Enlightenments* (New York: Vintage Books, 2005), she distinguishes French, British, and American enlightenments.

6. Helen Gilbert and Chris Tiffin, eds., *Burden or Benefits? Imperial Benevolence and Its Legacies* (Bloomington, IN: Indiana University Press, 2008).

7. *Ibid.*, 7.

8. Chris Tiffin, "Benevolence, Slavery, and the Periodicals," in *Burden or Benefit?*, 70.

9. Leigh Dale, "'This Nineteenth Century of Progress and Humanity': The Life and Times of Frederick Weld," in *Burden or Benefit*? 80.

10. Amartya Sen, in his "Introduction" to Adam Smith's *The Theory of Moral Sentiments* (New York: Penguin Books, 2009), draws a bold contrast between the Social Contract, or what he calls "transcendental institutionalism," tradition of democracy that includes Hobbes, Locke, Rousseau, Kant, and Rawls, and which envisions justice from a state of nature or veil of ignorance; and the "comparative realization" tradition that includes Smith, Condorcet, Bentham, Wollstonecraft, Marx, and Mill, and which determines justice more nearly in terms of a third party "impartial spectator."

11. See Charles Taylor's *A Secular Age* (Cambridge, MA: Belknap Press of Harvard University Press, 2007). See especially pages 75–81. See also Pemberton and Finn, *Toward a Christian Economic Ethic*, chapters 2 and 3.

12. *Ibid.*, 76.

13. The 1648 Treaty of Osnabruck, part of the Peace of Westphalia, specified three types of worship: "domestic devotion," *executum religionis publicum*, and *executum religionis privatum*, thereby tolerating private, family or individual devotion.

14. Locke, *A Letter Concerning Toleration* (Indianapolis, IN: Bobbs-Merrill Company, Inc., 9th Printing, 1975), 13. Locke wrote this *Letter* in Latin; it was translated into English by William Popple in 1689. It is well-known that for Locke religious toleration was not entirely

absolute. Toward the end of his *Letter* he discusses at least four (pp. 50–62) exceptions to toleration, including those whose beliefs jeopardize the interests of civil society, those who are intolerant, those who are subject to foreign powers (Catholics, Mohammedans), and atheists.

15. *Ibid.*, 17–19.
16. *Ibid.*, 13.
17. *Ibid.*, 16–17.
18. *Ibid.*, 14.
19. *Ibid.*, 34–46.
20. *Ibid.*, 17.
21. *Ibid.*, 17.
22. *Ibid.*, 47, 48.
23. *Ibid.*, 46–47.
24. *Ibid.*, 46.
25. *Ibid.*, 28.
26. *Ibid.*, 58–59; see also 27.
27. *Ibid.*, 46.
28. Recent scholarship is demonstrating quite conclusively, I think, that Smith's argument regarding the science of economics in *The Wealth of Nations* (1776) should be interpreted in the context of his argument in *The Theory of Moral Sentiments* (1759, 1790), such that the so-called "separation thesis," that the moral principle or virtue is and should be subordinate to the social principle or social science, is largely discredited and that Smith regarded virtue as playing a vital role both in economics and political. See, for example, Andrew Abela's "Adam Smith and the Separation Thesis," in *Business and Society Review* (2001) 106:3, 187–199; and Ryan Patrick Hanley's *Adam Smith and the Character of Virtue* (Cambridge: Cambridge University Press, 2009).
29. See fn5.
30. David Hume, *The History of England: From the Invasion of Julius Caesar to the Revolution of 1688* (Philadelphia, PA: McCarty & Davis Pub., 1832), 554–555.
31. Adam Smith, *An Inquiry into the Nature and Causes of the Wealth of Nations* (Oxford: Clarendon Press, 1976) Vol. II. V.i.g.6., 791.
32. *Ibid.*, Vol. II. V.i.g.1., 788.
33. *Ibid.*, Vol. II. V.i.g.1., 789.
34. *Ibid.*; This is Smith's general thrust throughout *Wealth of Nations*, 788–814.
35. Adam Smith, *The Theory of Moral Sentiments* (New York, NY: Penguin Books, 2009), 13.
36. Michel Zouboulakis, "On the Social Nature of Rationality in Adam Smith and John Stuart Mill" (Cahiers d'economie politiqu, Eeditions L'Harmattan, 2005), 53.
37. *Wealth of Nations*, IV.ii.9., 456.
38. See, for example, Ryan P. Hanley's argument in *Adam Smith and the Character of Virtue* (London: Cambridge University Press, 2009); or Rudi Verburg in "Adam Smith's growing concern on the issue of distributive justice," *European Journal of the History of Economic Thought* (Spring 2000), 7:1, 23–44.
39. Adam Smith, *An Inquiry into the Nature and Causes of the Wealth of Nations* (Oxford: Clarendon Press, 1976), I.ii.2., 26–27.
40. Adam Smith, *The Theory of Moral Sentiments* (New York: Penguin Books, 2009), VII.ii.1., 320–321.
41. See Rudi Verburg's discussion in "Adam Smith's Growing Concern on the Issue of Distributive Justice," in *European Journal of the History of Economic Thought* (Spring 2000), 7:1, 23–44.
42. *Theory of Moral Sentiments*, II.iii., 104.
43. *Ibid.*, 104.
44. *The Wealth of Nations*, V.i.g.3., 790.
45. *Theory of Moral Sentiments*, II.ii.1., 95.
46. *Ibid.*, 94–95.
47. Samuel Fleischacker, "Adam Smith's Reception among the American Founders, 1776–1790," *William and Mary Quarterly*, Vol. 59, No. 4 (October 2002), 897–924, 916.

48. Verburg, 25; Verburg notes that in "section 2" of *The Theory of Moral Sentiments* "Hume's theory of justice is briefly recapitulated," namely, that "wealth and virtue advance together with the civilization of society, irrespective of rules, and arrangements of distribution." Indeed, says Verburg, "Smith considered Hume's indifference to the issue of distributive justice far from justified."

49. *Ibid.*, 25.

50. I should note, to begin with, however, the role of Roger Williams, founder of Providence. Williams' life spanned most of the seventeenth century, overlapping the lives of Hobbes and Locke. His arguments for the separation of church and state and for religious freedom were largely theological and ecclesiastical and not philosophical. He argues, for example, that religion and not government should have authority over the First Table of the Decalogue and that government should ground itself on "a covenant without God." This immediately put him at odds with John Winthrop and the founders of the Commonwealth of Massachusetts. For Williams, separation benefits both church and state; each gaining stability and strength independent of each other. In his great work on religious toleration, W. K. Jordan says that for Williams "Religious toleration promotes the economy of a nation. The history of Holland has demonstrated this as axiomatic. . . . [It] has been the strongest citadel of religious toleration, [and] has reaped the richest material rewards." And yet, because his arguments were so narrowly theological and ecclesiastical, Williams seems to have influenced the Founders very little regarding the development of religious freedom. As Perry Miller puts it, "he actually exerted little or no influence on institutional developments in America; only after the conception of liberty for all denominations had triumphed on wholly other grounds did Americans look back on Williams and invest him with his ill-fitting halo"; see Perry Miller, *Roger Williams: His Contribution to the American Tradition* (New York: Atheneum, 1962), 29.

51. The Virginia Assembly received this bill in 1779 but did not enact it until 1786, after Madison's "Memorial and Remonstrance" (1785) was accepted. In fact, Jefferson's "Act," having been penned earlier, helped shape Madison's views on church and state.

52. Fleischacker, *Ibid.*, 897.

53. Madison, *Federalist* No. 10.

54. *The Wealth of Nations*, Vol. II, V.i.g.9., 792–793.

55. *Ibid.*, 793.

56. *Annals of Congress*, House of Representatives, 3rd Congress, 1st Session, page 170 (1974-01-10).

57. *The Second Treatise of Civil Government*, II.6., 123.

58. *Ibid.*, V.27., 134.

59. *Ibid.*, V.31., 136.

60. *Ibid.*, V.36., 139.

61. *Ibid.*, V.50., 145. See also V.46., 144.

62. This is a phrase C. B. MacPherson uses in reference to Locke and others in his classic *The Political Theory of Possessive Individualism* (Oxford: Oxford University Press, 1972).

63. See for example I.iii.3. and VI.

64. Verburg, *Ibid.*, 37.

65. *The Wealth of Nations*, 26; see also 456; *The Theory of Moral Sentiments*, 80–90, 227 237. See Fleischacker's discussion in "Adam Smith's Reception among the American Founders, 1776–1790," 916–917.

66. This phrase is used by Smith only twice; once in *The Wealth of Nations*, IV ii 9., and in *The Theory of Moral Sentiments*, IV.i.I.10, in an economic context.

67. "Sympathy," for Smith, is a dimension of human nature that allows for moral conscience and social unity. It is not just "sharing the sorrow of others," but also a "fellow feeling with any passion whatever" from the standpoint of a spectator (*TMS*, I.i.1.5); it energizes "original passions" rendering one person's happiness "necessary" to another's and "naturally" interested "in the fortunes of others," even though deriving "nothing from it except the pleasure of seeing it" (*TMS*, I.i.1.1).

68. *Theory of Moral Sentiments*, IV.ii., 43.

69. *Ibid.*, III.iii., 158–159.

70. See Giovanni Gullaci's discussion of these matters in "On the Moral Conception of the Enlightenment," *Journal of Value Inquiry* 27, (1993), 391–402; see esp., 393–397.

71. *Wealth of Nations*. IV.ix.51., 687.

72. Indeed, recent studies seem to refute Smith's assumption about "an invisible hand" and the altruism of its unintended consequences. See chapter 8 ("Economics as Moral Science") for a discussion of one such study.

73. See Rudi Verburg's discussion of this issue in "Adam Smith's Growing Concern on the Issue of Distributive Justice," *Ibid.*; see esp., 36–40.

74. *Theory of Moral Sentiments*, III.iii., 158.

75. Fleischacker, *Ibid.*, 916.

76. *Wealth of Nations*, I.ii.2., 26.

77. *Theory of Moral Sentiments*, II.I., 95.

78. *Wealth of Nations*, I.viii.15., 85.

Chapter Three

Benevolence as Public Virtue

What is God's and what is Caesar's? Smith, Jefferson and Madison answer decisively: religion, benevolence, and economics are private matters and exclusively God's, while justice as a public virtue belongs jointly to Caesar and God. This is orthodox dogma in the United States: justice established; religion and for the most part benevolence and economics disestablished. Historically, however, an alternative, parallel tradition developed that lays down philosophical conditions on which benevolence might be re-enfranchised as a public virtue. This tradition draws on the likes of Hume, Hamilton, and Mill and reflects, as I will argue, more nearly convictions embedded in biblical narratives. This tradition, however, is not without difficulty; for example, Hume argues for the establishment not only of benevolence but also of religion. The trick and task is to argue, as I do here, with Smith for the disestablishment of religion and to argue with Hume and Mill for the establishment of benevolence. My aim in this chapter is to investigate the philosophical roots of this alternate tradition.

How and why should benevolence be established? Under what conditions is this possible and desirable? What philosophical basis is there for establishing benevolence? In his *Second Treatise*, as already noted, Locke examines a natural, moral foundation for establishing benevolence, even though he is ambivalent about it as a public virtue. Along with freedom and equality, the state of nature, he argues, includes a natural "obligation to mutual love." This obligation includes a law of nature that instructs humans not to harm but to preserve self and others in "life, health, liberty, [and] possessions." Generally for Locke, natural law should be protected and promoted by civil law. Moreover, each human has a natural "property" in her own "person" (rights and liberties), and a property in labor and products of labor, at least as much as one needs for the sake of a sustainable livelihood.[1] Locke's catalogue of natural virtues includes both justice and benevolence. For Locke, which virtues are public and which are private is not as pressing an issue for him as it is for Smith and Hume. And yet Locke does argue that the aim of the social contract, of forming a government, is not only in order to protect and preserve "property" (rights and liberties) but also to practice benevolence, by protecting and preserving as far as possible a sustainable livelihood for others or, as he puts it, "the life, health, liberty, and possessions" of others. Smith, on the other hand, slices the virtues' pie thinly, insisting, as we have seen, that justice qualifies as a public, political virtue whereas benevolence along with religion does not. Why? Because, as already noted, for Smith the absence of benevolence does not result in any positive harm and evil. Hume, in contrast, argues that, along with religion and justice, benevolence also should be established, partly because of the good it does and partly because of the harm resulting from its absence.

Parallel to Smith's "fallacy of self-interest" is a "*fallacy of piety*" wherein Hume and others mistakenly believe that the establishment of religion somehow enhances public morality or at least minimizes harm to it. In contrast to both of these traditions, I argue for one in which religion is disestablished while benevolence is re-enfranchised as a public virtue, as a cornerstone of the "general welfare" which, according to the Constitution of the United States, is a responsibility of the federal government. What is the philosophical basis that makes this possible? What moral foundation might establish benevolence as a public, political virtue?

ESTABLISHING BENEVOLENCE: HUME

In contrast to his friend Adam Smith, David Hume argues for the establishment not only of religion but of benevolence. By advocating the establishment of religion he commits a "fallacy of piety" whereby religion, a properly private matter, is falsely believed to benefit societies that establish it. But by advocating the establishment of benevolence he avoids Smith's "fallacy of self-interest" wherein it is falsely believed that the unintended consequences of self-interest are beneficial to "the general welfare." I have already indicated Hume's reasons for establishing religion, which are perhaps just shy of cynical. He argues for religious establishment so that magistrates can exercise due power over clergy and church and thereby neutralize, or at least minimize, religion's deleterious effects. An established church and clergy, he argues, will more likely favor enlightened thinking, avoid factionalism and concomitant violence, and escape recalcitrant clergy activism by "brib[ing] their indolence."[2] But we can quickly discard Hume's establishment of religion while still endorsing benevolence as a public virtue. One trajectory of the Enlightenment's moral philosophy is humanistic. It argues that although historically morals may be rooted in religion, philosophically and logically they can emerge and flourish on the basis of reason and natural law, independently of religion, even though for many they remain firmly rooted in religious faith. What is equally important to my thesis is to discard Smith's propensity to toss the baby (benevolence) out with the bathwater (religion), and endorse an energetic role for benevolence in public and political life. To do so, I will examine Hume's notions of justice, sympathy, benevolence, and government.

First, Hume's notion of justice revolves around two foci, property and self-interest. Justice originates as a liberal sentiment of self-interest that respects the procedural rules of a system that protects an individual's "property" (i.e., rights and liberties). But justice, he insists, is and should be beneficial not only to the individual but to society as a whole. The need for government distributing goods justly depends on certain conditions obtaining, namely, conditions of moderate scarcity and of limited altruism. If there is little scarcity of goods and if humans are unlimited in their generosity, then conditions are absent under which the need for benevolence arises as a public virtue. Only when conditions of scarcity and limited generosity are present is there a need and demand for the benevolence of distributive justice as a public virtue.[3]

Although self-interest by itself is for Hume a natural sentiment, curiously, he argues that justice as the protection of mutual self-interests is not natural at all but a convention, a social construct, a virtue belonging not to individuals in some hypothetical state of nature but to societies. Protecting the property of a single individual is in fact more proximate to injustice than to justice, he argues, because the protection of a single individual's property, without regard to any other individual's welfare, without regard for the equitable, mutual self-interested protection of others, is morally bankrupt. "Were all society and intercourse cut off between man and man, by the primary intention of the supreme Creator: It seems evident, that so solitary a being would be as much incapable of justice, as of social discourse and conversation."[4] Justice arises only in the context of social units where the common, public interests of all are at stake; where the desire of several individuals for protecting the property of each requires a system of rules that regards the self-interest of each individual simultaneously and equally, as a common and therefore a public benefit. Often individual acts of justice are "contrary to public interest," Hume argues, and "prejudicial to society['s]" benefit as a whole.[5] Imagine, he says, a kindly person who finds and returns a lost fortune to a miser; this act is just and honorable, yet society as a whole is by this single act disadvantaged. Only a whole system of justice, only a structure of institutions that guarantees equal justice to all, only by "a kind of convention or agreement; that is, by a sense of interest, suppos'd to be common to all" can we claim that justice benefits society.[6] Although self-interest is a natural motive for seeking justice, justice is not itself natural; instead, it is constructed as justice only when it is transformed by sympathy into a useful convention, into an institution that benefits the public interest, the interest of the whole, of all citizens.[7] Justice, then, as the protection of the mutual self-interests for the common good is not a natural sentiment, according to Hume, and not the property of individuals in a state of nature, but the property of society, a public virtue.

Secondly, Hume contrasts sympathy as a natural sentiment with self-interest or "self-love." Sympathy cannot be reduced to the motive of self-interest as some of his peers argue. There is "a principle in human nature," namely, sympathy, that is of "such extensive energy," that "the interest of each individual is, in general, so closely connected with that of the community, that those philosophers were excusable, who fancied that all our concern for the public might be resolved into a concern for our own happiness and preservation." Besides Lord Bacon, Hume does not identify the errant philosophers he has in mind, but certainly his friend Adam Smith is one of them, one who is seduced by the strength of self-love, imagining it as "the *experimentum crucis*," an Archimedian point that resolves "any doubt or ambiguity" regarding human motivation. Indeed, for Hume it is an error of moral reason to imagine self-interest as the touchstone and motive of all sentiments, of all virtues and vices, pleasures and displeasures, private or public; it is an error to imagine all of these as no more than "modifications of self-love," modifications of a singular principle in terms of which we must account for every moral sentiment. This mistaken theory, according to Hume, entails the fallacy of self-interest by assuming "a confusion of interests," one that "we must renounce. . . ." Whatever self-love may account for it cannot account for the reality of public affections and virtues and the natural tendency of humans toward fellow-feeling, toward sympathy with others, even those we do not know, and toward acts of benevolence as manifestations of sympathy. Indeed, in sympathy, Hume insists, we have a principle of human nature "which accounts in great part to the origins of morality."[8] As such, sympathy is both natural and normative; as natural it is a sentiment prior to and independent of self-interest; and as normative it constitutes the basis for benevolence as a public virtue.

In contrast to Smith, for whom self-interest is most native and natural, sympathy is for Hume a natural capacity and pervasive in human experience. It is a sentiment prior to, more "vivid and lively" than, self-interest; a sentiment at the origins of morality. Indeed, the arts in particular manifest just how native and natural sympathy is; theater, poetry, narrative, histories, indeed, whatever humans do and wherever they travel they inevitably encounter "human happiness or misery," which "excites in our breast a sympathetic movement of pleasure or uneasiness. In our serious occupations, in our careless amusements, [sympathy] still exerts its active energy."[9] Hume concludes that "natural sympathy" is prior to and so much more basic than self-interest that even the most coldly insensitive and narrowly selfish are not unaffected by human misery and happiness, vice and virtue; even they are moved by "a warm concern for the interests of the species"; even they are capable of "a delicate feeling of all moral distinctions; a strong resentment of injury done to men; a lively approbation of their welfare"[10] that empowers humans to undertake projects of benevolence. For Hume, then, theater, poetry, art, stories, religions, and histories are indispensable to cultivating sympathy as a natural, moral sentiment; this is because adults and children alike naturally identify with characters and events and experiences that they feel are contiguous and in which they can imagine themselves. Recently, Martha Nussbaum has argued similarly, that sympathy and compassion are triggered by "the narrative imagination," by stories and dramas, which draw us sympathetically into the lives of others, into their joys and miseries, into their triumphs and tragedies.[11] Out of this empathetic, intersubjective experience emerges a normative principle and sentiment that inspires acts of compassion and benevolence.

Furthermore, sympathy, Hume argues, is not only natural but normative, not only naturally but normatively at the origins of morality. It is a primal sentiment able to overpower self-interest and persuade even the most indifferent and cold person to a fellow-feeling, to an emotional "contiguity" with others, such that one will feel persuaded to hail the joyful and virtuous and help the miserable and vicious. Sympathy's normative power, although not inevitable, nevertheless lies in its capacity for intersubjectivity, as we might say today; a capacity powerful enough to prevent or prevail over sentiments of self-interest that divide and individuate, powerful enough to produce "the great uniformity" upon which community, nation, and perhaps even global peace are possible: "No quality of human nature is more remarkable, both of itself and in its consequences," insists Hume, "than the propensity we have to sympathize with others, and to receive by communication their inclinations and sentiments, however different from, or even contrary, to our own."[12] The normative quality of sympathy lies in its power to persuade a person, who otherwise is predisposed to self-consciousness and self-interest, to interact with others because of the "vivacity" of their "resemblance and contiguity" with other selves. "We never remark any passion or principle in others of which, in some degree or other, we may not find a parallel in ourselves." Moreover, sympathy is a remarkable sentiment by which the self not only comes to greater understanding of others but also to a greater understanding of one's self.[13] As natural capacity and normative, accordingly, sympathy and its manifestation as benevolence is a moral catalyst of mutual understanding and interest that properly embodies itself in social institutions and public policy as benevolence. At least that is the conclusion Hume seems to draw, as we shall see.

It is perhaps beneficial to pause and appraise Smith's and Hume's views; to measure them against the canon of biblical narratives. In their origin story, goodness, sympathy, and benevolence are portrayed as primary, natural, and native to human creatures, as qualities of *pax Dei*. Indeed, all things are created by God "good." With God's own goodness refracted through *imago Dei*, sympathy and benevolence, as Hume insists, are natural endowments, virtues *sine qua non* of what it means to be human. They are therefore logically prior to humanity's Fall into pride and self-interest, which in the Genesis narratives are portrayed as functions of disobedience. Indeed, self-interest and pride are portrayed as fabricated, artificial human inventions; as the result of errant, unnatural motives; as curses, not as the natural, liberating blessings Smith makes them out to be. By insisting that sympathy and benevolence constitute the normative "origin of morality" Hume is more nearly in line with biblical narratives. The goodness of creation in general and of humans in particular establishes normative expectations of moral agents, of which benevolence is a social expression. In contrast, the self-interestedness on which Smith partly grounds his political economy marginalizes (e.g., from public life) the goodness that is primary in biblical narratives and magnifies the very evil of self-centeredness that those same narratives curse. Whether his views agree or not with biblical narratives is for Hume, of course, a matter of indifference. Nevertheless, for those who claim them these narratives are guides for private and public life. It is of utmost importance that benevolence is depicted by them as rooted in the goodness of God's creation and in the primal, natural, normative sentiment of sympathy. And it is of utmost importance to them that these same narratives depict the self-interestedness of fallenness as incommensurable with the normative expectations of humans as moral agents.

Finally, besides its character as natural and normal, Hume argues for benevolence as a public virtue. It is the primary public virtue whereby civil magistrates maintain social and moral order. Benevolence entails qualities that are "sociable, good natured, humane, merciful, grateful, friendly, generous, beneficent, or their equivalents,"[14] says Hume; it is a native human sentiment that, in contrast to Smith's view, is not only logically prior to humanity's Fall but expresses "the highest merit which *human nature* is capable of attaining."[15] "No qualities are more entitled to the general good-will and approbation of mankind than beneficence and humanity, friendship and gratitude, natural affection and public spirit, or whatever proceeds from a tender sympathy with others. . . ."[16] Before Hume, Locke had already identified "mutual love" and the preservation of the welfare of others as a "law of nature." For him this normative law, this sentiment of sympathetic benevolence, is in the state of nature inevitably violated because each individual human, in that state, possesses equal executive power to judge and punish any who threaten this natural desire for self-preservation. A state of war inevitably ensues, from which results the *raison d'etre* of a social contract. Although Hume is not so inclined as Locke to speak of "a state of nature" or of "a social contract," he agrees with Locke's emphasis on "mutual love" or the mutual welfare of others as a natural and normative sentiment that establishes the possibility of public and political order.

Hume, it seems, inverts Smith's view that self-interest is the natural, primary sentiment. For him, sympathy and benevolence are primal, natural sentiments and, as argued, prior to self-interest. Benevolence is for humans more significant than self-interest, moreover, because, as Hume argues, it is not self-interest but benevolence that distinguishes humans from "inferior creatures."[17] Whereas the sentiment of self-interest is common to all creatures, the sentiment of benevolence is uniquely human and uniquely suited to ordering human life. Benevolence, we might say, is the distinctive way in which humans and human morality has evolved beyond the rest of the animal kingdom of which it is one species. Accordingly, self-interest cannot and should not constitute the sentiment that most fundamentally defines, drives and determines human behavior and relations, private or public, political or economic. Indeed, benevolence, insists Hume, is so naturally and invariably "experienced to be a principle of human nature. . . . No man is absolutely indifferent to the happiness and misery of others";[18] so that "such as [it appears] to daily experience and observation, we must conclude it impossible for such a creature as man to be totally indifferent to the well or ill-being of his fellow creatures."[19] Hume grants to benevolence priority over self-interest, as Alain Marciano argues, because ". . . willingness to take another's welfare into consideration . . . [is] an 'original' feature of human nature. These principles are the basic characteristics of human nature, and benevolence is the most fundamental of these principles."[20] And one important way for Hume that it is fundamental is as a normative guide for ordering political and economic as well as private and personal life.

Hume's view of human nature assesses favorably, as already noted, when it comes to biblical narratives. Benevolence as the primary natural sentiment fits favorably with the original goodness with which God creates humans and the world, and with the imperative "love thy neighbor as thyself." If by "self-interest" as a natural sentiment Hume means, as I think he does, something like "love of self" qualified by "as one would love a neighbor," then it too is commensurate with the biblical tradition. But if one interprets self-interest as self-indulgent greed, as Smith's theory of economics seems to, then self-interest as a sentiment is not natural but artificial, a function of human fallenness and disobedience, an unnatural sentiment, an errant choice of human freedom, to be banned not burnished. Moreover, what is most uniquely natural to the human species, sympathy and benevolence, are by their very nature both communal and normative. Accordingly, they, and not self-interest, function as natural, normative guides for governments, for social and public endeavors and provide the basis on which "magistrates" should and must draw in order to fulfill the purpose with which they are entrusted namely, establishing and sustaining moral and social order.

Hume's argument for sympathetic benevolence, for love of neighbor, as natural and normative for magistrates and for civil order reflects, as we shall see in chapter 4, the spirit if not the letter of Paul's argument in Romans 13: 1–10. Government is endowed by God with the authority and power to resist wrongdoing and to promote good conduct, not only to execute punishment on wrongdoers but to promote what is good according to one's "conscience," which includes the command "to love one another; for the one who loves another has fulfilled the law." Hume's argument for benevolence as a public virtue seems to shadow, perhaps inadvertently and unintentionally, St. Paul's argument. How so?

Although Hume occasionally alludes to the notion of a state of nature,[21] he does not advocate the view, like Hobbes and Locke, that a "social contract" is ". . . a real or even a fictitious foundational event of civil societies."[22] Rather, humans are "governed by interest," first and foremost by the mutual interests of sympathy and benevolence. In order to avoid collapsing into "the wretched and savage condition" of a "state of nature," it is in their interest to uphold "society and the observation of the rules of justice. . . ."[23] For Hobbes and Locke the need for a social contract and government emerges from the disorder and chaos and fighting that are natural to the human condition. But for Hume it is not an artificial "social contract" that constitutes government; rather, it is constituted by what is most primal and natural to humans, namely, the power of sympathy and benevolence. Indeed, benevolence's power is of such a force that it is able to overcome the social and moral disorder produced by self-interest and to enable a genuinely civil society. The benefit of establishing institutions of government is explicitly for the purpose of executing what is natural and normative to humans, their common, mutual interests as citizens. These common interests include justice; "the observance of justice" is "the immediate interest" for which humans regulate not only their own conduct but also the conduct of others. Government (offices both civil and military) is established in order to assist in the execution of justice.[24] In addition to the execution of justice government provides another benefit to citizens, namely, what Hume calls "decisions of justice" or an impartial judiciary. Since passions inspire in humans "a remarkable partiality in their own favours" and prevent equitable decisions regarding disagreements over matters of justice, the advantage of government is that it provides an impartial means of judgment regarding such matters and is able to "decide them more equitably than every one would in his own case."[25] Government benefits society by working for justice, for the mutual self-interest of all and not merely for an individual's self-interest. But that is not all; political institutions have social utility for other purposes, according to Hume, but only if those other purposes prove themselves mutually beneficial to citizens and to moral order. Benevolence is a public virtue that qualifies for Hume; it contributes to the common, mutual interests of all citizens and to moral order.

Hume, in other words, does not limit government to matters of justice, as does Smith. Recall that Smith's argument for identifying the boundaries of government is based on averting malevolence. Thus, whereas justice is a legitimate duty of government because its absence is harmful to citizens, benevolence is not a legitimate duty, he insists, because its absence is not harmful; government is justified when preventing harm and not justified when not preventing harm. In contrast, Hume's argument includes benevolence as a public virtue; for him not only is the absence of benevolence harmful to citizens (poverty, illness, hunger, illiteracy), but whatever is of social utility, whatever benefits the individual and the mutual interests of citizens (even nullifying the adverse affects of religion) is at least in principle legitimate as public policy. Not only do matters of justice benefit citizens, so also do matters of general welfare, such as the benevolent distribution of social and economic goods. These are of mutual interest, benefit citizens and thus are properly matters of public policy. Catherine Wilson suggests that some such argument is at least Humean if not one Hume himself makes.[26] It is continuous and consistent with the trajectory of Hume's larger argument.

Since sympathy quite naturally leads to acts of benevolence and since acts of benevolence are mutually beneficial to citizens, then those acts, suggests Hume, are of *public interest* and potentially matters of public policy. By advocating the evolution of public virtue from mere justice to sympathetic benevolence Hume confers on government a moral integrity lacking in liberal traditions. He speaks of "public benevolence" as distinguished from "private benevolence" and argues that neither are nor can be the motive of justice, whose motive is self-interest. "A rich man lies under a moral obligation to communicate to those in necessity a share of his superfluities"; that is, the rich man, echoing Jesus and Aquinas, has a moral obligation to undertake acts of benevolence. To refuse to grant to those in need the necessities of life is harmful, Hume insists, even though not as cruel as dispossessing a man of what he already has.[27] Since for Hume the aim of government is for the mutual welfare of citizens, benevolence along with justice should be a public virtue, a collective moral obligation. Not only does benevolence prevent harm and positive evil to others, it beneficially distributes social and material goods, especially to the least advantaged.[28] What Hume argues of the virtuous person can equally be argued of the virtuous public.

> Here is a man, that does many benevolent actions; relieves the distress'd, comforts the afflicted, and extends his bounty even to the greatest strangers. No character can be more amiable and virtuous. We regard these actions as

> proofs of the greatest humanity. This humanity bestows a merit on the actions."[29]

From this and other similar passages, Rudolph Vanderpool insists that "Hume favors a policy of relieving persons in distress," favors public benevolence and "a developed 'sense of justice,' not derived from nature as such, but which arises artificially, though necessarily from education and human conventions."[30] Unlike Smith, who distinguishes quite sharply between public duties to justice and private duties to benevolence, Hume shifts the moral equation: just as public duties to justice, on the one hand, are as morally compelling as private duties to justice, so too, on the other hand, are public duties to benevolence as compelling as private duties to benevolence. Indeed, Vanderpool concludes that

> An immediate, practical advantage of Hume's theory of social justice is that through mutual consent it is possible to impose upon society, collectively, specific legislation having the purpose of remediating or at least relieving certain hardships among disadvantaged members of the citizenry. Programs of welfare, or social schemes of public wealth-redistribution are therefore fit candidates for worthwhile legislation.

Vanderpool argues that for Hume not only are individual acts of benevolence public duties, but "it would also be in order to 'roughly' require or make people, through government sponsored welfare legislation, 'duty-bound' to act as at least minimally decent, if not entirely good, Samaritans."[31] For Hume, benevolence is morally compelling for governments insofar as it prevents harm to citizens and contributes to their mutual welfare.

Since Hume argues for the establishment of religion, it is no surprise that he would argue for the establishment of benevolence. Benevolence in his day was rooted not only in the sentiment of sympathy but in the sensibilities of religion and religious practice. Just as today we instinctively separate church and state, my proposal separates benevolence from religion by disestablishing the later and establishing the former. European governments have struggled with such a separation and disestablishment, but most have managed in their own way to do so: disestablishing religion while still maintaining benevolence as a public virtue. Throughout the brief history of the United State separating religion as private virtue from benevolence as public virtue has been a contentious and continuing conflict.

ESTABLISHING BENEVOLENCE: U.S. CONSTITUTION AND BENEVOLENT EMPIRE

Since the American Founders argue for the disestablishment of religion, it is not surprising that some would also argue for the disestablishment of benevolence. Not surprising because benevolence historically and naturally is nourished by religion; so, in disestablishing the one the other quite naturally and spontaneously is disestablished. Hume himself was not without some influence on Jefferson and Madison, but his attitudes toward benevolence and its role in public life was not one of them.[32] The disestablishment of benevolence reflects more directly the influence of Adam Smith on the Founders. Hume's influence had more to do with the possibility of democracy in a country with a large population and a vast geographical territory. Against the received opinion of scholars at the time, such as Montesquieu's *The Spirit of the Laws*, Hume argues for the possibility and feasibility of democracy in a large country, an argument to which Madison subscribed in opposition to John Adams, Alexander Hamilton, and Patrick Henry.[33]

Also controversial was the extent of the federal government's constitutional power to enact policies of benevolence. Especially controversial is Article I, section 8, which reads:

> The Congress shall have Power To lay and collect Taxes, Duties, Imposts and Excises, to pay the Debts and provide for the common Defense and *general Welfare* of the United States; but all Duties, Imposts and Excises shall be uniform throughout the United States (my italics).

"General Welfare" is a phrase that ignited debate and dissension. This and the next fifteen clauses grant specific powers to the federal government,[34] and it is these "definite" powers on which James Madison, for example, bases his claim that the Constitution grants to the federal government only specific, definite, enumerated powers, on the one hand, and does not permit it any unspecified, unenumerated powers, on the other. Other founders, like Alexander Hamilton, claimed that granting the federal government power to provide for the "general Welfare" permits it unspecified powers, as long as those actions are for the "general Welfare" and "uniform throughout the United States."[35]

Madison's opposition to benevolence as a power enumerated and granted to the federal government favors Smith over Hume and disregards, in the view of some Founders, the substance and significance of "general Welfare." In addressing the issue as to whether the federal government should assume expenses for French refugees from the Haitian revolution (1794), as already noted, Madison famously says "I cannot undertake to lay my finger on that article of the Constitution which granted a right to Congress of expending, on objects of benevolence, the money of their constituents."[36] Madison explained his objection by stating, in *Federalist* No. 41, that the phrase "general Welfare" applied to and is limited by the specific powers enumerated in the subsequent clauses. Like Smith, Madison is eager to disestablish benevolence along with religion, although he seems willing to accommodate it as a power properly belonging to the states, as suggested in a speech before Congress: that, "The government of the United States is a definite government, confined to specific objects. It is not like the state governments, whose powers are more general. Charity is no part of the legislative duty of the [federal] government."[37] Madison's restriction of the Constitutional phrase "general Welfare" to definite, enumerated powers was at the time disputed by some, including Alexander Hamilton. He argues, in *Federalist* No. 33 (January 3, 1788), that the phrase is "perfectly harmless" and "a truth" that simply follows from forming "a federal government and vesting it with certain specified powers." Hamilton further insists that the definite powers enumerated do not form an exhaustive list and may include other powers benefiting the general welfare of citizens. Indeed, he states that this phrase is "as comprehensive as any that could have been used"; it "embraces a vast variety of particulars, which are susceptible neither of specification nor of definition."[38]

These two disputed interpretations of "general Welfare," represented by Madison and Hamilton, laid the foundation for the first two political parties in the United States; the Federalists led by Hamilton and the Republicans led by Madison and Jefferson. "[W]hether or not the federal government had the authority to subsidize various projects" of what were called "internal improvements," "on the grounds they promoted the general welfare," endured as an issue in the 1800s. In 1817, for example, President Madison "vetoed an act 'to set apart and pledge certain funds for internal improvements.' In doing so, he stated that the federal government did not have this power and to allow for it would require a distorted interpretation of the Constitution."[39] The Republicans, fearing excessive federal powers, were of a mind to leave such projects of "internal improvements" or benevolence to the states or private benefactors. This debate continues to this day: healthcare, gun laws, minimum wage, the role of FEMA are several of many examples. Running through the American body politic is a vibrant vein that like Smith and Madison promotes limited enumerated federal power, the disestablishment of benevolence, and some version of free market enterprise. Early on, in the late eighteenth century and through the nineteenth century, this disestablishment tradition seems to have dominated. And yet the federalist establishment tradition was a constant antagonist, always with advocates who, like Hamilton, promoted federal powers for the general welfare, for the establishment of benevolence. Eventually, gradually, the establishment of benevolence evolved and gained ground until in 2009, the federal government of the

United States spent 61 percent of its finances benevolently, on its citizens' general welfare, including housing, community services, welfare and social services, recreation and culture, health, education, retirement benefits, disability and unemployment benefits.[40]

Nevertheless, early in the Republic disestablishing benevolence dominated. In response, a plethora of private organizations emerged which together constituted what some historians call a "Benevolent Empire." Private "Reforming organizations and movements . . . harnessed the religious energies loosed by the Second Great Awakening . . . to bring about significant social reforms."[41] Indeed, reform organizations and movements so proliferated in the nineteenth century that not only did their significance not go unnoticed by Tocqueville, but he went so far as to identify what it means to be "American" partly by what he calls private, "voluntary associations." Some of these organizations and movements were para-church, like the American Bible Society and the Social Gospel movement, and some were church-based, like the Society of Friends (Quakers) and the Unitarians. The American Bible Society (1816) sought to distribute Bibles and tracts and by doing so promoted social reform through literacy and united Christians in common cause. It seems to have been relatively successful in accomplishing the former, but failed, as Edward Kilsdonk argues, in accomplishing the latter.[42] Congregationalists and Presbyterians also distributed Bibles and promoted literacy. Quakers seem to have been one of the earliest to link personal practice of religion with responsibility for reforming society; besides their ongoing witness for peace, they initiated efforts on behalf of the poor and imprisoned, temperance and the abolition of slavery. Unitarians were also active in public education and in providing care for the mentally disabled and for the deaf and blind.

Voluntary organizations, movements, and denominations such as these promoted and practiced benevolence as a private virtue; they have had enormous impact on American society and the general welfare. But for some they were and are not themselves sufficient to address the depth of damage and harm and need that threaten to irreparably wound the collective American soul, its civility and dignity. That the government should collaborate with private organizations to provide for the "general Welfare" not only does not transgress the spirit of the Constitution but more nearly affirms the letter of it: "provide for . . . the general Welfare." Some Americans were persuaded by this vision of the Constitution, benevolence as a public virtue; a tradition culminating with Franklin Roosevelt, who, faced with economic and social disaster, envisioned a "New Deal" in which government assumed greater responsibilities for the sake of the "general Welfare," for economic and social benefit. Indeed he employed policies of benevolence in order to bring moral and social order out of economic, political and social chaos. The New Deal included programs of benevolence that addressed poverty, jobs, disabilities, pensions, and other social and economic matters. These programs of public benevolence were supported by many mainline religious denominations, whose support partly earned them the label of liberal. Other religious groups came to be labeled conservative partly for their opposition to public benevolence.[43] Today, whether to establish policies of public benevolence or not remains a contentious issue. The current political and Constitutional debate over a comprehensive, public health care program, approved in 2010, is one of many examples.

ESTABLISHING BENEVOLENCE: MILL

Adam Smith argues, you may recall, that benevolence should not be "extorted by force" and made a matter of public policy, because its absence does not cause the same real harm and positive evil to citizens as does the absence of justice. Hume argues that benevolence should be legislated for its utility, for its benefits to mutual welfare, and for its power to provide social and moral order, without which follows much positive evil and harm such as economic inequalities, poverty, hunger, crime, illiteracy, and other deprivations. John Stuart Mill's *Principles of Political Economy* (1848) extends Hume's argument by establishing an additional moral basis for "extorting" benevolence "by force." In it he aims at "modernizing" Smith's (et al.) political economy, incorporating "the latest improvements which have been made in the theory of the subject," and bringing the results of the most recent "speculations . . . into harmony with the principles previously laid down by the best thinkers on the subject."[44] The "improvements" Mill makes in *Principles of Political Economy* are not only theoretical and speculative, nor are they only practical matters of application; they are also matters of morality and moral discipline that Mill believed to be vital to modernizing political economy.[45] He divides his analysis of political economy into two general economic phenomena, the production of wealth, on the one hand, and the distribution of wealth, on the other; a division that his contemporary, Karl Marx, articulates in terms of "mode of production" and "mode of appropriation." The former, Mill argues, is a matter of reason and scientific law, the latter a matter of will and moral judgment.

"The laws and conditions of the production of wealth," Mill says, "partake of the character of physical truths. There is nothing optional, or arbitrary about them. Whatever mankind produce, must be produced in the modes, and under the conditions, imposed by the constitution of external things, and by the inherent properties of their own bodily and mental structures." He goes on to insist that the production of wealth as a matter of "physical truths" (scientific laws) and "The opinions, or the wishes, which may exist on these different matters, do not control the things themselves."[46] The production of wealth is a function of certain scientific, economic laws; for a society to be economically successful, it will abide by these physical laws to which economic forces are in service. Production is not a matter of opinion or moral judgment; it is a matter of rational, scientific intelligence, implementation, and application. On this matter Mill is in agreement with Smith: that production and modes of production are a matter of scientific not moral judgment. The "scientific socialism" of Marx and Engels similarly anchors the economic "mode of production" in scientific laws. This argument in economics is analogous in politics to the discovery by reason of "property" (as Locke puts it), of certain rights and liberties. They are matters of rational analysis and natural law, not a matter of volition or personal preference or majority opinion. The identification of human rights and the democratic procedures suited to protecting and preserving them are property that all humans possess equally. They are not optional or arbitrary; all opinions and varying interpretations are subject to those rights and liberties as natural and objective law. So it is with the mode in which wealth is produced: rational, scientific, and objective.

"It is not so with the Distribution of Wealth," according to Mill, nor with the fair distribution of social goods for the general welfare. The mode of distribution "is a matter of human institution solely," insists Mill, and not scientific institution. "The things once there, mankind, individually or collectively, can do with them as they like. They can place them at the disposal of whomsoever they please, and on whatever terms."[47] Society can decide to place them at the disposal of forces of self-interest, as Smith does, or at the disposal of forces of benevolence, as does Hume. For Smith moral judgment and benevolence are not irrelevant to the distribution of wealth; but by disestablishing and privatizing them he leaves allocation to the vicissitudes of raw, fallen, self-interestedness, leaves them to the vicissitudes of an inscrutable law of unintended consequences, an "invisible hand" as if it were scientific instead of superstitious. In opposition to Smith, Mill, along with Hume, argues that the distribution and appropriation of wealth is a function not of physical laws but of human volition and moral judgment. More particularly, distribution is determined by two forces, says Mill, competition and custom, both of which are within the jurisdiction of humans to alter. They are powerful conditions that "infiltrate nearly all areas in which distributional decisions are made,"[48] and are therefore subject to volition and moral judgment. Since distribution is a function of competition and custom, and the latter are "subject to change at society's discretion,"[49] as Michel Zouboulakis puts it, then distribution is by implication subject to society's discretion. Smith leaves them to the discretion of self-interest, Hume and Mill to the discretion of intentional public benevolence. These two economic modes, of production and distribution, are perhaps somewhat analogous to two familiar political modes in democracy. The mode of producing and protecting rights and liberties as human "property" is a matter of reason and laws of nature. The mode of appropriating and distributing rights and liberties, in contrast, is a matter of custom, of volition and moral judgment, subject to society's discretion. In the United States these right and liberties are produced and protected in the Constitution; but for centuries the mode of distribution of these rights and liberties, as a matter of custom, volition, and moral judgment, was deliberately partial, unjust, and discriminatory (e.g., slavery, civil rights, Jim Crow); as a matter of majority opinion the distribution of rights and liberties manifested itself as public, institutionalized malevolence.

Mill's twofold analysis of political economy extends Hume's utilitarian approach by providing an argument for distributing social and economic goods, for institutionalizing benevolence as public policy. Following Hume and Mill, I distinguish liberal, procedural justice and distributive, egalitarian justice. The procedural principles of democracy (liberal justice) are of the character of scientific law and rational deliberation. In contrast, the principles of egalitarian justice aim at the fair distribution of goods for a sustainable livelihood for all; they are of the character of moral laws, subject to society's will, customs, and discretion. Mill seems to have understood that in modern societies the production of wealth is not the most urgent economic problem, but that the distribution of it is. Finding scientific ways of quadrupling production will not solve a distribution problem that at root is volitional and moral, not scientific. What are some of the discretionary policies that in the mid-1800s Mill recommends? An ongoing redistribution of wealth from rich to poor, experiments in profit-sharing cooperatives, and an inheritance tax to prevent a class of undeserving wealthy from evolving at the expense of the poor, are just a few policies. For Mill political economy is a discipline not only for scientists and mathematicians but a discipline for moral philosophers and ethicists; the former contribute scientific judgments, the latter contribute moral judgments, so that both the production and distribution of economic resources are not only efficient and effective but also moral and benevolent. Although humans are shaped by causal conditions, physical and social, they are not fully determined by them; they can also control and construct for themselves their own character and society; and it is this latter discretionary agency whereby a society can determine for itself a fair distribution of wealth, if it will, if it has character and courage.

BENEVOLENCE AS NORMATIVE

On what basis and to what extent is it possible to argue that biblical narratives envision benevolence as a public as well as a private virtue, a political orientation as well as personal one? To what extent, in other words, do biblical narratives tend to encourage benevolence as normative for public life? In the next section, "Theological Inquiry," I address these questions more fully and in detail. But for now I would like to address benevolence briefly, as a matter of religious faith and social responsibility.

It is clear, first of all, I think, that Jesus's embodiment of faith, hope, and love does not imply a specific political or economic system or ideology. In a neglected classic *Jesus on Social Institutions,* Shailer Matthews argues that the gospel of Jesus "has a message of hope born of its faith in God and the consequent practicability of goodwill. . . . Such a social gospel does not carry with it a program of economic or political activity. The church is not an economic or political institution."[50] Just as religious faith does not provide humans with scientific beliefs such as a general theory of relativity or quantum mechanics; and it does not provide humans with social scientific beliefs such as a democratic form of government, nor a capitalist or socialist economic system. Such matters are left to those who have mastered scientific knowledge and expertise. As Matthews explains, although Americans "enjoy—and endure—democracy, the sovereignty of the people; in the days of Jesus such a political conception was not even dreamed."[51]

Nonetheless, biblical narratives in general and the Gospels in particular contribute a normative principle of benevolence rooted in *agape*. For Christian communities this norm provides both spiritual identity and moral orientation, a kind of moral matrix on the basis of which to judge the moral and spiritual worth of a particular system or theory or ideology. Indeed, mercy and benevolence as normative "demands a choice," says Matthews, a choice "between a policy that is selfish and one [that is not] selfish, between one that seeks to give justice and one that seeks to maintain privilege."[52] Just as religion is unable and unequipped to provide guidance in all things scientific, so science is unable and unequipped to provide guidance in all things moral and spiritual. The very moral orientation in politics and economics that science is unequipped to provide invites the message and mission of faith traditions. "Self-interest" in economics as a social scientific observation, for example, does not thereby magically qualify it as normative economic guide. Christianity, as the embodiment and practice of the tradition inspired by Jesus, preaches freedom and liberation, justice and equality, grace and mercy; its gospel demands in public life what it practices as normative in private life; its calls for in political life what its cares for in personal life. Indeed, the private practices of disestablished religion, meekness and mercy for example, seamlessly produce certain public fruits of benevolence that shape the programs and policies of a politics that is morally and spiritually rooted. To abandon the distribution of economics goods to the vicissitudes and "invisible hand" of self-interest does constitute a moral judgment and orientation that obscures the horizon of expectation gospel sensibilities otherwise envision. To cast economic matters on stormy seas of self-interest, of private prejudices and gratuitous greed, redounds neither to a politics of mercy nor to the faith, hope, and love Jesus practiced. Rather, the entropy of economic self-interest defaults to forces of moral disorder and deprivation, which forces are reversed only by the intentional power of a collective volition willing in economic life to practice justice and benevolence. This is to say that granting Caesar what is Caesar's and God what is God's is not a way of justifying two different sets of moral values. What is good for God morally and spiritually is likewise good for Caesar. The politics that is Caesar's is to be shaped by the same power of justice, benevolence, and mercy that is God's. Perhaps Smith and his disciples would think differently about benevolence as a public virtue were they familiar with the notion of social evolution and the law of the survival of the fittest. Perhaps then they would not banish benevolence to the private domain and subjugate economics to the indiscriminate and corrupting forces of self-interest that determine that and who the fittest are who survive. As Matthews puts it:

> Why should the strong organize to care for the weak, or the fortunate to care for the unfortunate, unless there be some fundamental reason for this violation of the law of the survival of the physically fittest to survive? In humanity there must be something even more fit than strength, else our care for the weak and for the diseased, the depressed and the dependent, may be only a weakening of the race itself. Regard for human welfare implies that human welfare is worth preserving.[53]

The only force powerful enough to combat the strength of the self-interested fittest is the moral and spiritual force of sympathy that distinguishes, as Hume puts it, humans from the "inferior creatures." The social character of Christianity requires that it institutionalize the "mind of Christ" so that it is different than other vendors of social scientific technique. What it must institutionalize is a revolutionary attitude and activity of self-sacrifice represented by the cross and resurrection, by "not my will, but thine be done." This is the "leaven of sacrificial idealism," as Matthews calls it, which inspires Christianity and other faith traditions "to sacrifice social status or economic privilege in the interests of others less happily situated."[54] Benevolence entails self-sacrificial love practiced privately, publicly, politically, economically; it results from courage of will and not from adherence to scientific law; it entails faith, hope, and love for all and not just for the privileged fittest who because of advantage dominant economically and politically. This is to believe, as the followers of Christ should, that love in the form of benevolence can and should be public and in some significant way "institutionalized" in public policy, as Matthews insists, and that "the group as well as individuals can express the spirit of Jesus"[55] politically and economically, as well as ecclesiastically. Indeed, my thesis is that "the group" can and should evolve beyond a politics of self-interest and commit itself to a politics of mercy.

On what basis and to what extent, then, can and should the biblical story in general and the life and teaching of Jesus in particular manifest themselves publicly? To what extent should they be institutionalized as public policy? Under what conditions might and should they shape political and economic and social policy? Answering these questions provides a gateway to section 2, "Theological Inquiry," into justice, mercy, and compassion.

Much has already been said about benevolence as a private and public virtue. For the purposes of my argument here, I propose to construe benevolence even more specifically as a private and public virtue constituted by three values, namely, justice, mercy, and compassion. In the next three chapters I examine the relationship between these three qualities in some detail, especially as they express themselves theologically as the fundamental moral orientation of biblical narratives and faith traditions. Some such similar argument as I make here drawing on biblical narratives can very well be made, I would suppose, by drawing on the religious and theological resources of all religious and humanistic traditions.

Before proceeding, it might be well to summarize the gist of the argument thus far: first, that religion should be disestablished; secondly, that the aim of government is moral and social order and the mutual welfare of citizens; thirdly, that benevolence should be (re)established because it contributes to this welfare and order, that lack of which results in real, positive injury and evil; fourthly, that economics is not only a matter of reason and scientific law but equally a matter of will and moral judgment. What remains for examination? On what basis should economic and social goods be distributed and to what extent is it possible to do so?

NOTES

1. See *The Second Treatise of Civil Government*, chapters II–V. Locke was writing in the context of an agrarian culture and economy. He argues that there is a limit to how much one can "mix" his labor with; he has a property in (a right to) as much he can use before it "spoils"; anything beyond that is for the sustainability of others. But when it comes to money, Locke argues that a person can hoard as much as one can accumulate.

2. David Hume, *The History of England*, 554–555. Also, see chapter 2 of this book.

3. David Hume, *An Enquiry Concerning the Principles of Morals* (Oxford: Clarendon Press, 1975), III.I., 183–185.

4. *Ibid.*, 191.

5. *Treatise*, 497.

6. *Ibid.*, 498. This is the basis for Hume claiming that justice is not a natural virtue but an artificial one; because its utility requires the convention of public institutions to establish it.

7. *Ibid.*, 499 500.

8. David Hume, *Concerning the Principles of Morals*, V.II.

9. *Ibid.*, V.II.180–181.

10. Ibid., V.II.183.

11. See Martha Nussbaum, *Cultivating Humanity: A Classical Defense of Liberal Education* (Cambridge, MA: Harvard University Press, 1997), see especially chapters 2 and 3.

12. Hume, *A Treatise on Human Nature*, II.II.

13. *Ibid.*

14. By benevolence Hume refers to these qualities of benevolence as qualities "known in all languages. . . ." *An Enquiry Concerning the Principles of Morals*, II.I., 176.

15. *Ibid.*

16. *Ibid.*

17. *Ibid.*

18. *Ibid.*, V.II.n1.

19. *Ibid.*, V.II.

20. Alain Marciano, "Benevolence, Sympathy, and Hume's Model of Government: How Different Is New Political Economy from Classical Political Economy," *History of Political Economy* 37 (2005), Suppl. 1, 43–70, 54.

21. Hume, *A Treatise of Human Nature*, III.II.VII. For example, Hume says, ". . . it is impossible for men to consult their interest in so ineffectual a manner as by an universal and inflexible observance of the rules of justice by which alone they can preserve society, and keep themselves from falling into that wretched and savage condition which is commonly represented as the *state of nature*."

22. Marciano, 61.

23. Hume, *A Treatise of Human Nature*, edited by L. A. Selby-Bigge (London: Oxford at the Clarendon Press, 1888, 1948), III.II.VII., 497–498.

24. *Ibid.*

25. *Ibid.*

26. Catherine Wilson, "A Humean Argument for Benevolence to Strangers," *The Monist* (July 2003), 86(3), 454–468.

27. Hume, *Treatise*, 482.

28. Hume does grant that humans are more likely to want to show benevolence toward those who are near (family and friends) than to those who are distant (strangers and foreigners), yet he allows that moral conscience is not unacquainted with sympathetic benevolence toward the distant, even though the benefit may also seem remote.

29. Hume, *Treatise*, 478. Hume does argue that when it comes to benevolence the proximity of the other, including the stranger, is significant. "A man naturally loves his children better than his nephews, his nephews better than his cousins, his cousins better than strangers, where everything else is equal." See *Treatise of Human Nature*, 483–484.

30. Rudolph Vanderpool, "Hume on the 'Duty' of Benevolence," *Hume Studies* 16, 1 (April 1988), 93–110.

31. *Ibid.*, 106, 107.

32. See Craig Walton, "Hume and Jefferson on the Uses of History," in *Hume: A Re-evaluation*, edited by Donald Livingston and James King (New York: Fordham University Press, 1976), 389–403. Walton argues that although Jefferson initially admired Hume's *History of England* he became disillusioned if not "horrified" by it because of the "toryism" he found in it, a conspiratorial "toryism" that Jefferson thought was endangering the fledgling republic.

33. Hume sets forth this argument, for example, in "Perfect Commonwealth," published in his 1758 edition of *Essays: Moral, Political, and Literary*. Hume's argument is critically analyzed in an article by Douglas Adair titled "'That Politics May Be Reduced to a Science': David Hume, James Madison, and the Tenth *Federalist*," in *Hume: A Re-evaluation*, edited by Donald Livingston and James King (New York: Fordham University Press, 1976), 404–417.

34. Italics are mine. These definite powers include regulating international commerce, minting money, enacting immigration and bankruptcy laws, establishing post offices and courts, funding armies, declaring war, issuing patents and copyrights, and so on.

35. For the dispute between Madison and Hamilton on the issue of "general Welfare" I am indebted to James D. Agresti's article "Social Spending, Constitutional History," in *Just Facts*, December 5, 2007; updated 5/2/11; http//justfacts.com/socialspending.asp.

36. *Annals of Congress*, House of Representatives, 3rd Congress, 1st Session, page 170 (1794-01-10).

37. Speech, House of Representatives, during the debate "On the Memorial of the Relief Committee of Baltimore, for the Relief of St. Domingo Refugees" (1795-01-10).

38. Alexander Hamilton, "Report on Manufactures," December 5, 1791.

39. James D. Agresti, "Social Spending, Constitutional History," in *Just Facts*, December 5, 2007; updated 5/2/11; http//justfacts.com/socialspending.asp. Agresti notes that Jefferson wrote a letter praising Madison for his veto and insisting that Congress does not have "unlimited powers to provide for the general welfare, but were restrained to those specifically enumerated."

40. See Agresti's "Social Spending, Constitutional History."

41. Julia Corbett and Michael Corbett, *Politics and Religion in the United States* (New York: Garland Publishing, Inc., 1999), 91.

42. See Edward Kilsdonk, "Benevolent Organizations, and American Pluralism," in *The American Experience*, http://are.as.wvu.edu/kilsdonk.htm. "Benevolent organizations were also founded with the hope that by uniting all religious people in a common cause they could create a common Christianity. Paradoxically their overall effect was to strengthen denominational identity and denominational ties. This is because denominational leaders saw benevolent organizations as a threat to the ideas and practices of church members" (1–2).

43. Julia and Michael Corbett summarize the impact support of the New Deal or not had of religious groups. See *Politics and Religion in the United States* (New York: Garland Publishing, Inc., 1991), 103.

44. These "best thinkers" include especially Smith and Ricardo. See Mill's "Preface" to this work; wherein he praises Smith's *The Wealth of Nations* "because, in his application of Political Economy, he perpetually appeals to other and often far larger considerations than pure Political Economy affords—that he gives the well-grounded feeling of command over the principles of the subject for purposes of practice, owing to which 'The Wealth of Nations,' alone among treatises on political economy, has not only been popular with general readers, but has impressed itself strongly on the minds of men of the world and of legislators."

45. See Hans E. Jensen's article in "John Stuart Mill's Theories of Wealth and Income Distribution," in *Review of Social Economy* 59, 4 (December 2001), 491–507.

46. J. S. Mill, *Principles of Political Economy* (New York: Colonial Press, 1899), II.1., 196.

47. Mill, *Ibid.*, 197.

48. Jensen, *Ibid.*, 497–498.

49. Michel S. Zouboulakis, "On the Social Nature of Rationality in Adam Smith and John Stuart Mill," *Cahiers d'economie politique* 49, L'Harmattan (2005) 51–63, 55.

50. Shailer Matthews, *Jesus on Social Institutions* (Philadelphia, PA: Fortress Press, 1971), 144.

51. *Ibid.*, 146.

52. *Ibid.*, 144.

53. *Ibid.*, 138.

54. *Ibid.*, 134.

55. *Ibid.*, 135.

Part Two

Theological Inquiry

He hath shewed thee, O man,
what is good: and what doth the Lord
require of thee, but to do justly,
and to love mercy, and to walk
humbly with thy God.
(Micah 6: 8, KJV)

Chapter Four

Benevolence and Justice

"There was a man who had two sons" (Luke 15: 11–32). As sons will, each makes plans to dispose of his inheritance as he sees fit. The elder son, ever mindful of his inheritance, remains at home and works his father's estate. The more ambitious, if somewhat rambunctious, younger son decides to collect his inheritance and travel. And travel he does, to distant lands, squandering his inheritance on the proverbial wine, women, and song. Soon a famine devastates the land and the son finds himself destitute and on the ancient equivalent of skid road. To stay alive, he finds work slopping and then foraging with swine. No one comes to aid him in his need. Finally, the younger son comes to his senses; the prayer of every parent. He says to himself, "How many of my father's hired servants have bread enough, but I perish here with hunger! I will arise and go to my father, and I will say to him, 'Father, I have sinned against heaven and before you. I am no longer worthy to be called your son; treat me as one of your hired servants'" (15: 17–19). And so he makes ready to return home to ask forgiveness of his father and beg his indulgence to work as one of his servants. When the son arrives we discover what kind of man the father is; either he can sternly rebuke his son, as many a parent would do, and inflict the punishment he justly deserves; or he can have "compassion" on his son and in mercy restore their relationship. When the son is still some distance from home, the father sees him and rushes to receive and embrace him. The son tries to repent but the father hardly hears him; in his heart he has long ago forgiven him. He says nothing but does everything to show his son the depth of compassion and mercy he has for him and the joy with which he eagerly receives him. The father immediately instructs his servants to "Bring quickly the best robe, and put it on him; and put a ring on his hand, and shoes on his feet. And bring the fatted calf and kill it, and let us eat and make merry" (15: 22–23).

But what of justice? What of condemnation, at least of the sin if not the sinner? What about teaching the son a moral lesson? What about equal treatment of siblings? What about closure for the offended? These questions seem not to enter the father's mind. His heart is saturated with love and indescribable joy, "For this my son was dead, and is alive again; he was lost, and is found." Appropriately, "They began to make merry (15: 24)." How stunned the younger son must have been. "What is this that I should in my sin and squalor reap such unmerited benefits from my father?" he must have thought. "I deserve no more than to be my father's lowly servant, and yet he treats me lavishly, like a prince." The elder son, it should be noted, is also stunned and deeply offended. He hears the music and dancing and inquires as to the occasion. When he finds that it is a celebration in honor of the younger son's homecoming, he is furious and resentful and refuses to participate. The father comes out to entreat him, but he is stubborn and bitter in his animosity and angrily defames, "Lo, these many years I have served, and I never disobeyed your command; yet you never gave me a kid, that I might make merry with my friends" (15: 29). The father's heart is broken; he replies that his elder son's entire life with him is a celebration; that everything the father possesses is and always will be his and for his pleasure. We are left with the impression that still the elder son is not amused.

This parable has about it a ring of authenticity and authority; it is one of several stories Jesus tells dramatizing the strife between justice and mercy, between a Just man, the elder son, who demands justice; and a Righteous man, the father, who grants mercy. This conflict between elder son and father is precisely the primary global struggle today, a struggle of two virtues, of justice and righteousness (mercy), of reason and faith. Over the centuries this parable has been subjected to a wide variety of interpretations. It is common to allegorize each of the characters in the drama, as I do here. Primary focus on the son that is "prodigal," as is often done, misreads the parable. Of course, most humans are the younger son at one time or another: fallen morally and spiritually and lost in loose living. What is remarkable about the parable is not that the wayward son comes to his senses, repents, and finds his way home; most wayward children do. What is remarkable is the stark contrast between father's and elder son's responses to that homecoming. The father is commonly thought to represent God's response to fallen, sinful humanity; he is a Righteous man embodying the kind of merciful benevolence that Christians are emboldened by God's grace to practice. The father, so eager with mercy and forgiveness, shows little interest in inflicting just due, in punishing his son to teach him a lesson, even though moral law would demand it; that is easily enough done and indeed takes no thought or wisdom or courage of grace to do so. Instead of condemnation, the father's interest is the welfare of the son and his relationship with him. His desire is for redeeming, reconciling, restoring a broken relationship; his desire, in a word, is for fellowship. The elder son, a Just but not a Righteous man, represents, regrettably, the faithlessness of many Christian communities. They cry justice for others, for enemies, but for themselves eagerly receive the benefits of God's benevolence; mercy for themselves, condemnation and retribution for others.

Although justice is a virtue, it is sometimes itself not a solution to broken relationships, whether individual or social. The father in his wisdom understands this. Indeed, he seems to assume with Luther that justice strictly enforced produces injustice. From the ancients Luther quotes: "*Summum ius, summa iniustitia*, the most extreme justice is the greatest injustice."[1] The wayward son is reconciled by mercy and the elder son, for all his grumbling, perhaps learns from his father the power of mercy. Recall the "new commandment" Jesus gives his disciples on the night of his betrayal. Not only are they to love each other as they love themselves justly and fairly; but, says Jesus, "even as I have loved you [mercifully], that you also love one another." Indeed, it is by this very kind of merciful love that "all men will know that you are my disciples" (John 13: 31–35). What then are the spiritual and moral qualities that constitute merciful benevolence, that reconcile and restore, that make egalitarian justice a practical possibility?

My aim in these three chapters (4, 5, 6) is to clarify the inexorable intrinsic moral link between justice and mercy. Just as Newton formally united into a single law two separate fields of experience, i.e., the gravity of bodies on earth and the movement of the stars in the sky, compassion unites into a single moral equation what has more often than not been two separate fields of moral activity, i.e., the rational laws of justice in morality and the faith of mercy's benevolence in theology. In this chapter I examine justice in its relation to benevolence; in chapter 5 I examine mercy as the way in which benevolence subverts injustice and establishes justice; and in chapter 6 I show how compassion constitutes the practical moral power by which humans move from justice to mercy and back.

What then is the relation of justice to benevolence? In order to address this question I situate justice within the range of orders, Created, Fallen, and Redeemed. In so doing, I distinguish "liberal justice" and "egalitarian justice." Liberal, procedural justice establishes structures through which the mutual self-interests of individual rights are protected, retributive justice executed, and due process and equality of opportunity guaranteed. The Constitution of the United States and especially the "Bill of Rights" is a document dedicated largely to establishing liberal, procedural justice. Egalitarian justice, in contrast, aims at a "Bill of economic Rights," a "fair balance" of economic and social goods, that is able to produce a sustainable livelihood for all. Such an aim requires altruistic projects of merciful benevolence. Without a sustainable livelihood the dignity of humans created *imago Dei* is diminished. Egalitarian justice, accordingly, guarantees a livelihood that satisfies basic human needs—sufficient food, clothes, shelter, health, and healthcare, as John Locke suggests in his *Second Treatise*. Certainly, government's business is to guarantee liberal, procedural justice; this is one of the chief means by which its aim of moral and civil order is achieved, but it is not the only one. As Hume and Mill insist benevolent distributive justice, including a sustainable livelihood for all, is morally compulsory for any society claiming civility. In order for government to fulfill its primary role of moral order and the well-being of citizens it must promote and practice public policies not only of liberal justice but of benevolent, egalitarian justice as well. Religious and humanitarian communities assist governments in doing so. Although disestablished, their obligation is to help government implement policies of benevolent, egalitarian justice without which arises all manner of injustice, moral disorder, and social chaos.

CREATED ORDER AND STATE OF NATURE

The three moral/spiritual Orders (Created, Fallen, Redeemed), described in chapter 1, are mirrored in modern political theory: "the state of nature" parallels the Created Order *(pax Dei)*; the state of corruption, war, liberal justice and social contract parallel the Fallen Order *(pax Romana)*; and "the state of egalitarian justice" and peace parallels the Redeemed Order *(pax Christi)*. Contemporary politics and conceptions of justice are not fully understood without an appreciation of their relationship to these three Orders.

It would be difficult to overestimate the influence of the biblical tradition on early modern political thought and the development of the liberal idea of justice. Indeed, the ideas of Created and Fallen Orders are pivotal to understanding it. Whereas Hume and Smith speak of an original "natural sympathy," Hobbes, Locke, and Rousseau begin their political theories with the Created Order, with the "natural condition of mankind" in a "state of nature." These modern theories refract philosophically the Genesis account in which all things by a benevolent God are created "good." Especially humans, created in the "image" and "likeness" of God, possess certain natural endowments wherewith to fulfill their appointed purpose. Hobbes puts it in terms of the "felicity" of the Created Order and the "misery" of the Fallen Order.[2] Locke more than Hobbes examines the state of nature in specifically Christian terms;[3] but whether referring to God or to Nature, both assume an original condition in which humans are created with certain natural endowments,[4] including reason and knowledge of certain (divinely appointed) laws of nature, laws on the basis of which order, peace, and harmony is possible. These endowments, as set forth by both Hobbes and Locke, include freedom, equality of faculties, equality of ability, of power and jurisdiction, of hope, and equal executive power. Certain natural rights and liberties or *jus naturale,* as

Hobbes puts it, guide humans in the preservation of their own life; and certain prohibitions or *lex naturalis* forbid them from doing anything that might be destructive of their lives and the lives of others. These rights and duties comprise the basis of liberal, procedural justice. Locke largely agrees with this exposition of the state of nature by Hobbes. The law of nature obligates a person to preserve her own life, liberty, health, limb, goods, and possessions as well as the livelihood of others.[5] Even further, Locke insists that God benevolently grants to humans a natural endowment of "property,"[6] first of all in their own "person" (i.e., rights and liberties); second, in their "labor"; and finally in whatever they "mix" labor with, the products of labor. These properties or entitlements, granted by God to all humans naturally, are employed in service to the preservation and enjoyment of life, for oneself and for others. And when they are so employed, the intended original Created Order is propagated. For Locke and Hobbes, protecting and preserving these rights and liberties, as expressions of the laws of nature, constitute justice. Indeed they establish not only the original harmony and symmetry of God's Created Order but also the standard model whereby just, moral equilibrium is measured. Smith and Hume tend to avoid the contractual language of this liberal tradition. As noted earlier, they articulate their preferences in terms of "natural sympathy," moral sentiments, the mutuality of self-interest, and so on. More recently, John Rawls identifies his own "original position" with Hobbes and Locke's state of nature and perhaps inadvertently with the religious notion of an original Created Order.[7] "In justice as fairness," he says, "the original position of equality corresponds to the state of nature in the traditional theory of the social contract." In order to aim well at an ideal of just fairness, humans in this original position are located in relationship to each other behind a "veil of ignorance," a quintessential liberal, procedural condition.[8]

The question remains, how should liberal societies make judgments about what is just and fair? How are humans, so created and conceived, to determine what justice is and what the just thing to do is? For those, like Locke, Rawls, and countless theologians who subscribe to the liberal interpretation of justice, justice is best determined from a hypothetical, presumptive condition. Philosophically this condition is articulated in terms of a "state of nature" or "a veil of ignorance" or an "original position"; theologically it is articulated in terms of the original, created order of things, of a garden or primitive "paradise," a state of "innocence," from within which unadulterated, uncorrupted judgments can be made. So, from within a hypothetical "state of nature" or from behind a "veil of ignorance" all citizens are potentially and hypothetically more or less equal and equally endowed and entitled. Individual differences and local particularities, personal conditions and parochial needs are intentionally concealed and suspended as irrelevant to determining justice. From this "original position," "the symmetry of everyone's relations to each other . . . is fair between individuals as moral persons. . . ."[9] Thus, in order to make fair judgments regarding college admissions, for example, a committee would not consider the particularities of race, religion, nationality, location, economic status or needs, etc., but only qualities directly related to academic performance.

Amartia Sen, in contrasting Rawls and Smith on this point, notes that "the Rawlsian 'veil of ignorance' addresses the need to remove the influence of vested interests and personal slants of the diverse individuals within the focal group. . . ." But in doing so, "it abstains from the scrutiny of (in Smith's language) 'the eyes of the rest of mankind.'"[10] Along with Sen, I am critical of this contractarian approach to justice. Whether articulated in terms of "a state of nature" or "a veil of ignorance" or "a state of created innocence," this hypothetical procedure for determining justice succumbs to its own isolation. As Sen notes: "the procedure of segregated 'original position,' operating in devised isolation, is not conducive to guaranteeing an adequately objective scrutiny of social conventions and parochial sentiments, which may influence which rules are chosen in the original position." The original position, although hypothetical, is not without its own constellation of social conventions and prejudices, against which the procedure itself cannot protect. As Sen argues, "the door" to "open scrutiny" and uncorrupted judgment in Rawls's theory "is partially bolted by the procedural form of requiring conformity with the territorially isolated original position: 'and by assessing the arguments for them [exclusively] by the restrictions expressed by the conception of the original position.'" What of the personal prejudices and parochial conventions of the state of nature and original position itself? What of centuries of embedded patterns of prejudices by dominate cultures that skew allegedly objective judgments? Hypothetical "does not foreclose the possibility of group interests and perspectives. There is not only no procedural barricade here against susceptibility to local prejudices," insists Sen, "there is no systematic way of opening up the reflections in the original position to the eyes of mankind,"[11] to the scrutiny of other objective, third party interests. This hypothetical approach to justice fails because it attempts to determine justice unrealistically, abstractly; as if there exist no inequalities and deprivations, no advantages, selfish interests and group prejudices. Deny these, and you deny the very conditions of injustice without which a moral judgment regarding just and fair outcomes is largely inaccessible and unlikely. Instead, the legacy of moral chaos, the realities of injustice and oppression and not their hypothetical absence, is the proper context for making just and fair judgments.

FALLEN ORDER AND LIBERAL JUSTICE

The legacy of "the Fall" in Western political thought is profound. The natural, original harmony of the Created Order is corrupted and damaged by sin and self-interest, by injustice and oppression. Human Fall entails a heightened self-awareness, exemplified by Adam and Eve's acknowledgement of guilt; each human at some point is keenly aware of one's selfish interests, of evil motives and corrupt outcomes, of self-deception and guilt. A typical human response to such self-consciousness, as narrated in the *Genesis* story, is intriguing but not surprising: concealment and blame; concealment of wrongdoing and blame of others. The damage resulting from the Fall is legendary and insidious. God fairly curses humans with each other, with "wages of sin," with a moral law of entropy: cycles of retributive justice from whose iron grip justice cannot by itself escape. Humans inflict themselves with all manner of evil, with moral and social chaos, strife and suffering, struggle and deprivations, with racial, gender and class alienations that result in banishment from Eden's paradise. Some Christians forget that these blights (e.g., gender inequality) are curses and not blessings, scourges not salves, corrosive and not normative. As such they are not to be accepted but transformed so the original harmony of *pax Dei* is restored.

The impact of this biblical narrative on modern political thinking is legendary, from Machiavelli to Hobbes, from Locke and Smith to Rawls. Their secular, political versions of the story of the Fall is typically framed in two ways: first, as a transgression of the laws of nature, which, secondly, results in competition, exploitation, fighting, chaos, violence, war, and death. Hobbes argues that humans naturally possess "an equality of hope in the attaining of our ends" that inevitably pits one against the other. Desiring the same things and in competition for limited resources, fallen humanity finds itself violating Nature's laws, thereby placing themselves in a condition of war "of every man, against every man."[12] Similarly, Locke, who draws explicitly on the biblical narrative, argues that humans in the state of nature possess equal executive power, "whereby everyone has a right to punish the transgressors of [the law of nature]. . . . [For] if any one in the state of nature may punish another for any evil he has done, every one may do so,"[13] so that ultimately the state of nature degenerates into a state of chaos and war that is "a state of enmity and destruction."[14] Smith and Hume analyze human corruption in terms of self-interest and social class prejudice, but insist, along with Hobbes and Locke, that moral and social order is naturally and reasonably within human reach. For Hobbes, Locke, Smith, and Hume alike human Fall from grace, whatever its cause, results in "wages," in ruin and corruption: selfishness, competition, animosity, war, chaos, death, and destruction, so that, as Hobbes famously puts it: "the life of man, solitary, poor, nasty, brutish, and short."[15]

Rawls's theory does not occupy itself much with human fallenness *per se*, although it presupposes it. What he does say parallels Locke's analysis in significant ways. Implicit in his standard model of "justice as fairness" is an acknowledgement of injustices and inequalities that beg redress. He speaks, for example, of justice as "proper balance between competing claims,"[16] which presupposes an imbalance of competing claims, of injustices. If liberal justice requires social institutions to fairly "distribute fundamental rights and duties,"[17] injustice implies fallen human tendencies that unfairly and prejudicially distribute them. Perhaps Rawls's most explicit statement regarding injustice is in reference to Aristotle's notion of *pleonexia:* "gaining some advantage for oneself by seizing what belongs to another, his property, his reward, his office, and the like, or by denying a person that which is due to him, the fulfillment of a promise, the repayment of a debt, the showing of proper respect, and so on," and where justice, then, entails refraining from *pleonexia.*[18] For Rawls, "justice is the first virtue of social institutions, as truth is of systems of thought."[19] The aim of the original position and social contract, of government and social institutions, then, is to subvert injustice and to establish and sustain procedures of liberal justice.

So, on what basis can and should humans, laboring under conditions of injustice and corruption, make judgments regarding justice? If doing so from a hypothetical state of nature or behind a veil of ignorance is unrealistic and finally impossible, on what basis are they possible? Assuming corruption, injustice and moral chaos, how can humans decipher justice and just action? An answer is suggested by Adam Smith in his notion of an "impartial spectator." A third party, "impartial spectator" is crucial to Smith's moral philosophy in general and to his notion of justice in particular. Both Hutcheson and Hume employed it as a moral tool and it is likely that they are its origin for Adam Smith. Its benefits for making juridical judgments are, I think, obvious, and indeed, the American judicial system presupposes it. I will focus on three characteristics: the need for it, the context of it, and the use of it.

First, the need for such a spectator is no mystery, given Smith's emphasis on the role of self-interest in human experience and given the limitations of sympathy. A person's capacity for sympathy is limited, as already noted, because I cannot truly feel what another, even family or friend, feels; or because the other is "distant" or without personal interest for me. So, if I want to determine what I should do to act justly, or evaluate whether I have done so or not, then I should want to consult others who are apt to be neutral and impartial regarding my interests and whose moral judgments are not shaped and distorted, as mine are, by self-love and self-interest.

Smith argues that "There is no passion . . . concerning whose justness we ought to be so doubtful, concerning whose indulgence we ought so carefully to consult our natural sense of propriety, or so diligently consider what will be the sentiments of the cool and impartial spectator."[20] Because there are real obstacles to my being a disinterested judge regarding my own moral judgments, it behooves me to consult an impartial, third-party, a kind of objective, moral conscience. Secondly, the notion of an impartial spectator presupposes a realistic, fallen state of affairs instead of the presupposed innocence of an abstract, hypothetical veil of ignorance. The spectator need not and indeed should not ignore particular, local realities. Not only my own passions and propensities to self-interest must be acknowledged, but particular conditions under which other labor, conditions such as injustice and poverty and other burdens, physical and psychological. An impartial spectator functions within the reality of fallenness, of self-love and indifference to others, which can be corrected only by the eye of this "impartial spectator." No hypothetical veil of ignorance here, but an objective, third-party perspective that "shows us the propriety of generosity and the deformity of injustice; the propriety of resigning the greatest interests of our own, for the yet greater interests of others, and the deformity of doing the smallest injury to another, in order to attain the greatest benefit to ourselves."[21] In other words, deciphering justice begins for Smith concretely, with reality, with poverty and oppression and class prejudices. Only then is made possible informed, fair, and impartial judgments. Finally, "impartial spectator" entails not only a moral principle but a pedagogical mechanism that enables a person to become, as Ryan Hanley puts it, "a self-spectator and thereby promote the development of conscience." It encourages "our equality with others by teaching us to transcend self-preference."[22] The impartial spectator is "reason, principle, conscience, the inhabitant of the breast, the man within, the great judge and arbiter of our conduct."[23]

The persuasive strength of Adam Smith's "impartial spectator" is partly evident in its difference from the social contract's "veil of ignorance," a difference between what Sen refers to as "open" and "closed" impartiality. Whereas a "veil of ignorance" draws on "the views of people within a polity in which the contract is being made," an "impartial spectator" draws on resources "as readily from outside of a community as from within it." Although for Rawls "distant" perspectives can be invoked, the impartiality to which his "reflective equilibrium" lends itself is "closed," that is, "it is confined to the members of the contracting parties (or their 'representatives')."[24] In contrast, Smith's "open impartiality" requires enfranchising the perspectives of people at a distance, people beyond borders and regions and cultures. In order to make a fair judgment at a distance, i.e., impartially, in order to traverse the boundaries of parochialism, we must endeavor to make such a judgment "with the eyes of other people, or as other people are likely to [make the judgment]." Smith's rationale for the necessity of such distance is simply that humans "can never survey our own sentiments and motives, we can never form any judgment concerning them, unless we remove ourselves, as it were, form our own natural station, and endeavor to view them as at a certain distance form us."[25] Smith's open "impartial spectator" is superior, I think, to Rawls's closed "veil of ignorance," not the least because it presupposes what in fact is, namely, the fallen, corrupt, selfish conditions under which humans individually and collectively live and labor, conditions that the contractual veil of ignorance by design seeks to suspend.

For all of its benefits, Smith's notion of "impartial spectator" is not without difficulty. Smith assumes, first of all, that all humans are capable of the self-discipline necessary to acquire impartiality's "distance." Some people, perhaps even some communities, societies, and nations are so far corrupted, their capacity for the "distance" of impartiality so far damaged, that on at least certain issues they seem incapable of seeing with the eyes of a third party. Wall Street Capitalists, corporate CEOs, anti-Muslim/anti-mosque tea party ideologues, anti-Western terrorists, ideological Marxists exemplify groups of people who on certain issues seem incapable of impartial spectatorship. Smith assumes, secondly, that once distance brackets partiality and one occupies a space of impartiality and sees through the eyes of the other, everyone would and should make the same judgment regarding justice. Smith's "impartial spectator" and indeed Rawls's "veil of ignorance" assume a kind of cosmic, moral symmetry that, allegedly at least, is transparent to rational minds. Although both approaches have their strengths both approaches assume that justice should entail making a judgment based on detachment from human experience instead of interaction with it, based on an intentional nullification of empirical reality instead of engagement with it. I develop my suspicions regarding these assumptions in the next two chapters; I argue that the most sufficient, empirical, and realistic position from which to make judgments regarding justice is a sentiment Hume insists most clearly distinguishes humans from other creatures, namely, sympathy, compassion. Justice can best be discerned not from a "veil of ignorance" or the distance of an "impartial spectator" but from a "vale of tears." I will argue that only on the basis of compassionate, sympathetic engagement are humans able not only to see justice but to see when projects of benevolence are needed in order to establish and sustain justice. In chapter 6 I examine compassion in some detail, showing, among other things, that justice for all is more likely achieved not from behind a veil of ignorance or from the distance of an impartial spectator but from the heart of a person who weeps with those who weep and rejoices with those rejoice. First, I examine how it is that liberal justice and egalitarian justice are related to moral order and to each other.

SOCIAL CONTRACT AND LIBERAL JUSTICE

In biblical narratives, the Redeemed Order employs the mercy of *pax Christi* in order to retrieve some semblance of the Created Order (*pax Dei*). Those inclined toward drawing political parallels might be tempted to identify liberal justice and its social contract with the Redeemed Order. The logic is simple: the Fall produces projects and structures of injustice; programs of liberal, procedural justice aim at restoring a just moral order. But we should resist this temptation. For although liberal procedures are *necessary* for establishing a just moral order (e.g., fair opportunities, *lex talionis*, and equal treatment), they are not *sufficient* for doing so. Liberal justice is by itself incapable of establishing the substantive, fair outcomes of a sustainable livelihood needed for approximating the harmony of God's original Created Order. Doing so requires projects and policies of benevolence. By examining the relationship between liberal and egalitarian justice here we will be able to see that and how benevolence, how a politics of mercy, is sometimes necessary for establishing any society that can rightfully claim to be just and civil. The aim of justice, John Rawls argues, is "fairness" or "the symmetry of everyone's relations to each other."[26] By "justice as fairness" Rawls refers primarily to liberal, procedural justice, a structural symmetry in which all are treated impartially and equally. Its purpose is to guarantee in the midst of injustice some measure of moral equilibrium and social order. The question is, how do we realize such an ideal? By what criteria do we measure success? How measure the rational symmetry of each to each other?

Any conception of liberal, procedural justice presupposes a rational moral symmetry, a correlation of rights and duties. By correlating duties and rights and codifying that correlation in laws, policies, and institutions government establishes a structure of fairness necessary to a just social and moral order. Correlating rights and duties constitutes the deontological dimension of justice's standard model, and constitutes a rational symmetry that makes the idea of a social contract morally attractive. In biblical narratives "the government, more than any other human agency, is given responsibility for justice." Its first duty, Mott rightly insists, is liberal and procedural, that is, it "is to ensure the basic rights of living in community."[27] Given that human nature is fallen and susceptible to disorder, evil, and injustice, God institutes government to establish and enforce just and orderly laws. Indeed, a kind of double duty characterizes a good society, as the apostle Paul's notes in his Epistle to the Romans: the aim of government is to establish social and moral order and the duty of Christians is to obey the good and just laws government enacts (Romans 13: 4–7).

The justification for establishing government, according to both Hobbes and Locke, is rational, moral symmetry, duties correlated with rights, like the symmetry that parallels biblical narratives and *lex talionis*. Humans in the state of nature are endowed by God with a "property" in rights and liberties, as Locke puts it, or with mutual self-interests, as Smith and Hume put it. Accordingly, it is the duty of government and stewardship of religious communities to see that these procedural duties are preserved and protected.

Since fallen humans typically infringe each other's rights and liberties or mutual self-interests, the ensuing state of war and moral chaos constitute the rationale for forming civil government. Its aim, we know already, is to guarantee a just moral order, and it does so by executing a social contract whose duty is to protect and preserve rights and liberties and mutual interests, to correlate rights with duties. The role of government so conceived constitutes the standard political model of moral reason, a modern version of *pax Romana*. Although Hobbes (enlightened despot) and Locke (democratic republic) differ regarding the distribution of governmental power, both insist on a social contract as the legitimate means for establishing that power and for correlating duties and rights. Legitimate authority for governing is derived through due process from the consent of those who are governed. The sovereign, accordingly, has a political duty first and foremost to the welfare, peace, and security of those from whom authority is derived and for whose benefit justice is executed.[28] Hobbes puts it this way: "*that a man be willing . . . to lay down [his] right to all things; and be contented with so much liberty against other men, as he would allow other men against himself.*" His "renouncing" or "transferring" of right, according to Hobbes, is really nothing more than "that law of the Gospel; *whatsoever you require that others should do to you, that do ye to them.*"[29] In Hobbes' version of *pax Romana* a benign despot with absolute power is the best, most efficient means for achieving the aim of a just moral order. The sovereign's contractual duty is to guarantee for citizens their right to peace and security, to social and political order, to live free of a state of war. Their rights and liberties via the social contract are mutually "renounced" and "transferred" to the sovereign, whose property they now are and whose duty it is to exercise them in whatever, enlightened way he sees fit for the peace and security of Leviathan's citizens.

Locke's version of social contract differs considerably at this point from Hobbes. Two ideas are crucial to Locke's social contract: "consent" and "majority rule."[30] Like Hobbes, Locke insists on a liberal social contract wherein legitimate authority to govern is derived from the consent of those governed. Unlike Hobbes, this contract is a pact between citizens and government so that government is continually accountable, via majority rule, to those whose rights and liberties it is obliged to protect. "For when any number of men have, by consent of every individual, made a community, they have thereby made that community one body, with a power to act as one body, which is only by the will and determination of the majority."[31] As in Hobbes, so also in Locke's version of *pax Romana* duty is correlated to certain rights. The duty of government is to protect and preserve as much as possible the moral symmetry of the Created Order, "the liberty, health, limb, or goods of another,"[32] the rights and liberties with which humans are naturally endowed. Indeed, he argues that if government fails in this duty, it forfeits its authority to govern and must be dissolved. "The end of government," claims Locke (echoing the apostle Paul from Romans 13), "is the good of mankind,"[33] government's duty is "the preservation of their property,"[34] their rights and liberties. When governments "act contrary to their trust . . . when they endeavor to invade the property of the subject" then they must be dissolved.[35] Interpreting the biblical tradition, Locke is arguing that the fallen, chaotic condition of humans in the state of nature necessitates a social contract in which the governed grant government the authority to execute justice by protecting their rights and liberties. This liberal aim establishes the duty of government and its social contract. When government fails in that duty it forfeits its contractual authority to govern, and citizens from whom that authority originates, are entitled to dissolve it and form another.

John Rawls's secular version of liberal justice parallels in significant ways Locke's Christian version, as Harlan Beckley carefully demonstrates.[36] Already I have noted that Rawls's "original position" correlates, as he himself says, to the natural condition of humans in the original state of nature (Created Order). The fallenness of humans, the state of chaos and war in which they find themselves, correlates to the basic self-interest that drives the desires and intentions of each individual and drives them into conflict and apart. For Rawls the duty of political and social institutions is to find a rational, practical way to advance procedural justice for all, a way to correlate duty to rights and liberties. As already noted the best procedure,[37] according to Rawls, is to suppose (what he calls) the "original position," a hypothetical, imaginary condition that consists of rational citizens of average intelligence. This society supposes itself behind a "veil of ignorance" that prevents citizens from making judgments based on self-interest; this is because the veil of ignorance prevents them from knowing what intellectual and personal abilities and traits they possess, and prevents them from knowing what they will accomplish or how they will fare socially and economically. For example, suppose a mother gives a piece of pie to her two children to share, with the stipulation that one child gets to cut the pie in two pieces while the other gets to choose first which sliced piece she will eat. The first child in the original position will operate from behind a veil of ignorance, not knowing which piece of pie will be left for her to eat. So, as a rational being, that child will cut the pieces of pie equally out of self-interest, in order to guarantee that she will be left with a piece of the pie equal to what her sibling selects. Likewise, citizens of a liberal society, in the original position and from behind a veil of ignorance, will construct institutions and policies that guarantee that they will be left with roughly as many rights and duties for themselves as will be fairly available to others.

More specifically, Rawls argues that in the "original position" society's duty correlates to two procedural principles, what he refers to as the Liberty Principle and the Difference Principle. "First: each person is to have an equal right to the most extensive basic liberty compatible with a similar liberty for others." And "Second, social and economic inequalities are to be arranged so that they are both (a) reasonably expected to be to everyone's advantage, and (b) attached to positions and offices open to all,"[38] especially to the benefit "of the least advantaged members of society."[39] These principles are much discussed by Rawls and his commentators and critics. The point I want to draw attention to here is that these two principles establish two sets of rights that correlate, for Rawls, to the duty of any society interested in justice as fairness. They establish a standard model of moral and civil order that he believes is procedurally fair and rational. The challenge Rawls's two principles addresses is a dilemma common to all such attempts; as Arjun Appadurai puts it: it is "the challenge of squaring Enlightenment universalisms and diasporic pluralisms."[40] Justice addresses the delocalized, transnational universalism of moral reason, while benevolence addresses the localized particularities of diasporic pluralism. Both must be accounted for, as indeed Rawls's two principles endeavor to, albeit inadequately. His Difference Principle, it seems to me, remains aristocratic and plutocratic, privileging still the most advantaged in ways that fail to adequately address the needs of the least advantaged.[41]

Whether one prefers Locke's social contract version of democracy or Rawls's version of justice as fairness or indeed any other version, benevolent communities, as stewards of social and moral order, are obligated to insist that governments protect not only liberal, procedural justice but promote egalitarian justice; that they protect not only rights and liberties but promote the fair economic outcomes of a sustainable livelihood without which the actual exercise of those rights and liberties remains largely formal and fanciful.

REDEEMED ORDER AND EGALITARIAN JUSTICE

Given that the mode of economic distribution, unlike the mode of production, is a matter of will and not scientific reason, what principle pilots a community toward fair economic outcomes? Along with Rawls's Liberty Principle I propose a "Distribution Principle" to replace his Difference Principle. It submits that *social and economic inequalities should be addressed by policies that directly and primarily benefit the least advantaged members of society, while at the same time secondarily minimizing burdens and/or maximizing benefits for the most advantaged.* This Principle might very well be called the "the least of these," in reference to Jesus's parable of the sheep and goats (Matthew 25). By "distribution" I mean to include several normative characteristics: first, that it provide a specific guide for allocating social and economic goods among the people of a particular, designated community or society or nation; secondly, that it provide "regulatory" power, both interpersonally and structurally, and that it provide a "corrective" to inequities in either transactions or allotments; thirdly, that it provide a substantial measure of economic fairness, although not strictly equal outcomes in exactly the same measure of goods for all. Instead its aim is to provide a "fair balance" of social and economic goods so that all people enjoy a "sustainable livelihood," as we have defined it: namely, enduring employment and the basic needs of a humane life, including, food, clothes, shelter, and health care. This principle does not, of course, constitute the whole of benevolence and a politics and mercy, but it is central and vital to them.

Not only does this Distribution Principle manifest the spirit of Jesus's life and teaching, and his remarkable focus and care for the vulnerable, it also refracts a principle St. Paul establishes for the Corinthian Christians (II Cor. 8: 7–15, NRSV). Paul says that just as the Corinthians excel in faith, speech, knowledge, eagerness, and love, so they should excel in a "generous undertaking." The undertaking he has in mind is somewhat paradoxical; they should emulate both "the generous act of . . . Christ . . . who was rich, yet for your sakes became poor, so that by his poverty you might become rich." Their generosity should distribute resources to the needy according to their means; they should give for the "relief of others" without undermining resources sufficient to maintain themselves. Indeed, Paul insists on it as an egalitarian matter; a matter "of a fair balance between your present abundance and their need, so that their abundance may be for your need, in order that there may be a fair balance: . . . The one who had much did not have too much, and the one who had little did not have too little." This is the kind of "fair balance" that the Distribution Principle strives for: that the most advantaged do not have too much and that the least advantaged have enough.

Unless societies are willing to incorporate as moral guide some such Distribution Principle to benefit "the least of these," unless they are willing to restructure institutions and policies and habituate them to the normative contours of some such principle, I do not see how a society can be anything but hypocritical when (pro)claiming itself just and fair. Without practicing such a principle publicly and politically, structurally and systematically; without local, national, and global initiatives for a decent and sustainable livelihood for all; without deliberately enacting egalitarian justice's substantive economic outcomes, societies cannot with integrity profess let alone promise social and moral order, including the harmony and peace envisioned by faith traditions. A willingness of communities to do so, of course, requires an evolution of collective moral character in which a society aspires to practice the virtues of benevolence along with the virtues of justice, aspires not only to the elder son's desire for fair treatment but also to the father's gift of merciful benevolence, aspires to be a Righteous and not merely a Just community.

Not only the Liberty Principle of liberal justice, then, but the Distribution Principle of egalitarian justice are integral to realizing the original harmony of the Created Order and the promise of the Redeemed Order. Merciful benevolence is the indispensible moral means for fulfilling that promise and achieving that "fair balance." Indeed, it is for religious communities not only a horizon of expectation but a present way of living. How is it to be retrieved and re-established as the realization of divine will? What demands does it place on government and benevolent communities? Locke and Hume, we have seen, tend to insist on egalitarian along with liberal justice as a public virtue and on a politics of benevolence for achieving it. Smith and Rawls tend to favor liberal, procedural justice alone as a public virtue, although Rawls's Difference Principle moves minimally in the direction of egalitarianism. The view for which I argue, based on biblical narratives, is for practicing the "fair balance" of the Distribution Principle. In short, the common aim of maintaining moral/social order and of protecting the dignity of all humans requires practicing egalitarian as well as liberal justice as a public virtue, requires commitment to the asymmetrical power of merciful benevolence.

Already we have seen how in his *Second Treatise of Government* John Locke insists not only on self-preservation but also on altruism as a duty and as natural to the human condition. These duties are not only to self-preservation, which humans have in common with all creatures, but as far as possible to the preservation of a sustainable livelihood for others. Two natural laws in particular are relevant. First, Locke suggests that the state of nature includes not only justice's liberal duties, protecting "property," rights and liberties; but that it also includes altruistic duties of benevolence, protecting the property of others, preserving their health, possessions, food, shelter, indeed, protecting all that humans need to preserve themselves in their livelihood. Accordingly, when government contracts with citizens to rule, one of its duties is to preserve and protect as far as possible these natural, moral laws of reason. He argues that it is a duty of reason and nature that humans not only work to preserve their own liberty, health, limb, possessions and goods, but also a duty to do the same for others.[42] Moreover, a social contract, which establishes its possibility, obligates government to preserve and protect publically what reason's laws establish naturally. In short, government is obligated, according to Locke, to both liberal and egalitarian justice; and, as we shall see, projects and policies of benevolence are required in order for government to fulfill these obligations, especially projects that treat of basic human needs (health, possessions, food, shelter, goods, etc.) for all citizens. Civil law and policy, Locke believes, should not neglect but protect and preserve these "properties" of rights and goods established by nature and discovered by reason.

Moreover, for Locke obligations of egalitarian justice are rooted not only in moral reason but also in biblical tradition. He quotes favorably, for example, and at some length from "the judicious [Thomas]Hooker['s]" *Lawes of Ecclesiasticall Politie:*

> The like natural inducement hath brought men to know that it is no less their duty to love others than themselves; for seeing those things which are equal must needs all have one measure; if I cannot but wish to receive good, even as much at every man's hand as any man can wish unto his own soul, how should I look to have any part of my desire herein satisfied unless myself be careful to satisfy the like desire, which is undoubtedly in other men, being of one and the same nature.[43]

Humans should love others as much as they love themselves; we should desire for and grant to others the same substantive goods and benefits of life that we desire for and grant to ourselves. One might argue over precisely what beneficial outcomes are included within the scope of such egalitarian justice, but it seems it would include, at least according to Locke, a "fair balance" of those goods necessary for the dignified preservation of human life created in the image of God: decent shelter, food, clothes, employment, estate, property, and health, all of which Locke at one time or another suggests in *The Second Treatise*. That humans do not all equally share in these benefits of life originally provided in and by the Created Order is the tragic result of fallenness. The duty of government is to establish a social and civil order so that all humans are able to embody and practice the dignity of their Divine image. Locke's rationale for establishing benevolence is explicitly religious: for humans are all "the workmanship of one omnipotent and infinitely wise Maker . . . made to last during his, not another's, pleasure; and being furnished with like faculties, sharing in all one community of nature, there cannot be supposed any such subordination among us that may authorize us to destroy another, as if we were made for one another's use as the inferior ranks of creatures are for ours."[44] As benevolent stewards of egalitarian justice the state as well as faith communities must work toward a fair balance of social and economic outcomes. Such outcomes properly belong to all humans simply because they are created by God in God's image, are equal before God and of equal, intrinsic value. Although in his *Essay on Toleration* Locke tends to separate quite radically church and state, he nevertheless insists that along with justice both are obligated to practice what he calls "benevolence" and "charity." Locke is advocating at minimum, it seems, that justice and benevolence are interdependent and mutually established duties of government. Indeed, sometimes the former (egalitarian justice) requires the latter (benevolence) if it is to subvert injustice and sustain itself.

Secondly, Locke argues on the basis of natural law that moral reason limits the quantity of "property" any human has a right to. He makes this case in the context of his famous argument for property. The earth is given by God in common to all humans; and yet property is justifiable, because all humans have a property in their own person (rights and liberties), in their own labor, and in whatever they "mix" their labor with, the product of their labor. No one has a right to these properties, according to Locke and natural law, except oneself.[45] He goes on to argue, however, that there is a limit to the amount of property humans have a right to mix their labor with. "It will perhaps be objected . . . that 'if gathering the acorns, or other fruits of the earth, etc., makes a right to them, then any one may engross as much as he will.' To which I answer: not so. The same law of nature that does by this means give us property does also bound that property, too." The voice of Scripture and reason decrees that there is a limit to what humans can rightfully possess for themselves: "As much as any one can make use of to any advantage of life before it spoils, so much may he by his labor fix a property in; whatever is beyond this is more than his share and belongs to others."[46] Locke is writing in the context of an agrarian society, but his point is transferable to any economic system. Both Scripture and reason acknowledge a law of nature that limits the property to which any human has a right: only as much as I need to sustain my life and those lives dependent on my labor. I have no right, indeed it is an injustice, argues Locke, to possess more than this; and when we do it is an insult to God and an infringement of the rights of needy others to it. Americans especially have so apotheosized free market Capitalism and its alleged efficiency that its vice of self-interest (i.e., "greed") is treated, ironically, as an economic virtue; a kind of pyrrhic duty to engross to oneself for the sake of a vital economy as much of society's goods as possible. Locke rejects such reasoning as contradicting the laws of reason and nature established by God, for two reason; first, because one has a natural right only to so much as is necessary for a sustainable livelihood, and second, because humans are obligated not only to self-interest (preserving their own life) but naturally obligated to altruism, to assist in sustaining the lives of others. Accordingly, any social contract must protect and preserve not only the natural duty of self-preservation but the altruistic duty of helping others maintain something like a sustainable livelihood. This philosophical inquiry on behalf of egalitarian justice is consistent with theological inquiry and the biblical narratives.

Locke's philosophical argument for establishing egalitarian justice's fair balance parallels an ancient theological one, which I briefly sketch here and develop more fully in the remainder of this book.[47] As summarized in chapter 1, biblical narratives trace morality's evolution from tribal customs to rational law and finally to spiritual law. Most important for my purposes here is this latter evolution from the strict equal justice of rational law to the merciful benevolence of faith's egalitarian justice. A number of significant covenantal codes and public institutions, in ancient Hebrew tradition, promote egalitarian outcomes as a function of mercy. From Abraham and Moses, from Hosea and Jonah, from Amos to Jesus and Paul, mercy's transformative power calls the faithful to a law of liberty that distributes a "fair balance" of social and economic goods. The biblical narratives envision an egalitarian society established by a politics of mercy, by intentional policies and institutions crafted for the care of "the least of these."

First of all, the Distribution Principles' aim of fair balance is exemplified by the law of gleaning (Leviticus 19: 9–10), which requires that harvesting take place in such a way that food is made available to the poor and needy. The reaper is to leave unharvested the borders of fields and pickers are to leave grapes on the vines and on the ground "for the poor and the alien." Even further, the covenant permits the poor and hungry entering another's field and eating one's fill, although it prohibits abuse of this practice (Deut. 23: 24–25). Secondly, of the several kinds of tithes commanded in ancient Hebrew tradition, one of them was directed to assist the poor (Deuteronomy 14: 28–29; 26:12–14). Every third year, "the year of tithing," a tenth of one's possessions is required of Israelites as a contribution to the welfare of the poor, to Levites, to strangers, orphans, and widows. Thirdly, especially directed to the welfare of the poor is the law of usury (Leviticus 25: 35–38), which states that if a poor neighbor cannot maintain himself economically, then you, as his brother, have a duty to "maintain him" economically, and in doing so you are to "take no interest from him or increase. . . . You shall not lend him your money at interest nor give him your food for profit. I am the Lord your God that brought you forth out of the land of Egypt to give you the land of Canaan, and to be your God." God's covenant with Israel includes an economic trajectory as well as spiritual and political, a trajectory away from policies of self-interest and toward the interests of the vulnerable. The Israelite is protected from the prison of indebtedness by denying lenders the right to collect interest on borrowed money (Exodus 22: 25). Fourthly, the sabbatical year (Exodus 21–23; Deut. 15) includes the emancipation of slaves and their families, and by the poor and stranger the harvesting of crops that grow spontaneously in fallow fields (Exodus 23: 10–11). In the Deuteronomic version of the code, the sabbatical year care of the poor includes as a matter of public policy: cancellation of all debts (15: 1–6), lending to the poor (15: 7–11), and the liberation of Hebrew slaves (15: 12–18), with the stipulation that the freed slaves, including women, are to be sent away with provisions sufficient to establish a new life. This obligation of Israel to the economic welfare of freed slaves is linked specifically to God's mercy in freeing Israel from Egypt and providing for them. Finally, the provisions of the Jubilee Year (every fiftieth year), found in Leviticus 25, presupposes that the people of Israel are to be good stewards of what rightfully belongs to God, redistributing property in order to guarantee fairer outcomes so that land does not become the possession of a privileged few. These provisions include returning real estate to its original owners, the sale and redemption of land, and the redemption of slaves.

Collectively, these covenantal practices constitute a fairly elaborate system of distributive benevolence for the sake of realizing an egalitarian ideal of "fair balance." Indeed, they constitute a politics of mercy that obligates Israel to care for the poor, needy, and vulnerable in extraordinary ways. These covenantal practices establish political institutions that enfranchise procedures for achieving a "fair balance" of social and economic outcomes commensurable with the Distribution Principle: freedom from debts and fair distribution of land and economic resources. As Robert Kysar concludes about these ancient Hebrew provisions, God instructs Israel to "create a system whereby those [whose resources] are plentiful supply the needs of those who want. It is a system of welfare in the best sense of the concept—a social structure that enhances the welfare of those who have suffered misfortune."[48] In short, Israel as God's covenantal community is instructed to establish a benevolent as well as a just political and social system that guarantees a fair, minimum sustainable livelihood, and not only for all citizens but for immigrants and foreigners as well.

It is not surprising, accordingly, that a central message of the Hebrew prophets assumes something like the Distribution Principle and a politics of mercy; a common target of prophetic venom is Israel's failure to care for the needs and interests of the vulnerable. Amos, for example, is vitriolic: "They sell the righteous for silver and the needy for a pair of sandals—they that trample the head of the poor into the dust of the earth" (2: 6–7). He refers to the rich as "the cows of Bashan . . . who oppress the poor, who crush the needy"; wealthy women, so calloused that they luxuriate in self-indulgence while ignoring the needy, instructing "their husbands, 'Bring that we may drink,'" (Amos 4: 1) while the poor and needy in their midst suffer hunger and thirst. Prophets routinely excoriate the rich who exploit the poor in order to increase their wealth. Micah, for example, berates the unjust means by which those with power conspire to acquire land at the expense of others (2: 1–2). And Jeremiah denounces the rich who calculate to trap the poor, like animals, in order that they might increase their wealth (5: 26–27). The rulers of Israel, as representatives of the people, are given special responsibilities, and they too have failed miserably. Like the wealthy, they too have failed to fulfill the covenantal mandate of economic justice. Speaking to the "heads of the house of Jacob and rulers of the house of Israel" Micah charges them as ones "who abhor justice and pervert all equity"; rulers who "give judgment for a bribe," priests who "teach for hire," and prophets who "divine for money," all in the name of the Lord (3: 9–11). The Psalmists' message is similar, as noted by Kysar. In advocating for the welfare of the poor and needy. "God raises up the needy (107: 41) and is the savior of the poor (34: 6). The afflicted are defended by God (140: 12). God is present with the needy (103: 31) and reverses the human conditions of want and deprivation (113: 5–9), rescuing the needy."[49] The consensus of prophets and psalmists is that Israel is responsible for substantive—egalitarian, social, and economic—outcomes of its citizens and that mercy and generosity of benevolence is therefore necessary. As the prophet Amos suggests: in order to "do justly" one must "love mercy" and "walk humbly with God" (6: 8, KJV).

Jesus and Paul certainly promote, at least in spirit if not in all its specific codified details, Israel's obligation to egalitarian justice and something like the Distribution Principle. They call on Christians to show mercy and benevolence. Jesus intentionally extends the covenantal mandate of the Hebrew prophets, of which he is one, into the social and political culture of his day. Indeed, in his first reported public appearance he identifies himself with the economic and social message of the prophets when he reads in his home synagogue a passage from Isaiah (61: 1-2; Luke 4: 16–21):

> The Spirit of the Lord is upon me,
> because he has anointed me to bring good news to the poor.
> He has sent me to bring release to the captives
> and recovering of sight to the blind,
> to let the oppressed go free,
> to proclaim the year of the Lord's favor.

Jesus announces that this covenantal mandate is fulfilled in himself, in his own ministry and mission. His message really is unambiguous: "to be the fulfillment of God's concern to alter the physical conditions of the people of Israel,"[50] by advocating the "year of the Lord," which implies a system of benevolent political and social welfare that addresses in a egalitarian way poverty and oppression. So Jesus's intends outcomes, intends to actually alleviate the poverty of the poor and slavery of the oppressed; he does not intend in his ministry merely to establish liberal procedures whereby these accomplishments might be possible and nothing more. Jesus speaks of and to the poverty of his time and to the wealthy who he holds partly responsible for the plight of the poor. He praises the wealthy Zacchaeus who instinctively understands his conversion to mean that he should distribute his wealth for the care of the poor (Luke 19: 1–10). He tells the Rich Young Ruler that if he is to be a disciple and inherit life eternal he must "sell all that you have and distribute to the poor" (Luke 18: 18–25). The wealthy Dives is condemned to hell for not caring for poor Lazarus who sits at his gate (Luke 16: 19–31). In short, justice as economic fairness—fairness of substantive economic outcomes—is crucial to Jesus's gospel. For his hearers "The advent of the kingdom of God meant the transformation of the economic conditions of the nation and the poor in particular. It implied . . . the alleviation of poverty . . . a radical reordering of society." Jesus message of hope to the poor is good news to the poor only if their poverty is substantively alleviated; it had "a revolutionary quality that was directly relevant to those suffering impoverishment. This is the 'good news' the poor hear preached to them (Luke 7: 22) in the ministry of Jesus."[51]

This biblical view, that justice includes the benevolence of egalitarian outcomes challenges the separation of church and state. Because benevolence is rooted historically in religion, disestablishing religion while establishing benevolence is a precarious undertaking at best. We have already seen that Jesus sanctions the system of public benevolence long practiced by Judaism. The Apostle Paul, it seems to me, also explicitly argues for the establishment of benevolence and something like the Distribution Principle; in Romans 12 and 13, for example. Recall that in the modern Bible chapter "breaks" are later additions to the original texts. The moral principles advocated by Paul in Romans 12: 14–21 are guides for political authorities realizing the social and moral order for which purpose their offices are instituted. Many New Testament scholars would agree with John Yoder who in reference to Romans argues that "In the structure of the Epistle, chapters 12 and 13 in their entirety form one literary unit. Therefore the text 13: 1–7 cannot be understood alone."[52] Chapter 12 calls Christians to be non-conformist, independent of the "world," and to be fundamentally transformed. In the final eight verses of that chapter, Paul catalogues a series of moral principles that explicate what it means to resist worldly corruption and conform to Christ: bless and don't curse your enemies (meekness), rejoice with those who rejoice and weep with those who weep (empathy), live harmoniously with each other (peacemaking), do not be arrogant (humility), associate with the powerless and marginalized (compassion), reject retaliatory justice (vengeance) for it belongs to the Lord alone, help those in need, even enemies and wrongdoers (benevolence). These are the radical moral principles not only that the Christian community should practice but around which "governing authorities" should rule; it is this vision of social and moral order that governing authorities, "instituted by God," are to enforce. In other words, Paul's vision of benevolence for the Christian community is at the same time a vision of public virtue and policy.

Paul's *Letter to the Galatians* includes a sustained examination of the difference between "man's gospel" and "the gospel of Christ." Man's gospel is "a different gospel," and "pervert[s] the gospel of Christ" (Gal. 1: 6–11). And how does it? Man's gospel, we find out, is a legalistic gospel, Christ's gospel is one of grace and mercy. In the early church, certain Christian leaders were insisting on a gospel based on law, even of Gentile converts, especially on the practice of circumcision. In contrast, Paul was insisting on a gospel of faith, faith in the power of "grace" and "love." What redeems, what liberates is not some efficacy of works of the law, Paul argues, but the efficacy of works of mercy and love (Galatians 2–4). Not by submitting to some legalistic "yoke of slavery" are people and society redeemed, but by "stand[ing] fast" on behalf of freedom, on behalf of grace and mercy and love. Indeed, the "freedom" for which "Christ has set us free" (4: 1), according to Paul, is the freedom for Christian communities to practice the same grace and mercy and love that they receive from Christ. To restrict practicing this freedom of mercy to private personal life is a "yoke of slavery." So, it seems to me that the defining moment for Christian communities *qua* Christian is precisely those moments of freedom, those occasions, private and public, for practicing the freedom of mercy; those public and political occasions of freedom for acting not only justly and fairly but compassionately and mercifully; occasions of freedom for practicing benevolence in public life as well as justice; and freedom for practicing the asymmetry of faith's mercy in public life as well as the symmetry of reason's justice. So, this is one way, it seems to me, of faithfully applying the distinction Paul makes in Galatians between "man's gospel" and "the gospel of Christ."

There are practical reasons for believing that the ideal of egalitarian justice is unlikely to be realized without a substantial and sustained public commitment to policies of benevolence and something like the Distribution Principle. To subvert habits of social and economic injustice and transform them into just economic outcomes often requires projects of benevolence. When presupposing human fallenness, as do biblical narratives, we are presupposing at the same time a social and structural culture of fallenness, of injustice and discrimination. If in the midst of a social fabric of injustice the strict symmetry of procedural justice is implemented and practiced, then the inequities already present are simply perpetuated and preserved, not redeemed and changed. If a race is run in which one contestant runs fifty meters to the finish line and another seventy-five meters and another one hundred (culture of injustice), and all are now required to run at the same velocity (liberal justice) then the very inequalities at the beginning of the race remain at the end, albeit perhaps with some contestants feeling smugly that the race is fairly run (advocates of liberal justice) and with others feeling swindled by a race unfairly won (advocates of egalitarian justice). The need for affirmative action is a familiar case in point. Or recall the parable of the day laborers. Instead of treating all of the laborers procedurally the same (liberal justice), proportional to the hours worked, Jesus treats some of the laborers more generously and benevolently. Not to make day laborers feel unfairly treated, for Jesus has paid them a fair, agreed upon wage. Instead, Jesus generously provides the other hourly workers with a sustainable livelihood based, we can imagine, on their need. Jesus understands that to redress and redeem economic injustices he must act benevolently, by transcending justice's simple procedural symmetry and by faith practicing the "moral turbulence" of benevolence. This is the difference between a Just person and a Righteous one. The Righteous compensate for injustices embedded in the Fallen Order by granting the extraordinary generosity of benevolence in a way that eludes the Just man. The elder son, a Just man, in Jesus's parable, is confounded by the mercy granted by his Father, a Righteous man. But the Father knew, as apparently did the younger son, that justice would rightly reckon the prodigal a servant, and that only the benevolence of mercy could reconcile the prodigal to the Father and restore him as son.

Substantive and sustained historical examples of a politics of mercy are discussed in chapter 7. For now, an instructive example comes from a substantial historical event, namely, the Camp David Accords (1978) between Israel's Prime Minister Menachem Begin and Egyptian President Anwar Al Sadat, facilitated by U.S. President Jimmy Cater. The hostilities between the two governments were persistent and passionate. Begin and Sadat were not on speaking terms; each considered itself a victim and the other a vendor of injustice. Nevertheless, both sides thought that peace was in their mutual best interests, and so they were willing to forfeit the perpetual cycle of retaliatory, retributive justice that had for decades dominated their relationship; they were willing in good faith and with integrity to engage in negotiations that required of them a politics of mercy and the exercise of the Distribution Principle, which in the end yielded stunning results: sustained peace and the equal justice, a "normalization of relations." This normalization required both sides to forego customary habits of retaliatory justice and undertake projects of merciful benevolence. Both nations mutually contributed acts of benevolence; granting amnesty by withholding certain burdens, and generously granting unmerited benefits.

Israel agreed to withdraw its armed forces from the Sinai, evacuate its 4,500 civilian inhabitants, limit its forces near the border, and guarantee safe and free passage between Egypt and Jordan. Egypt agreed to normalize diplomatic relations with Israel (despite objections from Arab nations), guarantee safe and free passage through the Suez Canal and other water ways, such as the straits of Tiran, and limit the number of military forces Egypt could maintain on the Sinai Peninsula. For both Israel and Egypt good and just reasons could and were given for maintaining a status quo of reoccurring hostilities and injustices. These two leaders, however, with integrity of character, evolved beyond futile patterns of retaliatory justice that over decades proved themselves powerless to subvert the injustice people on both sides suffered. They drew on the transformative power of merciful benevolence, forfeiting moral reason and the demands of liberal justice, and in faith trusted that there is in a politics of mercy power sufficient to transform the alienation of injustice into a fair balance that eluded proposals rooted in the retributive cycles of liberal justice. The Camp David Accords represent one of many instances in which the transformative power of mercy was sufficient to subvert injustice and produce the "fair balance" socially and economically that habits of liberal justice themselves could not produce.

Proposals advocating benevolence as a public virtue are available. Kai Nielsen in *Equality and Liberty*[53] argues for such a benevolent system on a non-religious, philosophical basis; Robert Kysar in *Called to Care* argues for such a system theologically, on the basis of Christian faith. What I am suggesting here is that the image of justice that the Christian community must require of the state, in its efforts to establish a fair moral and social order, should include not only something like the procedural duties of Rawls's liberal justice but also something like the substantive outcomes of Nielsen's egalitarian justice. My aim in the next chapter is to show how mercy as the driving spiritual force of benevolence is able, in the midst of injustice, to establish and sustain a culture of egalitarian justice that is essential to the biblical vision of restoring the harmony and peace of God's Created Order.

NOTES

1. Quoted from *Shakespeare and Christian Doctrine* by Roland Mushat Frye (Princeton, NJ: Princeton University Press, 1963), 207.
2. See chapter XIII of *Leviathan.*
3. Both Hobbes and Locke are explicitly Christian thinkers and in their political works refer to the Christian sources and dimensions of their ideas and theory. However, Hobbes is typically thought of as being largely a secular thinker. The chapter immediately preceding his discussion of the state of nature is "of Religion," which provides the immediate conceptual framework for examining the natural condition of humans. Moreover, in both part II and III of *Leviathan* he relates his political theory explicitly to Christian ideas, such as the "Kingdom of God" and "Christian Commonwealth." Locke is perhaps even more "Christian" in that his political ideas seem to arise more naturally and logically from his Christian convictions. His *Second Treatise of Civil Government* is immediately preceded by the *First Treatise*, which is an extended theological examination of the emergence of Sovereignty in the biblical tradition and the relationship of Adam to it.
4. These classic sources of modern political thought are familiar. See especially Thomas Hobbes, *Leviathan*, chapter XIII, and John Locke, *The Second Treatise of Civil Government*, chapter II.
5. *Second Treatise*, II., 6.
6. *Second Treatise*, V., 27.
7. I do not mean to unfairly identify Rawls's views with any religious conceptions that he has no apparent interest in. His theory of justice is an entirely secular one, amazingly free of any reference to the role and significance of religion in political and public life. But the parallel to a religious version of justice is nevertheless apparent, the case for which Harlan Beckley has made persuasively in "A Christian Affirmation of Rawls's Idea of Justice as Fairness—Part I and Part II," *Journal of Religion Ethics* 13, 2 (1985); 14, 2 (1986).
8. John Rawls, *A Theory of Justice*, I., 3.
9. John Rawls, *A Theory of Justice*, I., 3.
10. Amartya Sen, *The Idea of Justice* (Cambridge, MA: Belknap Press of Harvard University Press, 2009), 126.
11. *Ibid.*, 127.
12. *Leviathan*, XIII.
13. *Second Treatise*, II., 7–8.
14. *Ibid.*, III., 16.
15. *Leviathan*, XIII.
16. Rawls, *Theory of Justice*, I., 2.
17. *Ibid.*, 7.
18. *Ibid.*, 10.
19. *Ibid.*, 3.
20. *Theory of Moral Sentiments*, I.ii.3., 47–48.
21. *Ibid.*, III.iii.158.

22. Ryan Patrick Hanley, *Adam Smith and the Character of Virtue* (Cambridge: Cambridge University Press, 2009), 136.
23. *Theory of Moral Sentiments*, I.iii.158.
24. Amartya Sen, "Introduction" to *The Theory of Moral Sentiments* (New York: Penguin Books, 2009), xvii.
25. *Theory of Moral Sentiments*, III.i.2. Amartya Sen, in his "Introduction" to Smith's *The Theory of Moral Sentiments*, indicates a couple of reasons why the "closedness" of Rawls's "veil" is problematic: "(1) the relevance of other people's interests—far away from as well as close to a given society—for the sake of preventing unfairness to those who are not party to the social contract for that society; and (2) the pertinence of other people's *perspectives* to broaden our own investigation of relevant principles, for the sake of avoiding underscrutinized parochialism of values and presumptions in the local community" (xviii). See also Sen's critique of Rawls's "closed" veil in his *Idea of Justice*, 128–130.
26. John Rawls, *A Theory of Justice* (Cambridge, MA: Belknap Press of Harvard University Press, 1971), I., 3.
27. Stephen Mott, *Biblical Ethics and Social Change* (New York, NY: Oxford University Press, 1982), 192.
28. Hobbes and Locke, as is well-known, differ as to who is party to the social contract. For Hobbes the contract is solely between citizens and not between the citizens and ruler. Hence, although the ruler is obligated to rule for the benefit of the citizens who mutually transfer their rights and liberties to him, the ruler has no legal or contractual obligation to act as representative of the people's will or desires, nor can the people dissolve the power of the sovereign. For Locke, on the other hand, the social contract is between citizens and government, so that government is obligated to do the will of the people, i.e., protect their rights and liberties; if the government happens to infringe these rights and liberties it is the obligation of the citizens to dissolve the government and form a new one.
29. *Leviathan*, XIV.
30. *Second Treatise*, VIII., 96–97.
31. *Ibid.*, VIII., 96.
32. *Second Treatise*, II., 6.
33. *Ibid.*, XIX., 229.
34. *Ibid.*, XIX., 222.
35. *Ibid.*, XIX., 221.
36. I highly recommend Harlan Beckley's two articles, "A Christian Affirmation of Rawls's Idea of Justice as Fairness," parts 1 and 2, *Journal of Religious Ethics* 13 and 14 (Fall 1985 and Fall 1986), 210–242, 229–246.
37. The summary of Rawls's theory that follows is found in chapter I, "Justice as Fairness" in his *Theory of Justice*.
38. *Theory of Justice*, II., 11.
39. *Ibid.*, 75.
40. Arjun Appadurai, *Modernity at Large: Cultural Dimensions of Globalization* (Minneapolis, MN: University of Minnesota Press, 1996), 172–173.
41. Rawls's Difference Principle establishes, it seems to me, a basis for something like the infamous "trickle down" economics of the Reagan presidency and in the United States' subsequent conservative economic policies.
42. *Second Treatise*, II., 6.
43. *Ibid.*, II., 5. Locke notes that this selection is from (*Eccl. Pol.* Lib.i).
44. *Ibid.*, II., 5.
45. *Ibid.*, V., 27.
46. *Ibid.*, V., 31.
47. For fuller treatments of egalitarian justice I point the interested reader to two accessible books: Robert Kysar, *Called to Care: Biblical Images for Social Ministry* (Minneapolis, MN: Augsburg/Fortress, 1991); and Kent A. Van Til, *Less Than Two Dollars a Day: A Christian View of World Poverty and the Free Market* (Grand Rapids, MI: William B. Eerdmans Pub. Co., 2007).

48. Robert Kysar, *Called to Care: Biblical Images for Social Ministry* (Minneapolis, MN: Augsburg Fortress, 1991), 17.

49. *Called to Care*, 23.

50. *Ibid.*, 33.

51. *Ibid.*, 39.

52. See John Howard Yoder, *The Politics of Jesus* (Grand Rapids, MI: Eerdmans Pub. Co., 1972), 197. See also Richard Hays, *The Moral Vision of the New Testament: A Contemporary Introduction to New Testament Ethics* (San Francisco, CA: HarperCollins Pub., 1996), 240–246.

53. Kai Nielsen, *Equality and Liberty: A Defense of Radical Egalitarianism* (Savage, MD: Rowman & Littlefield, 1985).

Chapter Five

Benevolence and Mercy

Consider the parable of the unforgiving servant (Matthew 18: 23–35). A king has a servant who owes him a debt the servant cannot pay. The king, wanting to settle the debt, decides that in all fairness the debtor must nevertheless pay, even if the servant must sell all of his possessions, including his wife and children. The debtor is understandably distraught and with great remorse falls on his knees, imploring "'Lord have patience with me and I will pay you everything.' Out of pity for him the king released him and forgave him the debt." Now, this same servant, who has been forgiven, comes upon a fellow servant who owes him a debt. He immediately assaults the servant, saying 'Pay what you owe me.' The second servant pleads with the first for patience and time to pay off the debt. But the first servant will have none of it and throws his fellow servant in prison until the debt is paid. When the king hears what happens he is furious and summons the forgiven servant to him and says "You wicked servant! I forgave you all that debt because you besought me; and should you not have mercy on your fellow servant as I had mercy on you?" Angered by the servant's arrogance and vengeful spirit, the king jails the servant until he pays his debt. Jesus ends this parable by declaring, so also will God do to every one who does not show mercy and forgiveness.

This parable penetrates to the heart of the thesis I am advocating, as does the parable of the prodigal. It challenges Christians with what appears to be a conflict between two virtues, justice and mercy; it confronts the reader with a decisive choice between two moral qualities: justice or mercy, reason or faith, law or grace, servitude or liberty. It is a challenge because mercy requires a more evolved moral character than does justice, a challenge because mercy grants unmerited benefits of amnesty to wrongdoers and enemies as well as generosity to the vulnerable; a challenge because mercy requires between donor and recipient moral reciprocity and social equilibrium. But this divergence between mercy and justice is in truth a distinction without a difference. For the aim of mercy is not for the sake of mercy itself but for the sake of establishing egalitarian justice. It has the power to subvert the injustice of poverty and need, just as did the ancient mercies of the Sabbatical and Jubilee Years. Under conditions of injustice, it alone possesses the power for establishing and sustaining the "fair balance" of economic outcomes. Even further, as in the parable of the prodigal, mercy has the power to redeem, restore and reconcile, to enfranchise the disenfranchised.

Mercy constitutes the subjective disposition of which benevolence is the objective, behavioral manifestation. For Christian communities mercy's burdens and benevolence's benefits are deeply rooted in the grace of Eucharistic gratitude. Without it, faith's "conviction of things not seen" and "assurance of things hoped for" seem irrational and inert. Without Eucharistic remembrance Christians typically emulate the debtor servant who prefers justice to mercy, reason to faith, law to liberty. Like the debtor servant, recipients of benevolence earnestly plead God's mercy and forgiveness; but too often as donors hypocritically grant others not mercy but justice and condemnation. Like the servant, they eagerly receive mercy with one hand but refuse to give it to others with the other hand; for example, by practicing mercy in private life but refusing to practice it in public life. When devotees perceive it is not to their advantage and benefit as donors, they refuse, like the servant, to grant mercy and instead in "bad faith" demand justice. But what if Christian communities take seriously their confession of faith? What if they actually believe that the world is fallen and that injustice is pervasive? What if they practice in public as well as in personal life the same benevolence and generosity that Christ grants them and which they claim for themselves? What if in social and political matters they grant to others the same compassion and mercy they have received? What if they really had "the conviction of things not seen" and "the assurance of things hoped for"? What if Christian communities understand themselves not as propagandists for any local nation-state but as patriots of God's transnational, peaceable Kingdom? What would result?

Recall the "new commandment" Jesus gives his disciples on the night of his betrayal. Not only are they to love each other as they love themselves; but they are to love, says Jesus, in a specific and unique way: "even as I have loved you [mercifully], that you also love one another." Indeed, it is by this very kind of merciful love whereby "all men will know that you are my disciples" (John 13: 31–35). This "new commandment" yields certain fruits, what I have been referring to philosophically as "benevolence." Benevolence entails activities and projects of mercy that under conditions of injustice are able to establish and sustain egalitarian justice. As the motive and power of will for practicing benevolence, mercy is constituted by two qualities; it is primarily altruistic and other-regarding, not egoistic and self-regarding; secondly, it situates itself asymmetrically in relation to justice's symmetry, entailing a duty, as we shall see, without a correlative right. The point and ultimately the result of practicing such mercy is protecting the dignity of humans created in God's image; and it does so by distributing social and economic goods so that at minimum a fair balance is established and sustained. What, then, are the spiritual and moral qualities that constitute mercy and make possible the practice of Jesus's new commandment? At least three qualities are crucial: gratitude, generosity, and remembrance.

GRATITUDE

Most Christians and I dare say most Christian ethicist would reply, when asked, that the central principle of Christian morality is love, Divine love, *agape*. They would be correct, of course. Yet saying so leaves a great deal of ambiguity; love lends itself to a wide variety of interpretations. These interpretations are noticeable when ethicists draw out love's moral and political implications. Does Christian love favor just war or just peacemaking? Does it favor libertarian or egalitarian economies? Does it favor strict fairness or affirmative action? Pro-life or pro-choice? And so on. Christian social ethics becomes as partisan and politicized as secular social and political ethics. What is often neglected, in such discussions, is the historical, theological, and sacramental anchor to which any viable and genuinely Christian conception of love is tethered. This is a point Joseph Fletcher made decades ago in *Situation Ethics*. He argues that gratitude or a feeling of thankfulness is at the heart of Christian love because the Eucharist is the sacramental heart of Christian experience. "The Christian ethic," he says, "is peculiar because it is a Eucharistic ethic, an ethic of thanksgiving. It comes from the compulsion to behave according to the belief of the Christian faith, Christian behaving according to Christian believing."[1] For the Christian community the Eucharist, the sense and sentiment of gratitude for the mercy that God in Christ has delivered to the world, shapes and sanctifies all that it believes and does, including most especially *agape*, Christian love. Indeed, Eucharistic gratitude (for God's gracious love in Christ) determines the version of love that the Christian community is obligated to preach and practice if it is to retain its identity as Christian. The sense of gratitude central to the Eucharistic experience channels any interpretation of Christian love in one direction and not in others. When it comes to ethics, the trajectory of Christian love is toward an ethics of mercy and benevolence; and its trajectory is away from any ethics that brackets or neglects them or that accommodates the fallenness of self-interest as a basis for allocating economic goods. Fletcher argues as much in *Situation Ethics*. For the Christian community, mercy is a more highly evolved spiritual quality than justice alone; it requires of the Righteous an integrity of character not required of the merely Just. Eucharistic gratitude requires the Christian community to practice, not only in its personal and communal life but also in its public and political life, a kind of righteousness, a kind of merciful benevolence without which the egalitarian harmony of *pax Dei* is impossible.

Assuming, as I think Christians must, then, that any ethic that is Christian must be shaped by Eucharistic worship, what is the nature of that gratitude and how does it shape Christian ethics and politics? To answer this question we must first identify the aim or *teleological dimension* of mercy. In contrast to *pax Romana*'s liberal justice, whose aim is to distribute burdens and benefits fairly, the aim of *pax Christi*'s mercy is to redeem, restore, and reconcile humans to God and each other. What results is not only the Liberty Principle's protections of rights and liberties but also the Distribution Principle's "fair balance" of economic resources. Gratitude's Eucharistic and reciprocal norm is "Do unto others as God in Christ has done to you." Eucharistic gratitude calls the Christian community to deliver to others the same mercy that God in Christ delivers to it, to the end that the world might be redeemed and the harmony of something like egalitarian justice realized. Just as Christians feel grateful for God acting mercifully toward them, so also they should act mercifully toward others, so that the recipients of mercy will feel toward the Christian community the same gratitude the Christian community properly feels for the mercy it has received from God. Any faithful, worshipping Christian community, any interpretation of Christian love, obligates it to such a notion of mercy. Eucharistic gratitude is a familiar Christian disposition in which the recipient of mercy's unmerited benevolence is genuinely thankful to a donor for graciously making the world of the recipient qualitatively better than it otherwise would be. Indeed, so grateful is the recipient community that now as donor it is inspired and empowered by God's grace to act similarly, to graciously give to the world unmerited gifts of mercy in like manner as it has received. What then is the nature of this Eucharistic gratitude?

First, gratitude involves a judgment made by a recipient that she is beneficiary of unearned benefits and unmerited mercy. The symmetry of justice establishes entitlement; a person merits the burden or benefit she receives. But it is precisely the asymmetry of mercy that invites gratitude; a recipient receives an unmerited gift that benefits her beyond what she deserves. The wrongdoer or undeserving, for example, receive amnesty, not the penalty they deserve; or the vulnerable receive the generosity of economic benefits to which they otherwise have no power of access. Feelings of thankfulness naturally follow and properly inspire and empower the grateful recipient to practice and deliver to others the same kind of mercy they have received, so that now she is not only a grateful recipient but a gracious donor. As Paul Camenisch says, in his careful analysis of gratitude,[2] the recipient believes that a gift or "an unearned benefit has been received from a donor." The gift is "not a windfall . . . [but] something of value given to one unearned and undeserved by another agent at some cost to that agent and for the benefit of the recipient."[3] So, Christians believe that God freely and graciously delivered to the world an unmerited gift in Jesus Christ, a gift of mercy and forgiveness to fallen humanity. In response, Christian's feel properly thankful for God's benevolent gift of mercy, a thankfulness expressed individually and communally and repeatedly in the Eucharist. It is this seminal experience of gratitude for God's mercy that shapes the nature and character of the love Christians ought to practice.

Secondly, implicit to gratitude is the principle of "moral reciprocity." Does the grateful recipient of an unmerited gift accrue indebtedness to the donor? If so, how can such mercy still be gracious and unmerited? Camenisch insists that the feeling and expression of gratitude necessarily entails certain kinds of "obligations or moral expectations." Consider again Jesus's parable of the unforgiving servant (Matthew 18: 23–35). Although the text does not explicitly say so, we assume that the servant who pleaded for and received mercy from his king judged himself to be the beneficiary of an unmerited gift. We also assume, as Jesus does, that the recipient's appropriate response to such a gift should be a feeling of gratitude. However, although the gift, insofar as it is and remains a gift, requires of the servant nothing in return that would preempt the gracious liberality of the gift. Still there are certain moral expectations, Camenisch insists, that the donor rightly expects of the recipient. This expectation is not for the servant to try to reward the merciful king with some comparable, compensatory gift. Mercy's moral expectation is not that; it requires no such repayment, which the servant is unable in any case to provide. Instead, the king expects of the servant "moral reciprocity," which is indeed within the servant's power to perform; that is, the king rightly expects the servant to imitate the benevolence of the donor. Just as the servant has received mercy so likewise should the servant show mercy toward others. Gratitude, in other words, involves a normative attachment that establishes between donor and recipient a reciprocal relationship of moral integrity. It is the moral quality of this relationship that justifies the donor's expectation that the recipient, if he truly judges himself to be the recipient of an unmerited gift and is genuinely grateful, will with integrity act similarly toward others. When in the parable the recipient does not meet the moral expectations of the donor, the donor is portrayed as justified in allowing the recipient to suffer the penalties of justice, namely, the just fate the fellow servant suffers at the hand of the ungrateful servant. But in the parable the default to justice, the king's condemnation and punishment, is portrayed as a kind of recessive moral entropy and not as a highly evolved act of moral integrity.

Embedded in the experience of gratitude, then, is a normative expectation and promise: the donor's expectation and the recipient's promise of moral reciprocity. In feeling gratitude, the recipient of an unmerited gift incurs a moral, even spiritual, attachment to the donor, what Camenisch refers to as "a relationship of moral community."[4] This relationship requires of the recipient of mercy a kind of righteous moral integrity, an act of faith whereby the recipient practices the same merciful benevolence that elicited her gratitude in the first place. Although the gift is freely given and freely received, Camenisch points out that a gift "is given for some reason. And in accepting the gift, the recipient cannot strip it of its connection to the donor's will and intention, of the donor's reason for giving it. To accept the gift is on some level to consent to that total complex reality and to consent to become part of it."[5] In receiving a gift gratefully, the recipient is promising to practice toward others the same benevolent mercy. The donor rightly expects the recipient to keep this promise, rightly expects the recipient to act with moral integrity. One might object that a gift graciously and freely given cannot be delivered with strings of obligation attached. But, as Camenisch points out, "Moral relations between mature agents will most often be reciprocal relations."[6] "Reciprocal" in this case does not mean that the recipient must somehow try to compensate the donor for the gift, which not only would discredit the gift as a gift but presumably exceed the servant's means. Rather, "reciprocal" in the sense that the recipient is rightfully expected by the donor to act similarly toward others, to practice mercy's benevolence. Upon feeling grateful for mercy received, a recipient is morally obligated to act mercifully toward others. The expectation of the king in Jesus's parable, that the servant act toward his fellow servant with the same unmerited mercy from which he has benefited, establishes a pattern of reciprocal moral integrity that, if neglected, defaults to the penalty (payment of debt) he justly deserves.

As the emotional experience central to Eucharistic worship, gratitude is the very heart of what is distinctive about Christian love. When Christians confess that in Jesus God freely and benevolently delivers to fallen humanity an unmerited gift of compassion, mercy, and reconciliation, they properly feel and express their gratitude in the Eucharist. But expressing thankfulness sacramentally does not exhaust the demands of gratitude, for gratitude is not only a sacramental feeling and act but a way of life. Genuinely felt gratitude entails, as we have seen, a moral obligation incumbent on the recipient, an obligation to act with moral reciprocity, with love and mercy equal to that which was received. Indeed, the thankful community, having received God's unmerited gift, is specifically empowered by faith to act mercifully toward others, just as God in Christ has acted mercifully toward it. Gratitude is inauthentic and disingenuous if the recipient of God's gift, such as the servant in Jesus's parable, does not in turn employ the power present in that gift to practice in equal measure the same benevolence of mercy toward others.

In the parable of the unforgiving servant we find contrasted the spiritual asymmetry of Jesus's mercy and the moral symmetry of justice: treating others as God has treated me, with mercy, or treating others with the justice they deserve and merit. What both servants in the parable deserve is that they pay their debts or suffer fair punishment. The gratitude of the servant to whom mercy and forgiveness are shown by the master, we know, is not genuine and authentic; for when opportunity arises, he refuses to act in faith; he refuses now as donor to benevolently bestow on his fellow servant the same mercy and forgiveness he receives from his master. What is graciously done to him he refuses to graciously do to another. As undeserving he nevertheless happily receives from his master the benefits of mercy. But when a similar occasion arises, the servant acts strictly according to the symmetry of justice's standard model. He acts in all fairness according to what his fellow servant justly deserves, payment of debt or punishment. The unforgiving servant is demanding of his fellow servant nothing more than what just fairness requires, what is owed. Indeed, he is behaving, as Archibald Hunter says, "as we do ourselves every day. Making his case on the basis of a contractual notion of justice, he sought to recover his debt in accordance with the law"[7] in accordance with the demands of equal fairness. But the touchstone of Christian integrity and love, I am arguing, is not fairness or just deserts but the asymmetry of mercy, the law of liberty. The Christian community, insofar as it is genuinely Christian, is obligated to treat others as God in Christ treats it, with undeserved, unmerited mercy.

Eucharistic gratitude, as the core of Christian ethics, embodies, I hardly need point out, the central event of the Christian faith and coheres with the teaching and practice of Jesus throughout his ministry. Recall the woman caught in adultery or the way Jesus concludes his prayer: "for if you forgive men their trespasses, your heavenly Father also will forgive you; but if you do not forgive men their trespasses, neither will your Father forgive your trespasses" (Matthew 6: 14–15). Elsewhere Jesus enjoins his disciples to "Be merciful even as your Father is merciful" (Luke 6: 36). For Jesus, as Hunter puts it, "'the quality of mercy,' so far from being something to be granted on single and exceptional occasions, had the nature of an ordinance, that is, something providentially written into the moral constitution of things,"[8] a quality of heart that constitutes the heart of Christian ethics. This is the force of the biblical injunction, "Freely you have received, freely give," or as Gustafson paraphrases it, "you have freely received, therefore you ought to freely give."[9] Eucharistic gratitude for God's mercy is a moral and spiritual disposition, a habit. It becomes, as Camenisch puts it, "the salient characteristic, the dominant mood or theme of a total way of life."[10] Eucharistic gratitude for God's mercy is the way a community lives Christianly *in* the world but not *of* the world.

I dare say that too often Christians and Christian communities, whether because of false prophets or perverse partisanship, fail to keep the moral promise of their professed faith. In biblical narratives the evolution of moral consciousness from justice to mercy's benevolence, from symmetry to asymmetry, from reason to faith, is clear and clearly normative. It is perhaps surprising, then, that many Christians and Christian communities, like the ungrateful servant, tend to default in their social and political lives to little more than liberal justice, which requires not grace and faith but law and reason, not the sacrifices of peacemaking but the retaliation of just warmaking. Bewitched by self-interest's invisible hand or paralyzed by the thought of "big government," they shrink mercy's benevolence to narrowly private affairs, as if benevolence contributes nothing to the moral and civil order for which government is responsible and ordained.

Implicit in mercy's gratitude is a relationship between "duties" and "rights." How does the asymmetry of mercy situate itself in relation to the notions of "duties" and "rights"? I have argued already that to each duty of liberal justice is correlated a right. The judgment of the Hodja in distributing walnuts unfairly to the children and the judgment of Jesus in distributing wages unfairly to the laborers and the gracious mercy the father lavishes on the wayward son stand asymmetrically to the way justice correlates duties and rights. What can we make of this?

GENEROSITY

Generosity is a quality essential to mercy's benevolence. By it I refer to a family of altruistic feelings—liberality, charity, magnanimity, kindness, graciousness, other-regarding—that underwrite habits of mercy. Jesus's mission and ministry certainly exhibit these qualities: from the kindness with which he treats enemies, the marginalized and irreligious to the meekness and forgiveness of his passion, death, and resurrection. The Apostle Paul calls generosity or kindness a fruit of the spirit (Galatians 5: 22) and elsewhere enjoins Christians to "Let all bitterness and wrath and anger and clamor and slander be put away from you, with all malice, and be kind to one another, tenderhearted, forgiving one another, as God in Christ forgave you" (Ephesians 4: 31–32; also Colossians 3: 12–13). Several questions arise. What is the nature of God's generosity to humankind? What does it mean to practice Christian generosity? What demands does it make on the Christian community and how are these demands related to duties and rights? What is asymmetrical about generosity and how is it apprehended by faith? Richard Stith identifies two ways that generosity situates itself asymmetrically in relation to justice. He argues, first, that generosity involves a duty without a right; and second, that it necessarily involves benefiting wrongdoers or undeserving or vulnerable. We shall find that although mercy's asymmetry distinguishes it markedly from justice, the power of its generosity is able to bring about fair egalitarian outcomes that contribute to restoring the just harmony of *pax Dei.*

First, Stith argues that generosity situates its duties asymmetrically in relation to rights. According to the symmetry of justice's standard model, duties correlate to certain rights. The duty to protect liberty is correlated, for example, to the rightful free exercise of religion; or the duty to grant due process correlates to the right of equal protection under the law. Such correlation of duties and rights is largely procedural and reflects the rational symmetry of liberal justice. In contrast, mercy's generosity deviates from the symmetry of this standard model, situating itself incommensurably to moral reason. Richard Stith insists that generosity entails a "duty without a right."[11] Feelings of generosity are initiated by a judgment that I have a duty to act kindly and mercifully toward the wrongdoer or undeserving or vulnerable, even though they are not entitled to any rights that correlate with that duty to act benevolently. Ordinarily we think of "duty" and "right" as corresponding; "that for every right there exists a correlative duty," as Stith puts it, "and that for every duty there exists a correlative right." But there are some duties which one should undertake in full knowledge that the recipient of our generosity can claim no right to the benefits of our action. In other words, there are morally compelling occasions when "'duties with rights' can and ought to be superceded in favor of . . . 'duties of generosity,'"[12] duties without rights. Sentencing a murderer to life in prison instead of to death is generous; it grants an unmerited benefit of amnesty to one who can claim no right to it. Such discontinuity between duties and rights is, of course, the benevolent heart of the Gospel. As a manifestation of God's *agape,* Jesus obeys mercy's duty to suffer the wages of sin and grant redemption to sinners even though they have no right to it. Only by faith, and not by reason, can one apprehend and accept such a merciful gift.

Secondly, Stith insists that generosity entails an attitude of merciful benevolence in which one grants amnesty from burdens by undertaking "a duty to benefit precisely and only those who do wrong";[13] along with those who are otherwise undeserving, the indolent or slothful who can lay no claim of entitlement to generosity's benefit. In addition to these, I argue that mercy's moral reciprocity includes a duty to grant unmerited benefits to the vulnerable and marginalized, who live under conditions that minimize their ability to earn a decent livelihood or who have little power of access to a sustainable livelihood.[14] Mercy's generosity necessarily benefits precisely those who have not earned that benefit,[15] even though each person's intrinsic worth as in God's image may be sufficient motive for acting generously. Similarly mercy's amnesty toward wrongdoers who have no claim to that benefit requires faith. Either act deviates considerably from the rationality of justice; so much so that generosity requires faith's assurance of things hoped for and conviction of things not seen. The symmetry of justice's moral reason, on the one hand, predicts and controls outcomes; it correlates duties and rights so that those who do wrong are burdened and those who do right are benefited; these are "things seen." Mercy's amnesty and generosity, on the other hand, supersedes justice's moral equilibrium; but it does so in order that justice might be somehow established. Faith apprehends mercy's moral asymmetry, apprehends, that is, a spiritual duty that correlates to no moral right, to "things not seen," namely, benefits to wrongdoer and undeserving and vulnerable that heal, restore, and redeem.

To illustrate these two threads of generosity Stith first employs a trivial example taken from etiquette. "Everyone has a duty to leave the last cookie on the table for someone else, and not to object when someone else takes the cookie." This duty to leave the cookie "cannot without contradiction be straightforwardly transformed into a statement of individual rights-claim,"[16] says Stith. The duty I have of leaving the last cookie for another transforms itself into an act of underserved generosity when I dutifully and graciously allow another to wrongfully (it violates rules of etiquette) take the last cookie, a cookie to which that person also has no right. Whether one is persuaded by Stith's illustration or not, his notion of generosity as a duty without a right is persuasive and can help illuminate, I think, the extraordinary character of generosity and the difference between a Just and Righteous community. I would only add to Stith's analysis that generosity as he understands it may not only be an act directed toward a wrongdoer or undeserving but also toward upright, vulnerable, marginalized persons who have little or no power of access to a sustainable livelihood. This benevolent character of generosity, taught and practiced by Jesus, constitutes the basis for distinguishing merciful benevolence and its Distribution Principle from justice as procedural fairness and Rawls's Difference Principle.

Consider Jesus's familiar illustration of this kind of extraordinary generosity, set forth in Matthew's version of the Sermon on the Mount. Jesus first makes clear to his listeners that the principle of justice as fairness is not a sufficient moral guide for citizens of his Kingdom.[17] "You have heard that it was said, 'An eye for an eye and a tooth for a tooth.' But I say to you, Do not resist one who is evil" (Matthew 5: 38–39). If justice as fairness, if justice as correlation of duty and right is considered by Jesus to be insufficient as a moral guide, what principle does he advocate? The answer explicit in Jesus's sermon is *agape*, which includes meekness (turn the other cheek) and benevolence (loving enemies). These values situate themselves asymmetrically in relation to moral reason's demand for symmetry. "If anyone would sue you and take your coat," Jesus says, "let him have your cloak as well; and if anyone forces you to go one mile, go with him two miles" are provocative injunctions that we can understand in terms of Stith's two traits of generosity, namely, (1) that it is a duty without a right and (2) that it benefits wrongdoer or vulnerable.

First of all, "let him have your cloak as well" and "Go with him two miles" and "Turn the other cheek" are commanded by Jesus as duties of generosity that his followers are to obey. They are imperatives and duties, not merely suggestions. And yet as duties they have no rights correlative to them. The recipients of "the cloak as well" and "the second mile" have no entitlement to these benefits; they have no rights on the basis of which to fairly claim them, even though Jesus commands his disciple, as venders of generosity, to nevertheless donate them. Because they are not correlated with any rights, these duties of generosity will sound dissonant in relation to the moral tonalities on which our rights-based culture nurtures us. Or they will seem to our rational, moral sentiments as "an impossible possibility," as Reinhold Niebuhr puts it in *An Interpretation of Christian Ethics*. Indeed, the rule implicit in Jesus's injunction that "Everyone has a right to more than they are allowed to sue for" is self-contradictory, if by "suit" we mean that to which another has a moral and legal right. By law, as one Matthew commentator puts it, a person did not have "to give as collateral an outer garment—more than what the law requires, which was merely an inner garment."[18] If one has a right *only* to X, then we cannot say that one also has a right to Y, without speaking at odds with ourselves. The one who has a right only to X cannot also claim a right to Y without violating the rights of another, namely, the other's right to Y. However, there is no contradiction or confusion in Jesus's injunction regarding generosity. He means that his disciples are to give not only what is due to others, what they have a right to, but also what is not due to them, what is not their right to claim. Even to those who treat them unjustly, his disciples' generosity is to be of this extraordinary, asymmetrical sort. Jesus's presumption is that even if one has a right to X (the first coat and first mile), one does not have a right to Y (the cloak and second mile). The generosity of the second mile, then, is a duty of faith that the Christian is commanded to undertake even though the recipient, who has no right to it, will benefit.

We are now in a position to see Stith's second point, that generosity is essential to mercy. It delivers an unearned benefit to those who according to the symmetry of justice can claim no right to that benefit—wrongdoers, the undeserving, and vulnerable. Merciful generosity, as an act of faith, involves a moral project where the undeserving and vulnerable benefit from the intentional kindness of another. Such generosity, taught and practiced by Christ, is extraordinary in that it benefits, as Stith says it, "precisely and only those who do wrong" or, as I argue, those who are vulnerable or otherwise undeserving of the benefit. It is extraordinary because it requires of the donor an act of faith and a measure of benevolence that exceeds common human expectations and ordinary capacities to grant. The context of Jesus's remarks about the second mile and cloak entails the virtue of meekness, a virtue almost entirely neglected in contemporary moral discourse. "Do not resist one who is evil," Jesus says. "But if anyone strikes you on the right cheek, turn to him the other also." *Pax Romana* allowed the first mile and coat; but, in addition, to grant the recipient the other cheek and the second mile and cloak will always benefit one who is at most evil or at least undeserving. Blomberg is right in concluding: "each of these commands requires Jesus's followers to act more generously than what the letter of the law demanded. . . . Not only must disciples reject all behavior motivated only by a desire for retaliation, but they must also positively work for the good of those with whom they would otherwise be at odds."[19] Paul similarly indicates that toward the enemies of God who treat us wrongly we should "not be overcome by evil"; instead, we should act kindly toward them, "overcome evil with good," benefit them even though they do not deserve those benefits (Romans 12: 20–21). Clearly, unmerited generosity of this sort presupposes that the donor is empowered by a measure of faith and grace to act generously toward others even as God in Christ has so acted toward humans.

What is extraordinary and asymmetrical about Christian generosity, then, is that no rights correlate to its duty; generosity benefits those who have no claim to it and in doing so affirms the dignity of all humans, guarantees the fair balance of a sustainable livelihood. Ultimately, the grace of mercy's generosity is the sole power able to redeem, reconcile, and restore the harmony of *pax Dei.*

REMEMBRANCE

"Remember" is one of the most fundamental and frequent biblical commandments that Israel and the Church are called to obey. What they are to remember is a history of Divine benevolence, a narrative of mercy. The purpose of remembering this narrative is twofold: self-identity and moral orientation. Remembrance reminds us of "who we are" and "what we are to do;" sacramentally the Christian community retrieves its identity; prophetically it retrieves its moral and political orientation; sacramentally its role is pastoral and prophetically its role is liberating. By thus remembering the benevolent community retrieves and practices "who it is" and "what it is to do." By remembering a community perpetuates in its own life the ancient narratives of mercy; by forgetting, as the servant in Jesus's parable, that narrative, that mercy, is in its own selfishness abruptly ended.

What does it mean to say that remembrance is sacramental and pastoral? What does it mean that remembrance retrieves a community's identity, reminds it of "who it is"? The biblical tradition assumes that remembrance is not merely informative, a recollection of a chronological *(kronos)* tradition;

but that it is formative and reformative, a sacramental and practical reenactment (*kairos*) of historical events through which God liberates, redeems, and reconciles. The habit of remembrance ancient Israel is commanded to cultivate is of this reformative sort. Israel is not simply to recall a historical event but it is, as Gadamer says, to "possess it as something that is absolutely its own,"[20] possess it sacramentally as something that unconditionally and irresistibly shapes and reshapes its identity. Remembrance, accordingly, involves imaginatively reconstructing past events on the basis of a community's present and future needs and concerns. Since remembrance is eschatological, "To remember is not to duplicate," insists Brynolf Lyon. "The events or impressions that we recall from the past are not exact reproductions of the 'original event.' They are interpretations or reconstructions of the 'original event,'"[21] communal reconstructions of "past experiences and impressions in the service of needs, fears, and interests."[22] In the act of remembering God's mighty acts of mercy, a faith community shapes and reshapes its present commitments and future prospects. Indeed, the very possibility of a community's present faithfulness and future hope is established by remembrance, by making itself vulnerable and accountable to the design and demands God has throughout history made on that community. The sacramental role of remembrance is not simply cathartic but *kairotic*, it is not to reenact or "relive the past," as Brevard Childs points out, "because much of what is remembered is painful."[23] Its role, rather, allows God's mighty and merciful acts to shape and reshape a community's identity, reminding it who it is.

What is the sacramental identity, then, that God's people "remember"? In a word "mercy"; that it is a community that inherits a legacy of Divine grace, of merciful benevolence. First, Israel is commanded to remember its identity, who it is. "Remember all the ways which the Lord your God has led you these forty years in the wilderness. . . ." Its identity is as a people who are liberated and redeemed by a benevolent and merciful God. It is true, God sometimes treats Israel justly, granting it what it deserves. Moses' banishment from the land of promise and Israel's experience of exile are such occasions. But justice is not God's final act, but the covenantal occasion for mercy, for redeeming and restoring relationships. This remembrance is pastoral; not condemnation, but compassion and care and comfort, so that God "might humble you, testing you to know what was in your heart, whether you would keep his commandments, or not" (Deut. 8: 2); so that you might obey God and live reciprocally, granting to others the same kind of mercy that God has granted Israel

Similarly for the Christian community Eucharist "remembrance" is equally central and provocative. By commanding "Do this is remembrance of me" (Luke 22: 19) Jesus forever calls those who claim to be his followers to return again and again to the central Christian event, so that they might not forget, so that they might remember their identity and orientation, who they are and how they are to live; so that they might remember that it is the grace of mercy and forgiveness with which God in Christ delivers redemption and reconciliation to the world, and not condemnation and punishment that humans justly deserve. The Apostle Paul preserves this command, "Do this in remembrance of me" (I Cor. 11: 23–26) as the primary way the church proclaims the gospel embodied by Christ and practiced by the community of faithful believers. "For as often as you eat this bread and drink this cup, you proclaim the Lord's death until he comes." What is to be remembered by partaking of bread and wine is not simply the passion and death and resurrection of Jesus, not only the meekness of "turn the other cheek" and "go the second mile," and not only the grace of mercy whereby God delivers healing and redemption to the world. What is Eucharistically remembered in Jesus's body and blood is the whole gospel: that in a fallen, unjust world, healing is not delivered to the world by retaliation, "an eye for an eye" or striking in return the aggressor's cheek, not by punishment and reward, not by hating enemies. Whatever value there is in justice, Jesus supersedes it with the benevolence of the amnesty of meekness ("turn the other cheek") and generosity of mercy ("love your enemies") in order to achieve the aim for which he lives, dies, and lives again, namely, redemption and reconciliation. He transforms justice; for, as the writer of John says (3: 17), he comes not to "condemn the world but that the world might be saved through him." The gift the church is to remember and reenact in an unjust world is the same unique gift it has received, namely, mercy, mercy, and nothing but mercy. In and through the Eucharist a community in gratitude reminds itself of who it is. In and through the Eucharist a grateful community reminds itself that it is the body and blood of Christ in the world today. Through Eucharistic remembrance Christian communities gratefully commit themselves to be who they are, missionaries of mercy, a benevolent community.

Secondly, remembrance is prophetic and liberating. Eucharistic gratitude orients Christian communities morally and politically; inspires them to do what God calls them to do, namely, practice the mercy for which in the Eucharist they have expressed their gratitude. As liberating and prophetic, Eucharistic remembrance entails what Metz calls "dangerous memory"[24] and Russell Butkus calls "the remembrance of suffering and freedom."[25] How so? How is remembrance liberating and prophetic? How is it "dangerous"? First, because prophetic remembrance requires suffering; secondly, because it requires liberation.

By remembering God's merciful benevolence the Christian community, imitating Jesus, makes itself vulnerable to sin and the wages of sin, to structures of injustice, to forces of violence and abuse and ridicule. In the biblical tradition, the demands of justice are not neglected. The writer of Hebrews, for example, speaks pastorally of the danger and vulnerability and violence to which the faithful are susceptible. He speaks of remembering the faith of patriarchs and matriarchs. "Recall the former days when, after you were enlightened, you endured a hard struggle with sufferings, sometimes being publicly exposed to abuse and affliction, and sometimes being partners with those so treated" (10: 32–33). The writer encourages his readers and insists that by remembering past sufferings of faithful people God will grant them faith, confidence, and courage to practice a life of compassion and mercy. "For you had compassion on the prisoners, and you joyfully accepted the plundering of your property, since you yourselves knew that you had a better possession and an abiding one. Therefore, do not throw away your confidence, which has a great reward" (10: 34–35). Remembering is dangerous because in so doing Christians make themselves vulnerable to the hardship and pain and ridicule of those for whose sake the faithful voluntarily suffer. And yet in so remembering Christians are thereby encouraged to take heart and have faith and courage just as multitudes of Christians before. That is why the author of Hebrews immediately retrieves a catalogue list of faithful, who suffered in the cause of God's awful love and mercy. We are to recall the faith of Moses who refused to exploit his inherited royalty but chose rather "to share ill-treatment with the people of God. . . . He considered abuse suffered for the Christ greater wealth than the treasures of Egypt. . . ." (11: 23–28). And we are to remember women and men who "suffered mocking and scourging, and even chains and imprisonment. They were stoned; they were sawn in two, they were killed with the sword; they went about in skins of sheep and goats, destitute, afflicted, ill-treated. . . ." (11: 36–38). And why is the church to remember such terrible suffering and hardship? Why is it to recall "so great a cloud of witnesses"? The writer tells us: so that Christians will "lay aside every weight, and sin that clings so closely . . . and run with perseverance the race that is set before us" (12: 1).

In sacramental remembrance, Christians are inspired, like Christ, to bear the burdens of (in)justice. The passion and pain of death that Jesus suffers reflects the symmetry of justice and God's demand for justice (e.g., see Romans 3). For the injustices of humanity justice (*pax Romana*) demands certain wages, including suffering and death (Romans 6: 23). This fair penalty and price is paid by Jesus, in his death and resurrection. In so doing repentant humanity is liberated from the necessity of suffering its just desserts. The asymmetry of God's benevolence grants amnesty by liberating humanity from the retribution of justice's symmetry, from sin and the wages of sin. Benevolent communities are reciprocally, morally required as *corpus Christi* to bear the burdens of justice in their own body and to grant even to enemies in Jesus's name the same grace of mercy that God in Christ grants them. By gratefully granting others, even enemies, the same grace of mercy granted them by Christ, Christians often must suffer; like Christ they accept the burdens of (in)justice for the sake of redeeming the sinner and liberating the oppressed. For example, Christians should be willing to suffer "reverse discrimination" for the sake of benevolently granting affirmative action to the vulnerable who because of centuries of oppression have no power of access to opportunities for a sustainable livelihood.

As prophetic and liberating, moreover, remembrance possesses the possibility and power of promoting in a new way "an emancipatory praxis of freedom . . . ," as Butkus puts it,[26] a freedom of grace, a liberation from oppression. God's mercy liberates both those remembering and those remembered, both people liberated by God's grace and people of God liberating the oppressed among them. For Jews and Christians Exodus is an ancient seminal act of liberation, when God saw the suffering and sorrow of his people and "on the wings of eagles" delivered them from bondage (Exodus 19: 4) and established them for freedom in a land of promise. The narrative identity of Jews and Christians is rooted deeply in remembrance, in the memory of being freed by God's mercy from exile and oppression. As the writer of Exodus says "I am the Lord your God, who brought you out of the land of Egypt, out of the house of bondage." As a result, Israel's identity, the writer insists, is to be shaped in terms of Yahweh alone: no other gods, no idols, no misuse of the Lord's name in magic, or divination, or false swearing (Lev. 19: 12). Keep instead a Sabbath, a separate holy day of remembrance dedicated exclusively to Yahweh (Exodus 20: 1–8; see also Deut. 5: 6–15). Israel's Sabbath, sacramental remembrance includes meditating on the fact that "You were a servant in the land of Egypt, and the Lord your God brought you out thence with a might hand and an outstretched arm" (Deut. 5: 15). In short, remember that you have been liberated by the power of God's grace and mercy. The ancient Hebrew prophets and the psalmists are messengers of remembrance, reminding Israel that the God they serve is a liberator of the oppressed and downtrodden (e.g., Psalms 10: 17; 69: 32–33). Furthermore, Israel is to remember that God has liberated it for the work of liberating others. "You shall not oppress a stranger; [remember] you know the heart of a stranger, for you were strangers in the land of Egypt" (Exodus 23: 9; see also 22: 21–24). A nations natural instinct is to preserve itself and its identity partly by protecting itself from strangers, foreigners, who threaten that identity. But Jews and Christians are called to "know the heart of a stranger" and to care mercifully for that stranger. So, that is its legacy and identity. To remember that they too at one time were strangers, oppressed and exploited, but nevertheless redeemed and liberated by the power of God's mercy.

Jesus appropriates this ancient Hebrew tradition of liberation and understands it to be fulfilled in himself, in his life, death, and resurrection. Exodus's "emancipatory praxis of freedom" is fulfilled in his mission of "good news to the poor," "release to the captives," "sight to the blind," "freedom to the oppressed" (Luke 4: 16–21). Accordingly, the Apostle Paul declares "For freedom Christ has set us free (Galatians 5: 1). Eucharistic remembrance retrieves this liberating power of Christ's body and blood and frees humanity from subjugating divisions such as male and female, Jew and Greek, slave and free (Galatians 3: 27–29). Remembrance, Eucharistic remembrance, in short, is indispensable to Christian identity and its moral/political orientation. It summons the Christian community to remain faithful to who it is (a merciful community) and to what it is to do (practice the liberating grace of mercy). Indeed, this identity and orientation imply moral reciprocity, imply a *conditio sine qua non* for receiving mercy and forgiveness. Jesus concludes his most famous prayer: "For if you forgive men their trespasses, your heavenly Father will also forgive you; but if you do not forgive men their trespasses, neither will your Father forgive your trespasses" (Matthew 6: 14, 15). If benevolence consists of that family of tender feelings that make genuine mercy and forgiveness possible, then that benevolence situates itself morally in private and public life is for the Christian community compulsory, not optional; indeed, it is the very identity of that community, an identity without which it has no claim to "Christian." Jesus is insisting that a kind of reciprocity exists between giving and receiving merciful forgiveness; one receives God's merciful forgiveness freely, but only if one is willing to practice it. God's mercy is freely given, no doubt, but it must also be freely received, which is to say practiced. Remembering and practicing mercy is *pax Christi.* In Ephesians Paul says, for example, that it is the mercy of Christ that restores peace, that "has broken down the dividing wall of hostility" between races and gender and classes. It is Christ's mercy and not mere justice that has the power to bring unity in the midst of hostility; "so making peace . . . [and] thereby bringing the hostility to an end (Ephesians 2: 11–16). The reconciliation and peace of *pax Christi* is possible, if possible at all for the Righteous community, by remembering a benevolence "rich in mercy" (2: 4–5).

MERCY AND THE OPPRESSED

Suspicions regarding mercy and benevolence no doubt remain. What about millions of innocent and vulnerable peoples who are disenfranchised, marginalized, and oppressed; who have little power of access to the "fair balance" of a sustainable livelihood? What about those exploited and subjugated by poverty, sexism, racism? What about immigrants and homosexuals and mentally disabled? What about those innocent victims who suffer the violent and vicious wars of the rich and powerful? What about millions who rightly desire and deserve justice? Are they to practice mercy and benevolence and not seek and demand justice? Are they to wait passively, suffering anonymously while the wicked prosper? To those suffering discrimination and oppression the call to mercy and benevolence may seem a cruel joke, a betrayal. "Turning the other cheek" and "Going the second mile" are for the craven and cowardly. Indeed, to show benevolence in the midst of injustice, to confront power with mercy, to show generosity to the oppressor, seems counterintuitive and counterproductive. For the oppressed, doing so seems only to tighten chains of injustice and lengthen shadows of despair.

Any response to these questions must not dilute the dignity of the oppressed or diminish in any way the weight of horror they suffer. Already implicit in my argument is a twofold response that revolves around the words "substantive" and "subversive." Mercy is "subversive" by refusing to play by the exploitative rules of the oppressor's game; and it is "substantive" by advocating new rules that liberate the oppressed from their oppressor's power and indeed places the oppressor at and in the mercy of the vulnerable.

First of all, mercy is subversive and not submissive; it refuses to accommodate and collaborate with oppressors but confronts them; it is not cowardly or craven, but courageous and defiant. How so? We have inherited in our American tradition an image of Uncle Tom; one who submissively collaborates with the oppressor. This is not an image consistent with mercy. Mercy is provocative and powerfully subversive. The oppressor wants nothing more than that the oppressed play his game by his rules. Black Nationalists, whose agenda Dr. King rejects, calculated that they would play by the same militant, violent rules of the oppressors; they got what they bargained for. Dr. King bet on the potency of *agape*'s mercy, and got the justice mercy aims at. Mercy, in its form as meekness, turns the other cheek; it refuses to play by the unjust rules and structures whereby the oppressor in the first place subjugates others. In a world already saturated with patterns and habits of injustice, to seduce the oppressed into playing by the rules established by the oppressor guarantees the oppressors perpetual social, political, and economic advantage. Even liberal justice by itself tends to perpetuate unjust conditions already embedded in a society; without a radical, asymmetrical act of amnesty or generosity, embedded structural injustices tend to remain unaltered and entrenched and benefit only those already advantaged. Enforcing *Brown v. Board of Education* (1954), the Civil Rights Act (1964), and the Voting Rights Act (1965), for example, has not alleviated among the disadvantaged discrepancies in education and economic outcomes. Although these official acts of procedural justice are necessary and beneficial, by themselves they are insufficient for realizing egalitarian outcomes, insufficient for redeeming and reconciling relationships. Although they treat individuals fairly, by themselves they are unable to subvert the patterns and momentum of injustice already present. By turning the other cheek, mercy simply refuses to play by rules that perpetuate the injustices already inherent in the game. Mercy establishes new rules by which to play the game. Such is the case, as we shall see in chapter 7, with Dr. King's campaign of nonviolent, civil disobedience, a campaign based explicitly on the power of Christian grace and mercy.

Secondly, mercy is a substantive and not a superficial response to oppression. It possesses practical social and political power. In the midst of fallen, unjust conditions merciful benevolence alone possesses the substantive, practical power capable of establishing and sustaining the "fair balance" of egalitarian outcomes, without which the full, intended dignity of humans cannot be restored. Not only is the benevolent community not content with the procedural rules of liberal justice, it invents a new, more radical moral game. That game requires the Righteous to live by faith's law of liberty, not by reason's law; by the awful grace of God's mercy and not merely by structures of liberal justice. In this chapter I have sketched the rules and requirements of its game. It requires communities of faith to live mercifully, to nurture a character courageous enough to turn the other cheek and travel the extra mile. It requires communities to fulfill duties of generosity that correlate to no rights. It requires distributing to enemies mercy instead of vengeance. It requires the other, the enemy, the oppressor to play a new game by new rules. In this game, the oppressed, who suffer unmerited evil at the hands of the oppressor, suddenly, unexpectedly grant the oppressor the benefits of unmerited generosity, thereby making themselves neighbor to the oppressor and in so doing co-opting them, placing them in their power and on equal ground. Affirmative action, as an act of merciful benevolence is a case in point. Its aim is a "fair balance" for the vulnerable who, marginalized by centuries of racial, gender, and class injustice for centuries, are guaranteed equal educational, professional, and economic outcomes for the sake of the fair balance of a sustainable livelihood. The dominate group, on the other hand, is granted amnesty by the oppressed, granted the benefits of unmerited mercy by the oppressed refusing to subjugate the oppressor to comparable centuries of exploitation and marginalization, a burden they justly deserve but which is mercifully withdrawn.

As we shall see in chapter 7, Gandhi and King demonstrate precisely this power of merciful benevolence to subvert injustice and establish egalitarian outcomes. But for now, consider again the Magnificat of Mary, whose life symbolizes for all the oppressed peoples of the world "the lowliness of God's servant" on whom nevertheless God "has looked with favor" (Luke 1: 46–55). Her proclamation manifests these two qualities of mercy—subversive and substantive. As subversive, the Magnificat represents Mary's life as the triumph of humility over humiliation, of the oppressed over the oppressor, of mercy over the merciless. "The assertiveness in the wording of the Magnificat shows Mary," as Jane Schaberg says, "to be 'one who has triumphed over her enemies, one to whom God was merciful, one for whom there was a radical overturning of social expectations.'"[27] Mercy is the subversive force and fulcrum; it is what shows "the strength of God's arm," scatters "the proud in the thoughts of their hearts," brings down the powerful from their thrones," and lifts "up the lowly." Secondly, Mary's Magnificat, "in remembrance of God's mercy," results in substantive fair balance of egalitarian outcomes, a vision of *pax Dei* in which God "has filled the hungry with good things, and sent the rich away empty." In short, mercy unleashes an awful power that in an unjust world subverts the oppressor, as Mary proclaims, and liberates the disadvantaged to live full, dignified lives.

In chapter 7 these subversive, substantive qualities are exemplified in the lives and labors of Gandhi and King; and in chapter 8 they are applied to contemporary social and economic praxis. But first, in chapter 6, I answer the question: How can moral agents, nurtured on liberal justice, evolve psychologically and spiritually from justice to mercy? My answer is in terms of compassion. I examine its role as a bridge between liberal justice and egalitarian justice, as a power of will that propels a community to migrate morally from the symmetry of liberal justice to the grace of mercy's benevolence.

NOTES

1. Joseph Fletcher, *Situation Ethics: The New Morality* (Philadelphia, PA: Westminster Press, 1966), 156.
2. Paul F. Camenisch, "Gift and Gratitude in Ethics," *Journal of Religious Ethics* 9 (Spring 1981), 1–34.
3. *Ibid.*, 2.
4. *Ibid.*, 3.
5. *Ibid.*, 2.
6. *Ibid.*, 9.
7. Archibald M. Hunter, *The Parables Then and Now* (Philadelphia, PA: Westminster Press, 1971), 69.
8. *Ibid.*, 69.
9. James Gustafson, *Can Ethics Be Christian?* (Chicago: University of Chicago Press, 1975), 101.
10. "Gift and Gratitude," 23.
11. Richard Stith, "Generosity: A Duty without a Right," *Journal of Value Inquiry* 25, 3 (1991), 203–216.
12. *Ibid.*, 203.
13. *Ibid.*, 208.
14. A question might be raised regarding the "vulnerable," whether in meeting their basic needs they are recipients of merciful gifts or of basic rights to which they are justly entitled. All humans, created in the image of God, I believe, are entitled to basic human rights, including a sustainable livelihood. The vulnerable are those who are oppressed by structures and policies and social habits that leave them involuntarily at risk; they are those who do not have the capacities to voluntarily extricate themselves from adverse conditions and by and for themselves meet their basic needs. Children and mentally disabled are obvious examples. But in a fallen and structurally unjust world, many vulnerable poor and marginalized are involuntarily, and often temporarily, unable to meet what they are entitled to, a sustainable livelihood. According to the strict rationality and symmetry of liberal justice, however, they should labor for themselves to appropriate those goods essential to a sustainable livelihood. The vulnerable have a right to them, but not for them to be freely given. I consider these vulnerable recipients of mercy's unmerited benefits when faith communities and governments nevertheless guarantee for them, through private and public policies, a sustainable livelihood.
15. Mercy's benefit includes withholding burdens or granting benefits.
16. Stith, *Ibid.*, 206.

17. Harlan Beckley acknowledges this fact when he says that "Christian love, as equal regard, 'affirms each of the beliefs that underlie Rawls's original position, even though Christian love requires more than justice.'" See "A Christian Affirmatiion of Rawls's Idea of Justice as Fairness," part 2, *Journal of Religious Ethics* 14, 2 (Fall 1986), 229.
18. Craig L. Blomberg, *Matthew*, in *The New American Commentary*, vol. 22 (Nashville, TN: Broadman Press, 1992).
19. *Ibid*., 113.
20. Hans-George Gadamer, *Truth and Method*, 2nd rev. ed. (New York: Crossroads Press, 1989), 15–16.
21. K. Brynolf Lyon, "The Unwelcome Presence: The Practical Moral Intention of Remembering," *Encounter* 48, 1 (Winter 1987), 139–140.
22. Ernest G. Schactel, *Metamorphosis* (New York: Basic Books, 1959), 284.
23. Brevard Childs, *Memory and Tradition in Israel* (New York: Alec R. Allanson, 1962), 51.
24. Johann B. Metz, *Faith in History and Society: Toward a Practical Fundamental Theology*, trans. David Smith (New York, NY: Seabury Press, 1980), 88–99.
25. Russell Butkus, "Dangerous Memory and Social Justice Education," *Religious Education* 82 (1987), 427.
26. *Ibid*., 438.
27. Traci C. West, *Disruptive Christian Ethics: When Racism and Women's Lives Matter* (Louisville, KY: Westminster/John Knox Press, 2006), 106.

Chapter Six

Benevolence and Compassion

When the lawyer asks what he must do to inherit life eternal, Jesus tells him he must love God and neighbor as himself. When the lawyer, clever fellow that he is, asks "Who is my neighbor?" he gets a narrative earful from Jesus. A man, a Jew, is assaulted on his journey from Jerusalem to Jericho; his money is stolen, he is beaten and left along the road for dead. Who would help? Who would be neighbor to the injured man? By chance a priest happens along, sees the suffering man, but passes by. Next a Levite comes upon the injured man, but he too continues on his way. In contrast, a hated, heretical, unneighborly Samaritan comes to the place where the injured Jew lays dying; "and when he saw him," Jesus says, "he had *compassion*, and went to him and bound up his wounds, pouring oil and wine on him; . . . he brought him to an inn, and took care of him." The Samaritan pays the innkeeper and asks him to care for the injured man, and upon his return says he will reimburse him for any additional expenses. Jesus then asks the lawyer, "Which of these three, do you think, proved neighbor to the man who fell among robbers?" The lawyer answers, correctly as it turns out, "'The one who showed *mercy* on him.' Jesus replies 'Go and do likewise'" (Luke 10: 25–37). The point to which I want to draw attention is the place and role of "compassion" in the parable, in life, and how it situates itself in relation to justice and mercy. Compassion, in fact, enfranchises into the experience of mercy the kind of caring feelings and emotions that are largely absent from justice.

Jesus praises the Samaritan for feeling "compassion" for his Jewish enemy and for the mercy he shows. The Samaritan, a foreigner, a heretic, is nevertheless a truly Righteous man. He is willing to bear undeserved burdens and grant unmerited benefits to a vulnerable enemy. The results are astounding; the Samaritan's compassion and mercy instantaneously, miraculously, it seems, transform him into neighbor to his Jewish enemy. In an instant, centuries of prejudice, hostility, animosity, retaliation, and violence are incinerated in a blaze of compassionate mercy. As Jesus tells the story, "compassion" inspires the Samaritan's "mercy" toward his enemy. Without feeling compassion it is unlikely that he would be moved to care so selflessly and benevolently for the injured man; without feeling compassion it is unlikely that the Samaritan would have desired to deliver so passionately to the vulnerable enemy the unmerited benefits, spiritual, economic, and medical, that he did. On the other hand, we see priest and Levite, Just men as they are but void of feelings of compassion, passing indifferently and callously by.

Christian communities too often emulate, perhaps unwittingly, priest and Levite instead of compassionate Samaritan. Scattered along the byways of church history are countless enemies, countless injured, marginalized, and vulnerable who the church for "good" moral and just reasons despises, ignores, or neglects. Some neglect the needy by believing that benevolence is strictly a private and not public matter; others neglect the needy by disregarding the necessity of public benevolence for realizing the egalitarian justice envisioned by God's kingdom. In either case, this neglect is unwarranted. The intrinsic worth of those created in God's image, not to mention Jesus's care for them, is sufficient reason for benevolent communities to care, as did the Samaritan, mercifully and publicly for all humans, including enemies. But too often Christian communities, lacking Samaritan compassion, are merely Just instead of compassionately and mercifully Righteous. Just as for priest and Levite "remembrance" fails them; they excuse themselves from mercy with "God helps those who help themselves" or "mercy is a personal and not public matter." They deceive themselves, believing that by acting justly they are acting Christianly, when in fact they are vacating the very compassionate mercy they preach and that ought to distinguish them as Christians. Whether he was inspired to "Go and do likewise," I suspect many Christians, like the lawyer, are unwittingly scandalized by Jesus's parable; not because religious leaders are disparagingly depicted, nor because Jesus commands help for an enemy. What bothers him, I suspect, is a gradual realization that, even though justice is his professional and personal conviction, what is required of him is not simple justice but righteousness; what is required of him is an integrity of moral character in which he must habituate himself to his enemy's reality, thereby not only making him neighbor to his enemy but making his status equal to his enemy's. In abstract theory or in story, of course, equality is acceptable, but in the reality of local, neighborly compassion, it is often for many intolerable.

This is perhaps why most modern people would prefer "veil of ignorance" or "impartial spectator" to compassion's "vale of tears." The implicit, abstract "distance" protects the moral agent from the challenges and burdens of compassion's sometimes stark Samaritan encounters. As the Christian axis for making moral and political judgments, compassion and mercy forsake the position of those who, like Rawls, make moral judgments from the "distance" of a hypothetical veil; a state in which the moral agent (the priest) retreats from the reality and burdens that compassion invites. Nor does compassion permit the Samaritan the "distance" of Smith's impartial third-party spectator (Levite). Instead compassion thrusts moral agents into the midst of suffering and deprivation and calls them to undertake projects of benevolence that grant to the vulnerable benefits to which he may otherwise have no power of access. Whether by bracketing the moral agent or by bracketing the burdens of the other, reality is circumscribed and responsibility neglected. Neither the one (veil) nor the other (spectator) of these positions is finally satisfactory, at least for Christians. Both methods suffer the distance of abstraction. The former brackets reality from the moral agent; the latter brackets the agent from reality; the former nullifies the other, the latter nullifies the self. Indeed, both abstractions are at bottom based on doubt, doubt of self and doubt of the other. Like Descartes' project they systematically degrade doubt, an otherwise useful activity, to the function of method; a kind of "comic method," as Unamumo calls it, "a doubt purely theoretical and provisional,"[1] not the genuine, tragic localized doubt of compassion that, like Hume's sympathy,[2] embeds the self intensely and passionately in a vale of tears, in joys and sorrows, in burdens and benefits that humans actually encounter. More importantly, neither of these two abstractions, when conditions of injustice are present, tends to produce egalitarian justice and the "fair balance" of a sustainable livelihood for all envisioned by God's peaceable kingdom.

I begin by examining the premise that compassion is the moral and psychological bridge or nexus coupling justice with mercy; that it constitutes a bridge between liberal justice and egalitarian justice. Compassion is that powerful moral and emotional fulcrum by which a community of character evolves organically from Justice to Righteousness, from mutual self-interest to benevolence, from reason to faith, from the moral entropy of law to the moral integrity of mercy's law of liberty. Secondly, I show how the compassionate self and the other interact; thirdly, how to educate for compassion; and finally, how compassion catapults Christian communities beyond the fallenness of self-interest to redeemed transnational world-citizenship. In chapter 3 I examined the nature and role of justice and in chapter 4 the nature and role of mercy, my focus in this chapter is compassion as the moral, spiritual, and psychological bridge between the two.

FROM JUSTICE TO MERCY

I assume in this chapter the evolution of moral consciousness and character described in chapter 1, specifically its evolution from justice (rational law) to mercy (spiritual law), from a Just to a Righteous community. The cognitive, emotional condition that makes possible this transition is compassion, the capacity of humans for emotional intersubjectivity. So, how is compassion an emotional and moral bridge between justice and mercy? Recall the analogy, taken from physics, set forth in chapter 1 and extended in chapters 4 and 5: symmetry and reason represent justice, asymmetry and faith represent mercy, and supersymmetry represents compassion. In physics SUSY or supersymmetry refers to two phenonmena: first, to an underlying unity and wholeness that supercedes traditional dichotomies, like subject/object, mind/body, self/other; and secondly, to the experimenter who by "peeking" at the experiment actively contributes to the construction of reality and the outcome of the experiment (i.e., the direction of the particle). Compassion, I am suggesting, functions analogously in moral practice; first, it provides a moral unity and wholeness, superseding dichotomies such as divine/human, faith/reason, grace/law, mercy/justice; and secondly, the compassionate moral agent contributes to the reconstruction of reality by acting mercifully and benevolently. In so doing she transforms herself, transforms the other, transforms the relation between the two and thereby transforms reality.

This evolution of moral character parallels a double theological and existential progression from human fallenness and (in)justice (reason's symmetry), to the incarnation of a divine/human being (compassion's incarnation), and finally to redemption (mercy's benevolence). The equation is simple: healing human fallenness and (in)justice requires of moral agents compassionate incarnation so that mercy's power of redemption and reconciliation is possible. Mercy's redemption presupposes compassion's incarnation; and compassion's incarnation presupposes human corruption and injustice. Compassionate incarnation and merciful redemption are required in order to reestablish and sustain the promise of *pax Dei*, its harmony and justice. They constitute the righteousness of *agape* the way God practices it. In his parable of the Good Samaritan and Sermon on the Mount, Jesus commands his disciples to make this transition in moral practice; commands that they evolve morally from justice to mercy, from the values of *pax Romana* to the values of *pax Christi*. The passage from Matthew's gospel (5: 38–48) is familiar but worth quoting for its regard of this transition.

> You have heard that it was said, "An eye for an eye and a tooth for a tooth." But I say to you, Do not resist one who is evil. But if any one strikes you on the right cheek, turn to him the other also. . . . You have heard it said, "You shall love your neighbor and hate your enemy." But I say to you, Love your enemies and pray for those who persecute you, so that you may be sons of your Father who is in heaven; for he makes his sun to rise on the evil and on the good, and sends rain on the just and the unjust. For if you love those who love you, what reward have you? Do not even the tax collectors do the same. . . . You, therefore, must be perfect, as your heavenly Father is perfect.

Jesus's culminating command for perfection, for full realization of moral integrity, indicates his central concern, namely, that his disciples evolve spiritually and morally; and that they do so by making the transition from justice to mercy. When it comes to an axis for moral judgment there is here no veil of ignorance or impartial spectator, only the compassionate mercy of *agape*. Unless his disciples distinguish themselves morally and spiritually, unless their righteousness exceeds that of even the most religious (v. 20), unless they practice mercy instead of mere justice, then the salt of their lives will lose its savor (v. 13), the light of truth will dim (v. 14–16), and God's Kingdom in them will come to an end. Piloting this transition, it turns out, entails an intermediate stage represented by compassion in Jesus's parable and by meekness in Jesus's Sermon. Although not named in Jesus's Sermon as it is in his parable, compassion very often entails meekness, which functions as a catalyst of moral evolution from justice ("An eye for an eye") to *agape*'s merciful benevolence ("Love your enemies"). How then can we characterize this transition from justice to mercy? What are the moral and psychological conditions that make it possible? Three features of compassion address these questions and facilitate this transition to benevolent community: emotional intersubjectivity, self-transformation, and other-transformation.

Emotional Intersubjectivity. Compassionate incarnation, or Hume's "natural sympathy," entails one of the most profound and powerfully unique human experiences, the experience of emotional intersubjectivity, which for Hume distinguishes humans from inferior creatures. "Intersubjectivity" refers to a common human experience wherein humans share specific emotions and emotional experiences. As Solomon suggests, in emotion "we 'open ourselves' to others, allow ourselves to share their experiences and opinions, their world views, and, ultimately, their other emotions."[3] In so doing, the moral agent situates himself *with* the other, creates between self and other a social and moral equality. Similarly, Blum states that "compassion involves . . . a sense of shared humanity, of regarding the other as a fellow human being. This means that the other person's suffering is seen as the kind of thing that could happen to anyone, including oneself insofar as one is a human being."[4] What compassionate intersubjectivity calls for, then, is a self "engrossed"[5] in the experience of the other. The "other" may be a wrongdoer or vulnerable other, but in any case a human of intrinsic worth to whom compassion is a compelling moral response. "Engrossment," as Jean Grimshaw explains, involves the self in a process of equilibrium, of "apprehending the reality of the other, . . . a putting aside of self and an entering into the experience of another as far as possible."[6] What is the significance of this emotional intersubjectivity for benevolent communities?

Jesus's incarnation establishes the supreme paradigm of compassionate meekness, of emotional intersubjectvity and engrossment. Paul is little short of rhapsodic in his epistle to the Philippians (2: 5–11), when he entreats Christian communities to have in themselves the same mind, the same compassionate meekness and mercy that Jesus incarnates. For Paul, Christian conversion and benevolent character are not primarily matters of doctrines or creeds or sacraments or morals or politics; rather they are a matter of a spiritual disposition of mind, a disposition of *kenosis*. What are the features of this disposition, this *kenosis*? Paul tells us. First of all, the *kenotic*, compassionate disposition of mind is humble, not haughty. Jesus, "in the form of God," as Paul says it, possesses all the power and privileges thereto appertaining. Jesus is not tempted, however, by his ontological status, his equality with God, nor is he tempted to exercise his rightful executive power, his authority to judge and condemn humans. As Divine Jesus has the authority and every right to do so, to execute justice. The symmetry of justice and the duties of moral reason require even the divine to repay an eye for an eye. But for the sake of compassionate incarnation Jesus's humility supersedes the otherwise legitimate claims of justice. Secondly and concomittantly, the *kenotic* disposition of mind entails self-emptying. Paul says Christ "emptied himself," a phrase that has produced more than its share of interpretations. For my purposes here the *kenosis* of "emptied himself" entails not only a spiritual disposition of self-denial but also a legal one. Even though Jesus as Christ has authority and every right to execute justice, he is willing for mercy's sake to forego that right and the demands of justice and to "meekly" turn the other cheek. For the sake of humanity Jesus "empties himself" of his authority to execute judgment on fallen humanity. Instead, thirdly, Jesus's *kenotic* disposition of mind inspires compassionate incarnation. Paul puts it this way: "Jesus takes 'the form of a servant, being born in the likeness of men. And being found in human form he humbled himself and became obedient unto death, even death on a cross.'" Jesus's *kenosis,* his compassionate incarnation entails an inversion of the original "likeness of God" in which humans are created. Now in Jesus God transforms the divine self and recreates Him in the "likeness of humanity," in the form of a servant so that the relationship of God and humans might be redeemed and restored. Through incarnation Jesus experiences and does what compassion requires, namely, *kenotic* engrossment in the joys and sorrows, desires and despairs of Fallen human beings. Engrossment is the sacrificial suffering that Jesus embodies in his ministry and that his disciples struggled to apprehend for themselves. What is important to note here is the significance compassionate engrossment has for the church's social and political obligations. By requiring it to share in the emotional life of another, by requiring the experience of another to become its own, compassion equalizes the two identities. Perhaps this is why compassionate incarnation in public life is rare; it undermines entrenched social hierarchies by presupposing a fundamental equality amongst humans. As Blum observes, the practice of compassion promotes "the experience of equality, even when accompanied by an acknowledgement of actual social inequality. Compassion forbids regarding social inequality as establishing human inequality. This is part of the moral force of compassion: by transcending . . . social inequality, it promotes the sensed experience of common humanity."[7]

The parable of the Good Samaritan similarly suggests that social distance between moral agent and other is mediated by a disposition of *kenosis* and the egalitarianism implicit in incarnation and compassion. The Samaritan is justified legally in disregarding the injured Jew. Codes regulating relations amongst Jews and Samaritans included mutual laws of dissassociation; indeed, they were forbidden to engage in formal and informal relations at all. As Jesus tells it, the Samaritan nevertheless has *compassion* on the injured enemy. He "empties himself" of his right to justice and to his culture's laws of disassociation and engrosses himself in the suffering of the injured man. In so doing the Samaritan situates himself spiritually in such a way that he can now forswear reason's just laws and care for the man with the mercy of unmerited physical and financial generosity; indeed, he is able to care in a way he could not if he adhered to justice's laws of disassociation. The resulting social equilibrium between moral agent and enemy supersedes the callousness of justice (priest and Levite) and prepares him for unsurpassed works of mercy.

Similarly, in the Sermon on the Mount, the *kenotic*, compassionate disposition of mind is implicit in Jesus's comments about meekness, "turn the other cheek, etc." Although "meekness" as a value has largely been lost to contemporary moral discourse, it is crucial to the evolution of moral practice. For Jesus justice's *lex talionis* represents the entropy of an old moral dispensation; for his disciples at least, the old is superseded by a new dispensation of meekness and mercy, by a new vision of a righteous, benevolent community. Indeed, practicing meekness is the way Jesus's disciples are to begin to distinguish themselves spiritually from others and to perfect themselves, as Jesus commands. Moreover, the compassionate meekness of "turn the other cheek" mediates the evolution of moral consciousness by superseding justice and inspiring mercy. "You have heard it said, 'An eye for an eye and a tooth for a tooth.' But I say to you do not resist one who is evil. But if anyone strikes you on the right cheek, turn to him the other also" (5: 38–39). The meekness of turning the other cheek entails the humility of self-denial and the compassionate self-emptying of *kenosis*. In turning the other cheek the moral agent denies or empties himself of his right to execute the benefits and burdens of justice. Justice's symmetry precludes the meekness of turning the other cheek, precludes the self-denial of *kenosis;* it eclipses the evolution of moral consciousness, eclipses the disposition of mind "which is yours in Christ Jesus" (Philippians 2: 5–7), as Paul says it. Moral entropy ensues. Justice requires of the moral agent no emotional intersubjectivity, no act of incarnate compassion with the other, only a simple, disinterested rational calculation, "An eye for an eye," burden for burden, benefit for benefit. Justice requires it, moral reason justifies it; a person reaps what he sows. Not only is compassion not necessary, it is irrelevant if not intrusive to calculating moral symmetry.

But meekness, "Do *not* do unto others what they do to you," "turn the other cheek," entails a disposition of *kenosis* that both forswears and supersedes justice. Its command stands asymmetrically in relation to justice's "Do unto others what they do to you." Compassionate meekness grants to the other what he *needs* for healing and not what he *deserves* as punishment. Jesus himself is the paradigm. He refuses to execute the justice humanity deserves. Through incarnation, compassion and the meekness of turning the other cheek, he embodies *kenosis*, emptying himself of the temptation to retaliate, to repay humanity with justice punishment. The meekness of turning the other cheek engages Jesus in the emotional intersubjectivity of compassion. By refusing to execute justice he is able to feel for humanity in its temptation and weakness; and in so doing he situates himself in such a way that he can show mercy and forgiveness. Jesus requires as much of his disciples. He commands them to situate themselves compassionately and meekly in relationship to the other; feeling for the other the same compassion that God in Christ feels for them. The disciple now is in a position to empty himself of justice's retaliatory demands and with the courage of meekness to "turn the other cheek," so that works of mercy are now possible. Jewish and Samaritan laws require mutual disassociation. By acting meekly, by transforming "Do unto . . ." into "Do not do unto . . ." the moral agent supersedes justice so that he is able to engross himself compassionately with the pain and plight of the other.

Self-transformation. The transformative power of a *kenotic* disposition and compassionate incarnation, is first of all self-regarding; it transforms the moral agent from a Just to a Righteous self. Only after transforming the self is the other, the recipient, the enemy, transformed. Practicing compassion entails an act of faith in which the moral agent by the power of grace transforms himself into neighbor to the enemy or vulnerable other. The locus of compassion's transformative power is most profoundly the moral agent himself. Being "neighbor" is not the prerogative of the enemy or wrongdoer or vulnerable, in Jesus's view, but the prerogative of the Righteous agent. He is responsible for showing compassion, thereby transforming the relationship, transforming himself into the other's neighbor. This is clear from the parable of the Good Samaritan. The lawyer asks "Who is my neighbor?" In answering Jesus inverts the question? "Who is neighbor to the injured man?" That is, "To whom am I to be neighbor?" The question is rhetorical. It is obvious; the neighbor is the one who acts neighborly, compassionately, mercifully to the other. Whether the other, the enemy, consents or cooperates or not, the agent who by faith empties himself and acts compassionately automatically makes himself neighbor to the other and makes the other his equal, or the self the other's equal. Rather than allowing the enemy or vulnerable other to establish the rules of the relationship—"An eye for an eye, Do to others as they do to you"—the moral agent establishes the rules for conducting the relationship. By compassionate incarnation, by transforming himself into neighbor to the other, the moral agent transforms himself and the relationship so that the benevolent, unmerited benefits of mercy are possible. The enemy or vulnerable other is granted the benefit of neighborliness, quite irrespective of his volition or justice's correlation of duties and rights. Even though moral reason comprehends it not, compassion transforms the relationship between self and other, transcends the limits of justice and rejoices in the liberality of mercy. Nothing the enemy does can diminish the benevolent neighborliness of a compassionate, incarnate moral agent. Whether the enemy likes it or not, whether he accepts benevolent treatment or not, the compassionate moral agent nevertheless (Jesus says it this way) transforms himself into neighbor to the enemy. The community that by faith empties itself and acts compassionately in that very act redeems hostile relationships and invites reconciliation and restoration.

The practical power of compassionate meekness should not be underestimated. In its self-emptying asymmetry, meekness co-opts moral initiative and power, snatching it from the hands the wrongdoer, from "the one who is evil" as Matthew puts it. The wrongdoer's action, the second "eye," no longer determines ("Why should it?") for the meek the quality of moral response. Meekness's resistance to the first "eye" places it asymmetrically in relation to the second "eye" and to justice. It refuses subservience to the second "eye"; refuses to permit injustice or wrongdoer the power to dictate terms of moral engagement. As St. Paul puts it, "Repay no one evil for evil. . . . Do not be overcome by evil, but overcome evil with good" (Romans 12: 17a, 21). The resistance to "Do not be overcome by evil" reflects the asymmetry of meekness that Jesus expects of his followers. Although meekness does not yet fully manifest *agape*'s mercy, "overcome evil with good," it nevertheless opens wide the door to it. By granting the unmerited benefits of turning the other cheek the moral agent is granting a quality characteristic of mercy, namely, delivering unmerited benefits to wrongdoers or vulnerable others.

How is it that meekness is necessary for mercy? Why must compassionate incarnation precede redemption? The answer in a word: "recapitulation." Of the many ways biblical writers understand and interpret Christ's incarnation, one of the most common and compelling is in terms of compassionate recapitulation. God enters human life, shares emotionally and spiritually in its joys and sorrows, benefits, and burdens. As Irenaeus long ago suggested, by recapitulating human experience in his own life, and doing so meekly, without submitting to justice's demand for condemnation and punishment, Christ places himself in a position to show mercy's benevolence and thereby to redeem humanity. The author of the epistle to the Hebrews explicates this relationship between incarnation and redemption, compassion and mercy. Jesus "had to be made like his brethren [humanity] in every respect, so that he might become a merciful and faithful high priest in the service of God, to make expiation for the sins of the people. For because he himself has suffered and been tempted, he is able to help those who are tempted" (2: 17–18). With compassion Jesus becomes incarnate, courageously and meekly he turns the other cheek enabling him to "sympathize with [human] weaknesses" so that they "may receive mercy and find grace to help in time of need" (Hebrews 4: 15–16). Martha Nussbaum acknowledges compassionate, incarnate recapitulation as a necessary condition for merciful redemption. "In order to imagine a god who is truly superior, truly worthy of worship, truly and fully just, we must imagine a god who has actually lived out the non-transcendent life and understands it in the only way it can be understood, by suffering and death. . . ."[8] Compassionate incarnation liberates the benevolent mind from justice's judgment and condemnation. It is the supreme recapitulative event through which God and the benevolent community suffer the fullness of the human condition. Doing so meekly, compassionately not only satisfies the demands of justice but summons one to the duties of mercy. Nussbaum notes this fact: "The universal compassion for human suffering which one associates with Christianity at its best is difficult to imagine apart from the paradigm of human suffering and sacrifice [meekness] exemplified in Christ."[9]

Other-transformation. Compassion's emotional intersubjectivity necessarily yields other-regarding, altruistic behavior, projects of merciful benevolence. As Snow suggests, a "concern for the other's good . . . expressed in benevolent other-regarding . . . actions" partly distinguishes compassion from related experiences like sympathy.[10] "It is not enough," insists Blum, "that we imaginatively reconstruct someone's suffering: for, like belief, such imagining is compatible with malice and mere intellectual curiosity." Hence, the self and object are related not only emotionally but altruistically, not only by feeling for an other but also by undertaking benevolent projects on behalf of the other. Compassion is not therefore "a momentary feeling of concern, it is rather to act consistently and reliably in such a way calculated to relieve the other's distress."[11] Jesus's identification with human suffering and weakness was not simply sympathetic feeling, as the writer of Hebrews makes clear, but practical, so that he might help those who are in need (see Hebrews 2: 17–18; 4: 14–16). All this is provocatively portrayed in the parable of the Good Samaritan, where compassion involves not only incarnation, not only imagining and feeling what the injured man must be suffering. For all we know the priest and Levite might well have imagined this and still passed by.

As altruistic, compassion ultimately includes other-regarding projects, compels us to grant mercy and to act benevolently to alleviate the other's suffering. Indeed, "compassionate acts often involve acting very much contrary to one's moods and inclinations. Compassion is fundamentally other-regarding; [and] its affective status in no way detracts from this."[12]

Mercy as *agape* constitutes the evolved way Jesus's disciples vindicate themselves as a Righteous and not merely as a Just community. It is how they distinguish themselves from other moral agents; it is how they are commended "to be perfect, as your heavenly Father is perfect." Not only is Jesus the embodiment of that perfection, of *agape* and mercy, moral reciprocity requires the same perfection of his disciples. Moral practice now evolves from meekness's "Do *not* do unto others what they do to you," to mercy's "Do unto others as you would they do to you," or more precisely "Grant unto others the same mercy God has granted you." "Love your neighbor with the same mercy with which you have been loved and love yourself." "Love your enemies and pray for those who persecute you"; not that they may be condemned or defeated but that they might be transformed, redeemed, reconciled. The evolved power of *agape*'s mercy transforms the other, even enemies, even tax collectors, Gentiles, the merely just, scribes and Pharisees into the Righteous of God's Kingdom. Jesus's command to practice *agape* and mercy, to "Do unto others as you would they do to you," not only has the power to liberate the moral agent from bonds of judgment and condemnation but also the power to deliver from bondage the other, the enemy. It is a command that for Christians emerges in the specific context of Eucharist gratitude and remembrance. By God's grace and in gratitude perfect yourself by granting to others, including enemies, the same mercy, the same unmerited benefits of *agape*, that God in Christ grants you and all humanity.

The aim of such mercy, of course, is reconciliation, healing, restoring relationships with God and others, as suggested by the Apostle Paul. God "reconciles us to himself through Christ and gave us the ministry of reconciliation. . . . And he has committed to us the ministry of reconciliation" (i.e., mercy) (II Corinthians 5: 16–21). Elsewhere Paul enjoins Christians to have in yourself the same love, joy, affection, sympathy and humility of mind as does Christ Jesus. He goes on to argue that Christians are to do so by becoming compassionately incarnate. Even as Christ empties himself and takes on the form of a servant, a servant even to enemies (Philippians 2), so too are Christians to empty themselves. By doing so Christians situate themselves spiritually so that there follows spontaneously and inevitably the healing balm and benevolence of mercy whereby broken relationships are reconciled. As noted already, the parable of the Good Samaritan dramatizes the way compassion has the power to invite works of mercy. Estranged by ancient habits of racial, religious, and cultural animosities Jew and Samaritan protected themselves from each other legally, by fair and equal laws of disassociation. The behavior of priest and Levite merely reflects these juridical habits of disassociation. The Samaritan, in contrast, is apparently a righteous man; his spiritual sensibility is anchored to feelings of compassionate meekness and not merely to his culture's code of justice. Because he has nurtured habits of compassion and meekness he is able to empathize with the plight of his enemy and turn his other cheek to justice's suffocating laws of disassociation. Feeling compassion spontaneously inspires and invites the Samaritan to perform acts of mercy to which the Jew, from the perspective of law, reason, and justice, has no right. He devotes time, energy, and resources to comprehensive care of the Jew; he cleans and binds his wounds, transports him to an inn, cares for him, and pays for the Jew's board and medical expenses. The Samaritan's goodness, his meekness and compassion clears the way for the healing of merciful redemption of the other. Without Jesus's incarnation there is no mercy of redemption; and without mercy there is in a fallen, unjust world little possibility of the harmonious and just egalitarianism of *pax Dei*. Without cultivating habits of meekness and compassion it is unlikely that the Christian community will practice toward enemies the same benevolence of mercy, the same *pax Christi,* which shapes its own spiritual and moral identity.

I have sketched the evolution of moral consciousness as reflected in Jesus's Sermon and parable: from justice via compassion to mercy; from fallenness via incarnation to redemption; from "Do unto others as they do to you" (justice), to "Do *not* do unto others what they do to you" (meekness), and finally, to the moral reciprocity of "Do for others according to the same mercy that God has done for you." Jesus does not suffer persecution, torture, and death, he does not rise again merely to inspire followers to do no more than execute the same justice to which his enemies subject him. Fallen humanity executes justice frequently and sometimes fairly. Christ expects and empowers his followers to practice mercy and peace and reconciliation; anything less forfeits grace as well as redemption; anything less than mercy is less than the perfection that *agape* demands.

In the following chapters, I show what practicing benevolence means for a politics of mercy. Suffice it to note here that Christian tradition officially identifies certain "works of mercy" as the heart of Christian ethics. These works are customarily distributed in two divisions, spiritual works of mercy and corporal works of mercy. Spiritual works include "instruct the ignorant, counsel the doubtful, comfort the afflicted, admonish the sinner, forgive offenses, bear wrongs patiently, and pray for the living and the dead."[13] Corporal works of mercy include "feed the hungry, give drink to the thirsty, shelter the homeless, clothe the naked, visit the sick, visit the imprisoned, and bury the dead."[14] Insofar as these works contribute to social and moral order they are properly entrusted not only to private endeavors but to public ones as well.

EDUCATING FOR COMPASSION

One of the great moral and spiritual tasks of Christian and indeed of all benevolent communities is to educate for compassion and thereby for mercy and benevolence. Educating for compassion is especially difficult; for compassion requires strengthening not only individual moral character but communal character as well. What pedagogical techniques are best suited to the spiritual formation of a compassionate character and benevolent community? At least three techniques are essential: narratives, apprenticeship, and diversity, all of which Jesus practices.

Educating for compassion involves narratives. Most religious prophets are justly famous for their storytelling. Often, when questioned or challenged, Jesus engages his listeners with stories, like the parable of the Good Samaritan. When it comes to storytelling, however, Jesus is not alone. He stands in a long line of Jewish rabbi's for whom storytelling is central. Jesus's own followers resort mostly to storytelling when trying to communicate the meaning and significance of his ministry. Indeed, all of the world's great religious founders are master storytellers, so much so that one wonders whether without stories their movements might not have withered and died. Why is this so? Why is narrative, why is storytelling such a powerful tool for educating the heart? The answer lies partly in the fact that narrative provides access to the emotional life of humans and thereby to nurturing emotions conducive to feeling compassion. Martha Nussbaum makes this point forcefully when she insists that our moral emotions very often "are not taught to us directly through propositional claims about the world. . . . They are taught above all through stories. Stories express their structure and teach us their dynamics. These stories are constructed by others and, then taught and learned. But once internalized, they shape the way life looks and feels."[15] If compassion is to shape the way humans live out their personal and public lives, then, narratives in general and stories of compassion in particular are crucial.

What is it about narratives that conduce to shape and inspire habits of compassion? The short answer is that narratives embody a logic of emotions; they are equipped with tools that shape and reshape emotions either into habits of virtue or habits of vice. Upon ending his parable of the Good Samaritan, Jesus enjoins his listeners to "Go and do" what the telling of the parable partly empowers them to do, that is, "likewise"; imitate the Samaritan; go imitate the plot of the story; go act compassionately toward all peoples including enemies. If a central task of Christian education is fostering compassion, then a central means for doing so is by and through what Martha Nussbaum calls "the narrative imagination."[16] For Plato the narrative imagination is unsurpassed in its power to shape the moral character of children. That is why in the *Republic* he has Socrates set forth strict guidelines for censoring both the moral content of stories and the pedagogical method for teaching them.[17] For him stories do not merely transmit values and wisdom, they awaken and activate the heart; they possess power to shape for good or ill the very marrow of a person's character and a community's moral habits. Put another way, as Mary Moore does, "narratives are an important source of imagination,"[18] and imagination is a key dimension of a community's capacity for experiencing compassion. The capacity for benevolence and malevolence, for virtue and vice, lies dormant in the human heart. Stories possess an imaginative power capable of nurturing the greatest virtues and the greatest vices. The story's secret lies in the power of the narrative imagination "to make the characters of the story so alive and human that those who hear it live with them and enter into their experiences."[19] Drama, as Aristotle teaches us, engages the imagination, invites the audience "to identify with the tragic hero"; when that "hero is a relatively good person, whose distress does not stem from deliberate wickedness," then, says Nussbaum, "the drama makes compassion for suffering seize the imagination. This emotion is built into the dramatic form."[20]

Educating for compassion can and must begin early in childhood, as soon as a child begins to listen to stories and to engage in storytelling herself. "The basis for civic imagining must be laid in early life," as Nussbaum says it, for "as children explore stories, rhymes, and songs . . . they are led to notice the sufferings of other living creatures with a new keenness."[21] Doing so educates the child's heart for compassion in several ways. First, many stories tell a tale of compassion as a desirable, noble habit of heart: narratives in which the compassionate hero (or community) is praised and the mean and unforgiving anti-hero is condemned or punished. Jesus's parables very often include such a scenario; for example, the story of the unforgiving servant. Secondly, it is important that the child learns and tells stories of compassion that originate in traditions other than her own. In doing so, she learns compassion for "alien" others not only through the story's content, not only through entering into and empathizing with compassionate characters, but by attending to the other's narrative tradition in the first place. As Nussbaum suggests, "As soon as children engage in storytelling, they can tell stories about other lands and other peoples,"[22] the very telling of which is itself an exercise in compassion. In hearing and telling compassionate stories from other traditions the pupil is vicariously expanding the range of her own capacity for feeling compassion for peoples amongst whom these other stories originate. And third, by engaging in the act of creating stories of compassion from her own imagination, the pupil begins to enter into the experience of compassion at a profoundly powerful and personal depth. Young pupils might tell stories, imagined or real, in which they help someone in need, and try to imagine what would happen if help was unavailable or denied. For the more advanced, students might reimagine actual historical events in such a way that reconciling compassion instead of hostile revenge is pivotal. Each of these narrative techniques possess a power to begin to habituate the child's heart to compassion as a virtue greatly to be desired, a virtue she must expect not only of herself but of other citizens as well.

Educating for compassion involves apprenticeship. Moses and Jesus, Mohammed and Buddha, and other great prophets taught their disciples as much by apprenticeship and association (what today is sometimes called service learning) as by story and discourse. It is rapidly becoming a pedagogical truism that a teacher teaches moral character as much by doing as by saying. Jesus calls his disciples with "Follow me," rather than "Listen to me," not because he disparages listening but because practicing a particular pattern of life is of more profound significance for moral and spiritual formation than is mere listening. He calls disciples so "they might first be 'with him,'" as H. H. Horne puts it, "and then that he might 'send them.'"[23] A central technique Jesus uses for training disciples, accordingly, is apprenticeship, on-site training in the art of compassionate, global citizenship. Early in his public ministry Jesus takes his disciples with him throughout Galilee and has them practice with him the techniques of compassion and mercy, healing, feeding, and helping. So although storytelling is necessary and essential to educating the heart, it is by itself insufficient. Storytelling "feeds the desire for experience,"[24] argues Cather, and that desire is to participate in projects of compassion that stories and storytelling inspire but cannot themselves fulfill. Educating the heart for compassion naturally and logically embraces a kind of collective, pedagogical apprenticeship in which pupils, under supervision, engage in benevolent projects involving experiences of compassion.

The fact that Jesus trains disciples as apprentices is continuous, of course, with the Christian understanding of incarnation. Mary Moore makes this point in a chapter entitled "Incarnational Teaching." "Incarnation is God's enfleshment or presence in the world. [So, incarnation] can be expected in the teacher-student relationship . . . in acts of compassion and acts of anger toward injustice."[25] Incarnational teaching includes apprenticeship because teaching God's presence in the world must involve actually "Caring for others [as] part of teaching" and not merely as "an extracurricular activity that some do because they are 'nice.'" Indeed, "caring for others is an important quality in the teaching-learning process and an important goal"[26] whereby teacher and student train together, participating in projects of compassionate service, as did Jesus and his disciples. Similarly, Pablo Freire seems to insist on the necessity of pedagogical apprenticeship when he speaks of "the word" as an event able to "transform the world." Within the word, he says, "we find two dimensions, reflection and action, in such radical interaction that if one is sacrificed—even in part—the other immediately suffers. There is no true word that is not at the same time a praxis."[27] When it comes to moral and spiritual pedagogy, accordingly, there is no true teaching and learning that does not at the same time include active apprenticeship. To make this claim is to imply at least two things; first, that any true word is at the same time communal, and secondly, that any true word is "not the privilege of some few men, but the right of every man." As Freire says, "no one can say a true word alone—nor can he say it for another, in a prescriptive act which robs others of their words."[28] The teacher's task, then, includes incarnational training, practicing with pupils the ancient art of acting compassionately in the world. In so doing not only pupils but also teacher and world are transformed. Indeed, we learn from the world's great moral and religious leaders that compassion as public virtue and apprenticeship as pedagogical technique are interdependent and compelling. Moses, Confucius, Buddha, Jesus, Paul, Mohammed, Gandhi, and King, all cultivate a group of disciples or "intimate learners" so that they might "learn not so much the lessons as the way of their teacher, so that by personal witnesses the blessed truth might be passed on to others and so on to others."[29]

Educating for compassion involves unity in diversity. Jesus was famous for stories and projects that challenged beliefs and behaviors that were otherwise taken for granted as "neutral, necessary, and natural," as Nussbaum puts it.[30] Of course, Jesus is not challenging beliefs and behaviors simply to defy them, but in order to teach what it means to love compassionately and act benevolently. To do so, Jesus realizes he must confront his disciples with difference. When he has Jewish religious leaders pass by the injured man with apparent disregard and has a despised Samaritan show compassion and mercy, for example, Jesus confronts his disciples with diversity and challenges their racial and religious and moral prejudices. Yet, he also suggests, in this parable, a way in which a benevolent community might be one in which difference enhances identity and diversity enhances unity. What challenges Jesus's listeners most profoundly is the realization that despite thinking of themselves as superior and privileged, foreigners and enemies may very well equal or exceed them morally and spiritually. Potential exists in the common experience of compassion for peoples of differing faiths and no faith to share moral ground, creating therein unity in plurality. The nature of emotions is that they can be shared transculturally and thereby function as the basis for unity and universality. Compassion's narrative imagination (imagining the other's plight) and empathetic emotion (feeling for the other) are capacities belonging to every human, every benevolent community; they provide the basis for unity in diversity. Indeed, compassion by its very nature as compassion presupposes harmony in the midst of difference. It presupposes, ironically, that wherever there is difference and diversity among humans there can and should be identity and unity (i.e., incarnation). Compassion's character is to preserve and perpetuate what is distinct and different while at the same time mediating and harmonizing.

Any community, religious or secular, that deigns to call itself benevolent and civil ought to be about the business of compassionate global citizenship. Any genuinely moral community by its very nature as moral will show compassion to communities distinct from itself. The most profound and permanent way of opposing immoral communities, like Fascists and Nazis, imperialists and terrorists, Islamists, and Islamiphobiacs, is by educating the communal heart for compassionate global citizenship. Not surprisingly, then, the primary aim of Jesus's calling apprentices is to teach compassion and mercy, and he does so by keeping company with sinners and outcasts and foreigners, by breaking Sabbath laws, by healing the distressed, by opposing injustice and oppressors. Indeed, Jesus practices a hermeneutic of suspicion. Questioning his own tradition (Sabbath laws), appreciating the traditions of others (the good Samaritan, Samaritan woman), socializing and caring for the despised and disinherited (publicans and sinners) often produces, as Nussbaum points out, "a widespread fear—reflected for example in the argument of Allan Bloom's book *The Closing of the American Mind*—that critical scrutiny of one's own tradition will automatically entail a form of cultural relativism."[31] No doubt such fear contributed considerably to the deaths of Socrates, Jesus, Gandhi, and Martin Luther King Jr. But as I argued earlier, relativism is not the inevitable consequence of difference and plurality. Human emotions in general and compassion in particular possess the power of intersubjectivity, of traversing while yet preserving difference and of establishing those universal truths that are presupposed in the compassionate judgments we make and benevolent projects we undertake.

If communities intentionally and systematically educate for compassion and mercy then peacemaking and world citizenship is possible. Mercy as the axis of moral judgment is available to all humans created in God's image; the capacity is natural; the practice is volitional and makes possible peace and world citizenship.

COMPASSION AND WORLD CITIZENSHIP

What does it mean to be a citizen of the world? How is compassion critical to securing that citizenship? An easy way of answering is to note that the Kingdom of God, of which Christians are primarily citizens, is global, transnational, and transcultural, even transreligious. By its very nature compassion calls a Righteous community to world citizenship and calls it in a way that seems inaudible to the merely Just community. Compassion is the passport to world citizenship; it inspires mercy and a politics of mercy; it inspires a willingness to turn the other cheek, execute duties without rights, benefit enemies, wrongdoers, and vulnerable others. Because compassion by its very nature involves shared emotional experience it traverses (not transcends) that which distinguishes and distances one person or community from another. By feeling compassion for the other, like the Samaritan in Jesus's parable, personal, cultural, national, and religious differences are superseded, differences that otherwise puts distance between self and other. Compassion possesses a power that inspires people, who are otherwise profoundly different in their national and religious cultures, to participate in common emotional experiences, mutually undertaking moral projects of great and lasting good. Gandhi's *satyagraha* and Martin Luther King Jr.'s nonviolent, civil disobedience campaigns are two examples. Compassionate incarnation and meekness possess an evolved spiritual quality whereby diverse peoples are empowered to become what Martha Nussbaum refers to in *Cultivating Humanity* as "world citizens." "Habits of empathy and conjecture conduce to a certain kind of citizenship and a certain form of community: one that cultivates a sympathetic responsiveness to another's needs, and understand the way circumstances shape those needs, while respecting separateness and privacy."[32] "The world citizen," in other words, "must develop sympathetic understanding of distant cultures and of ethnic, racial, and religious minorities within her own."[33] Compassionately entering into the experience of other communities traverses distance and difference and establishes on the authority of *pax Christi* a common global citizenship.

Jesus's encounter with the Samaritan woman at the well is illuminating in this regard. The differences between Jesus and the woman could hardly be more stark and striking. Both are members of cultural, religious, and national communities between which roil ancient animosities and hostilities. Differences in race, nationality, religion, culture, gender, and social status together create a seemingly unbreachable abyss. The woman is surprised that Jesus, a Jew, asks her, a Samaritan, for a drink of water (John 4: 9). And when they return from town Jesus's disciples marvel that he is talking to a woman (John 4: 27). Jesus manages these differences of race, gender, class, nationality, and religion, not by dissolving or disowning them, not by yielding or surrendering to them, not by transcending or surmounting them, but by compassionately traversing them. Jesus does not attempt to discover some common, universal beliefs by which to connect with the woman; but by incarnate, compassionate love for the woman he traverses the distance created by their differences. Indeed, Jesus treats her with such tender acceptance and intimate vulnerability that despite the distance she is drawn into the comfort of the mercy he offers. His loving care establishes with the woman a relation of spiritual intimacy that makes them vulnerable to each other's joys and sorrows. The intimacy of conversation between Jesus and the Samaritan is really quite remarkable. Their openness to one another diminishes the distance and draws them progressively into a relation of personal disclosure and emotional fellowship, but without dissolving their differences. When questioned about her relationships with men, the woman feels no need to defend herself. Instead, she is drawn by Jesus's accepting care into a relation of self-disclosure and transformation.

In another sense, however, compassion does concern itself with distinctions, by affirming and loving difference between peoples. By conversing with a Samaritan and a woman Jesus breaks traditional law and in so doing accepts and affirms her in her racial, national, and gender difference. Jesus also affirms the woman in her religious difference, acknowledging and accepting that she worships in a place and way that differs from his own (John 4: 20–22). And he does so without condemning or disowning her in her religious difference. Jesus recognizes that what distinguishes him from the woman most particularly, religious faith, is also what makes it possible for both of them to affirm and care for each other most profoundly. That which inspires Jesus and the Samaritan women, that which inspires diverse communities to practice compassion toward one another is precisely that which distinguishes them from the other, namely, their own uniquely local religious dialect, beliefs, and practices. Those communities that are truly and authentically compassionate toward others different from themselves will fairly acknowledge for those others what they insist on for themselves, namely, that their own distinctive religious beliefs and practices are indispensable for practicing compassion, for participating as world citizens in a global community. Accordingly, incarnate communities are benevolent; insofar as they are compassionate, they will not only affirm but love affirming the differences and local dialects of peoples of other faiths, of other traditions.

Jesus and the Samaritan woman acknowledge and affirm their religious differences, mutually accepting the fact that the woman's community worships at Mount Gerizim and that Jesus's community worships at Jerusalem. Jesus moves this interreligious conversation about interreligious cooperation a step further, however. He places worship at Mount Gerizim and worship at Jerusalem on equal footing when he exclaims that the day is coming when devotees of these two different religious traditions will recognize that true worship of God is a matter of spirit and truth and not merely of sacred place and time (John 4: 20–24). There will come a time, says Jesus, when Samaritans will not worship at Gerizim and Jews will not worship at Jerusalem. Yet that does not mean that true worship comes to a halt. For wherever there is sacred place and whenever there is sacred time, and however a community ritualizes that place and time, authentic worship is a matter of spirit and truth, grace and faith, compassion and mercy, incarnation and redemption. Insofar as any form of worship, however alien to me, inspires the faith and grace of compassion that leads to mercy, then that worship is authentic, is "in spirit and in truth."

The practice of compassionate incarnation and merciful redemption is the singular way a benevolent community worships God in spirit and truth. It need not be only a Christian version of compassion and mercy; any religion's compassion will do (e.g., the parable of the Good Samaritan). All else is important and necessary but procedural, a method. True worship through distinct, local dialects and at unique sacred places aims at protecting, preserving, and promoting compassionate incarnation and merciful redemption whose very spirit and truth is necessarily and universally common. These practices require benevolent communities to share, in the midst of difference, a transnational experience of such spiritual depth and profound truth that as world citizens they are able to traverse differences while at the same time embracing them. Jesus does not mean that devotees should forsake worship at Gerizim or Jerusalem. He himself continues to worship in Jerusalem and in synagogue, and he does not ask the woman to forsake her worship in the temple at Gerizim. But he is insisting on faith, on the grace of mercy and compassion, on incarnation and redemption; he is insisting that worship at Gerizim or Jerusalem does not empower and transform a community, but that worshipping God in spirit and truth, in compassion and mercy, empowers and transforms Gerizim and Jerusalem into authentic, sacred space and time.

How, then, does compassion and mercy situate Christians, as world citizens, in relationship to other faiths? Typically, the metaphor that is compelling for many is an image of multiple religious roads, all of which lead to a common end: God, Nirvana, Heaven, the Ultimate, the Humane, the Real, the Just. Each road requires of its travelers beliefs and practices distinct to that road, but ultimately all travelers arrive at the same destination. This metaphor, however, is too weak to bear the weight of what I am trying to argue. I prefer instead a metaphor suggested by Kierkegaard in his analysis of the parable of the Good Samaritan.[34] Represented in this parable are devotees of at least two religions who are traveling only one road. The road these devotees walk is one and the same road, not different roads. The parable tells of a single road, between Jerusalem and Jericho, and of five travelers (the injured man, the thieves, the priest, the Levite, and the Samaritan) all of who are walking the same road physically but who spiritually are walking that one road differently. The injured man, a Jew we presume, walks the road peacefully; the thieves walk the same road violently; the priest walks the road indifferently; the Levite walks it selfishly; and the Samaritan, the other, the enemy, the heretic, the foreigner, walks it compassionately and mercifully. Of the Samaritan Kierkegaard says, "He found the poor unfortunate man on the road of mercy. He showed by example how to walk the road mercifully; he demonstrated that the road, spiritually speaking, is precisely this; how one walks. This is why the Gospel says, 'Go and do likewise.'" The road everyone walks is the same road; but the difference, that for Jesus makes all the difference, how each person walks that one road. All walk the same road; but all religions embrace devotees who each walk that road differently—some violently, some indifferently and callously, some selfishly and self-righteously, some compassionately and mercifully. The traveler that is acceptable to Jesus, the one who walks the road truly, is not a devotee of Jesus's own religion but of a hostile religion.

For Jesus, then, the critical issue and criterion is not which religious tradition the devotee happens to claim; it is not what one claims that demonstrates how one walks the road; it is not that the road is walked in the garb of this religion or that, intoning this belief or that, but how devotees of any or no religious tradition walk the road. Does their religion, does their faith inspire them to walk the road in self-righteousness enmity and violence? Or does their faith inspire in them the grace and power with which to walk the road compassionately and mercifully? Does it inspire them to walk it indifferently and negligently? "Worldly sagacity," as Kierkegaard puts it, "teaches that the road goes over Gerizim, or over Moriah, or that it goes through some science or other, or that the road is certain doctrines, or certain behaviors," or all of these magnanimously embraced together. But not according to the life and teaching of Jesus, who repeatedly rails against such worldly wisdom even when it happens to be the wisdom of priests and professors of religion. "But all this is a deception," insists Kierkegaard, "because the road is how it is walked." As Scripture says, "two people can be sleeping in the same bed [religious tradition]—the one is saved the other is lost. Two people can go up to the same house of worship—the one goes home saved and the other is lost. Two people can recite the same creed—the one can be saved, the other is lost"[35] (Luke 17: 34–37). How can this be? How can devotees of the same religious tradition not all be acceptable to God? How can devotees of different traditions be acceptable to God? The deception of worldly wisdom is twofold: first, to believe dogmatically and exclusively that the key to transformation is for all to walk the road in the same religious garb in which I walk, and secondly, to believe benignly and naively that any road you walk, as long as you walk it earnestly, suffices. Jesus rejects both of these deceptions, as do all the great prophets. Knowing that all humans of all religious traditions walk the same road, Jesus preaches what he lives, namely, that it is not what road you walk that matters, but how by God's grace you walk the only road there is, whether by incarnate compassion and redemptive mercy or not. Spirit and truth consists not in whether "I speak in the tongues of men or of angels" but whether I walk in a "Love [that] does not insist on its own way" (I Cor. 13: 1–7). This is the "how." And this "how," this awful grace of compassion, this self-same mercy and benevolence constitutes worship in spirit and in truth and justifies in the only way possible any claim to citizenship in God's transnational, global Kingdom.

NOTES

1. Miguel de Unamuno, *Tragic Sense of Life*, trans. J. E. Crawford Flitch (New York, NY: Dover Publications, Inc., 1954), 107.

2. Hume's notion of sympathy is comparable in many ways to compassion and the moral orientation I am arguing here. Despite his reputation as skeptic and even atheist, there is evidence that in his personal life Hume manifested more nearly than many of his Christian critics the moral integrity of sympathy and compassion characteristic of a Christian character. Adam Smith eulogized his close friend as exemplifying, more than any person he knew, the qualities of a Righteous man.

3. Robert Solomon, *The Passions* (Notre Dame, IN: University of Notre Dame Press, 1976), 171.

4. Lawrence Blum, "Compassion," in *Exploring Emotions*, edited by Amelia Rorty (Berkeley: University of California Press, 1980), 511.

5. "Engrossment" is a word Nel Noddings employs to describe the profundity of emotional intersubjectivity required between the one-caring and the one-cared-for. See Noddings et al., *Caring: A Feminine Approach to Ethics and Moral Education* (Berkeley: University of California Press, 1984), 19.

6. Jean Grimshaw, *Philosophy and Feminist Thinking* (Minneapolis, MN: University of Minnesota Press, 1986), 216.

7. Blum, "Compassion," 512.

8. Martha Nussbaum, *Love's Knowledge: Essays on Philosophy and Literature* (New York: Oxford University Press, 1990), 375–376.

9. Nussbaum, *Love's Knowledge*, 375–376.

10. Nancy Snow, "Compassion," *American Philosophical Quarterly* 28, 3 (July 1991), 197.

11. Adrian Piper, "Impartiality, Compassion, and Imagination," *Ethics* 101 (July 1991), 743.

12. Blum, "Compassion," 511; see also 513.

13. James F. Keenan, *The Works of Mercy: The Heart of Catholicism* (New York: Rowman & Littlefield, 2005), 61.

14. *Ibid*., 9.

15. Nussbaum, *Love's Knowledge*, 287.

16. Nussbaum, *Cultivating Humanity: A Classical Defense of Reform in Liberal Education* (Cambridge, MA: Harvard University Press, 1997), chapter 3.

17. See books II and III of *The Republic*.

18. Mary E. M. Moore, *Teaching from the Heart: Theology and Educational Method* (Minneapolis, MN: Fortress Press, 1991), 139.

19. Katherine Cather, *Religious Education through Story-telling* (New York, NY: Abingdon Press, 1925), 26.

20. Nussbaum, *Cultivating Humanity*, 93.

21. Nussbaum, *Cultivating Humanity*, 93.

22. Nussbaum, *Cultivating Humanity*, 69.

23. Herman Harrell Horne, *The Teaching Techniques of Jesus* (Grand Rapids, MI: Kregel Publications, 1920), 143–144.

24. Cather, 25.

25. Moore, *Teaching from the Heart*, 92.

26. Moore, 93.

27. Pablo Freire, *Pedagogy of the Oppressed*, trans. Myra B. Ramos (New York: Continuum, 1990), 75–76. Freire states in a note that sacrifice of action equals "verbalism" or "idle chatter" and that sacrifice of reflection equals "activism" or an unwillingness to engage in genuine dialogue.

28. Freire, *Pedagogy of the Oppressed*, 76.

29. Hermann H. Horne, *The Teaching Techniques of Jesus* (Grand Rapids, MI: Kregel Publications, 1920), 143.

30. Nussbaum, *Cultivating Humanity*, 32.

31. Nussbaum, *Cultivating Humanity*, 33.

32. Nussbaum, *Cultivating Humanity*, 90.

33. *Ibid.*, 69.

34. Soren Kierkegaard, *Upbuilding Discourse in Various Spirits*, ed. and trans. Howard V. Hong and Edna H. Hong (Princeton, NJ: Princeton University Press, 1993), 289–291.

35. *Ibid*., 291.

Part Three

Moral Integrity

Help me, O Lord my God:
O save me according to thy mercy;
That they may know that
This is thy hand; that thou, Lord
Hast done it.
(Psalms 109: 26, 27, KJV)

Chapter Seven

Benevolence as Historical Praxis

Judas and "a great crowd with swords and clubs" come to arrest Jesus. They brandish not only weapons but the authority of "the chief priests and the elders of the people" (Matthew 26: 47–56). They come provocatively, prepared to use force and violence to seize and arrest Jesus. Judas, a disciple who has been with Jesus for some time, perhaps should have known better; so should have the other disciple who "stretched out his hand and drew his sword, and struck the slave of the high priest, and cut off his ear." Just the sort of response Judas and friends are hoping for. All the more reason to arrest and charge Jesus: assault and resisting arrest by a member of his entourage. But Jesus has none of it and surely wonders about his disciples, "Have I been with you so long, and still you do not understand what my peace is and is all about." Jesus says to the one who drew the sword and to a militaristic church tradition, "Put your sword back into its place; for all who take up the sword will perish by the sword." This incident is not just a private, personal confrontation with a disgruntled follower; it is a public and political encounter, eventually an international event, insofar as Roman authorities are drawn into it. And yet Jesus maintains his cool and his peacemaking habits. Indeed, he refuses coercion and the sword, even though it is available to him: "Do you think that I cannot appeal to my Father, and he will at once send me more than twelve legions of angels?" Jesus overcomes the temptation of fear and force and violence; he refuses the priorities and strategies of *pax Romana.* The peace he delivers, as he shows his disciples, is a different kind of peace than that delivered by the world. Peter takes up the sword because of fear; he has not yet learned to cultivate habits of compassion that inspire mercy instead of retaliatory justice.

Feeling compassion, as argued in chapter 6, is how Christian communities must first situate themselves strategically so that habits of mercy and generosity displace fear and retaliation. Most of Jesus's disciples eventually learn this lesson, as do the emerging Christian communities in the first several centuries. But the unique ecclesiastical tradition originated by them suffers defeat at the hands of Constantine's version of *pax Romana,* one consequence of which is a form of "Christian Realism" that, like Judas, betrays a gospel of mercy and peace, betrays the power and efficacy of love's benevolence. It opts instead for co-dependency, especially in national and international politics, on retaliatory justice and military might. Such "Christian realism" is in truth a failure of faith and courage parallel to the sword wielding "other disciple." Because they default so easily to intimidation and military might, Christian Realists make little room for compassion and the persuasive power of merciful benevolence, little room for the asymmetry of faith, for the conviction of things not seen or assurance of things hoped for; little room for turning the other cheek, for incarnation and redemption. Indeed, in national and international politics, Christian Realists prefer reason's predictability, the certainty of outcomes seen, the guarantees of superior military engagement that undermine the peace and harmony hoped for. The material powers of *pax Romana* are seductive indeed. Realists presuppose the very kind of values and priorities that Jesus rejects; favoring an "eye for an eye" instead of "turning the other cheek"; taking up the sword instead of putting it away, eliminating enemies instead of loving and transforming oneself into their neighbor. But the power of grace that Christian communities can access is not a result of a spirit of fear and timidity, as St. Paul puts it, but of a spirit of love and its persuasive power (II Tim. 1: 7). Ironically, the Constantinian model of Christian Realism has so bewitched Western Christianity that to resist is often to invite charges of betrayal, of being "unchristian" as well as "unpatriotic." Daily in the lives of tens of thousands of Christians, and indeed people of all faiths, in contrast, anonymous acts of compassion, mercy and benevolence are performed and many lives transformed. And yet very often these same Christians, who know the meaning and power of God's benevolence in their personal lives, fail to translate that benevolence of mercy into public and political life. This amounts to a collective failure of nerve and faith; Christians convinced of the power of God's grace in their personal lives are often insufficiently convinced of it in their public, political lives. The potency of faith, the grace of *pax Christi*, "of things not seen," often does not get transferred into national policy and international politics, because Christian communities tend to default in their social and political lives to the Christian Realism of *pax Romana,* a kind of power and peace from which Jesus distinguishes his own peace (John 14: 27).

In our own time we are not left without witnesses who, in national and international affairs, reject *pax Romana* and Christian Realism in favor of *pax Christi*, in favor of the potency of God's merciful benevolence. I examine two historical examples here—Mohandas Gandhi and Martin Luther

King Jr. Both understand the necessity of practicing in the midst of gross injustice a politics of mercy. Both understand that the reality of injustice liberates politics from the symmetry of justice so that justice might flourish. Like Jesus, they did not opt for physical violence and military might, but intentionally rejected it. As a result, all three died for mercy's sake. Many other heroes of mercy could be included: Mother Teresa and the Sisters of Charity; Nelson Mandela, Bishop Tutu and the Truth and Reconciliation Commission, the Dalai Lama, the Amish of Pennsylvania. This examination of Gandhi and King is to persuade Christians that a politics of mercy, that benevolence as a public virtue is more powerful than Christian Realism; more powerful and efficient in restoring the harmony of *pax Dei* and in civilizing societies.

MOHANDAS GANDHI

Gandhi is perhaps the most influential spiritual and moral leader of the twentieth century. His successful nonviolent campaign for India's freedom embodies works of mercy, embodies the benevolence of performing duties without correlative rights, of granting unmerited benefits to enemies. Born in India in 1869 and assassinated in 1948, he emancipated his people from the bondage of British imperialism by employing weapons of spiritual warfare exemplified in *pax Christi*[1] and not weapons of military might exemplified in *pax Romana*. He was educated in India and in England as a lawyer. He returned to practice law in India for two years, then traveled to South Africa in 1893 and became a successful lawyer and moral leader of the Indian community. While there he fought successfully to end legal discrimination against the Indian minority and nurtured seeds of his method of *satyagraha* ("holding to the truth"). In creating his benevolent community he drew inspiration from a curious diversity of sources, including the *Bhagavad-Gita*, *New Testament*, Jesus, Leo Tolstoy, John Ruskin, Ralph Waldo Emerson, and David Thoreau. Eventually, he abandoned European lifestyles and lived ascetically (from c. 1905), including celibacy. In 1907 he organized the first *satyagraha* campaign of nonviolent, civil disobedience against South African laws that discriminated against Indians, and by 1914 he and his movement had persuaded the South African government to abolish these laws.

The following year he returned to Indian with a reputation among the Indian people as a great moral and spiritual leader. His relationship with the British colonists was bittersweet. During WWI he actively supported British efforts, believing this might hasten India's freedom. But he also led labor and agrarian reform movements that mortified the British. In 1919 the Amristar massacre triggered Indian nationalism and in response Gandhi organized several *stayagraha* campaigns, which he subsequently discontinued because, against his desires, they resulted in violence. Nevertheless, Gandhi continued to promote his program of nonviolent, civil disobedience: to restore a free and united India, including efforts to regain economic self-sufficiency (e.g., revival of industries like spinning and the production of handwoven cloth) and moral integrity (e.g., the abolition of the untouchable caste). In protest of the British's salt tax, Gandhi led (1930) the renowned two hundred mile march to the sea to extract salt. For this he was imprisoned.

In 1942, Gandhi called for *satyagraha* and inaugurated the Quit India movement, for which action he was again imprisoned until 1944. Gandhi was influential in the postwar discussions with Lord Mountbatten and Muhammad Ali Jinnah that eventually led to India's independence and to a separate state (Pakistan) for Muslims, a partition which Gandhi passionately opposed, praying, fasting and traveling to regions disturbed by violence. While holding a prayer and pacification meeting at New Delhi (January 30, 1948), Gandhi was assassinated by a fanatical Hindu angered by Gandhi's care for the Muslim community. In life Gandhi achieved only one of his three goals, independence for India. The other two (Hindu and Muslim reconciliation and abolishing the caste system) remain unfulfilled to this day. Gandhi's influence, nevertheless, continues both inside and outside Indian. His model of a benevolent community, his method of nonviolent, civil disobedience, was adopted by civil right activists in the United States and by other protest and rights movements throughout the world. *Satyagraha* exemplifies for Christians the kind of compassion and merciful benevolence in politics that is sometimes required in order to subvert injustice and establish a just, egalitarian moral order.

The aim, duties, and consequences of *satyagraha* are clearly taught and practiced by Gandhi, and demonstrate for Christian Realists and other skeptics the power, locally and globally, of a politics of mercy. Gandhi is well aware of *satyagraha* as a gift that requires faith to apprehend and grace to practice. For him its *aim* is "holding to the truth of love"; its *duties* entail self-sacrifice, a commitment to nonviolent, and civil disobedience; and its *consequences* consist of freedom, self-determination, justice, and reconciling peace, both for the individual and for the community.

1. Gandhi explains the aim of his campaign by employing the word "*satyagraha*." While in South Africa, when he first developed his activist method, it was suggested by a cousin that he use the word "Sadagrah" which means "firmness in a good cause." Gandhi liked that word but it did not quite capture the whole meaning he wished to convey. So he altered it slightly, he says, "to 'Satyagraha.' Truth (Satya) implies Love, and Firmness (Agraha) engenders and therefore serves as a synonym for force . . . that is to say, the Force which is born of Truth and Love or Nonviolence. . . ."[2] Truth and Love, for Gandhi, are not means to achieve some other political or social or philosophical aim. Rather, they incorporate the justice that is aimed at; they

are the goal of mercy's benevolence. Commenting on Christianity, Gandhi says, "'I do not seek redemption from the consequences of my sin' (i.e., death, hell), as do many Christians. 'I seek to be redeemed from sin itself. . . . Until I have attained that end, I shall be content to be restless.'"[3] Sin rightly represents for Gandhi a broken relationship with God and others, a broken relationship based on falsehood and hatred. *Satyagraha* aims at Truth and Love, which for Gandhi by their very nature possess the power of mercy to redeem and restore broken relationships. The aim of *satyagraha* is not to establish a moral order based on enforcing the benefits and burdens of justice. In that case the British would have to be severely punished for more than a century for their atrocities against Indians. Its aim, rather, is the redemption and reconciliation that Truth, Love, and Mercy alone can deliver. As a result and even in the midst of hostilities and imprisonment, Gandhi took extra care to maintain redemptive, peaceful relationships with Englishmen and Europeans; not by retaliating but by "keep[ing] an open mind and seek[ing] every opportunity of serving his opponents."[4]

By respecting the dignity of his opponents (i.e., the British) instead of retaliating, by redeeming instead of punishing, by self-sacrifice instead of self-interest Gandhi reconciled them not only to India and to themselves but, as he says, to their own God. This strange asymmetry of mercy deviates in its aim from the symmetry of justice's standard model assumed by the colonists themselves. Truth and Love seeks to reconcile (through mutual respect and self-determination) India with the British, he says, in the same way the self-sacrificing German Jew, for example, is instrumental in reconciling German gentiles to Jews and indeed to all humanity. "The German Jews will score a lasting victory over the German gentiles," he insists, "in the sense that they will have converted the latter to an appreciation of human dignity. They will have rendered service to fellow-Germans and proved their title to be the real Germans as against those who are today dragging . . . the German name into the mire."[5] Similarly, Gandhi and his followers, by practicing *satyagraha*, render service to the British by restoring not only the dignity of Indians but also to the British their own dignity. Indeed, *satyagraha* will reconcile the British to themselves and to the Christian God they claim to serve.

2. *Satyagraha* inspired Gandhi and his benevolent community to commit themselves to certain duties of mercy, duties without correlative rights. "Holding to the Truth of Love" necessarily implies a duty to the principles of nonviolence and civil disobedience, a duty to which no British, according to the standard model of justice, had a right. If one is devoted to Truth then one is obligated to subvert the falsehood of injustice; and if one is devoted to Love's mercy then one is obligated to act benevolently, nonviolently, turning the other cheek to those who pretend truth and power lies in force and violence. Accordingly, *satyagraha* is constituted by mercy; it requires the benevolent community to exercise a duty of nonviolence that benefits unjust,

violent wrongdoers (the British) even though no right to those benefits correlate with that duty. *Satyagraha* requires faith. Nonviolence as a response to violence and meekness as a response to the insult of injustice deviate considerably from the standard model, namely, force and violence countered by force and violence. Indeed, persistent injustice empowers a community with a freedom to pass beyond the limits of liberal justice to practice a politics of mercy moral reason itself cannot comprehend and cannot justify. Moral reason employs what Gandhi calls "Body Force" while faith's asymmetry employs "Soul Force." Body Force uses fear and intimidation and violence (*pax Romana*) in order to secure some temporary moral order; Soul Force (*pax Christi*) admittedly involves self-sacrifice. In fact, Gandhi believes it is a trait of the evolved moral consciousness. "The law of the survival of the fittest is the law for the evolution of the brute," he argues, "but the law of self-sacrifice [mercy] is the law of the evolution of man."[6] How so?

Consider *lex talionis*, the law symbolizing "body force" and the symmetry of justice: duties are explicitly correlated to rights; each has a right to repay the other in kind: evil for evil, violence for violence, injury for injury, benefit for benefit. One only half awake will realize the endless, inexorable cycle of retaliation duty to such a law of justice lends itself. Even though fair burdens and benefits are important to social order, it is not within the nature and power of retaliatory body force to resolve conflicts already shaped by inequalities and to heal relationships defined by injustice. "Brute force will avail against brute force," argues Gandhi, "only when it is proved that darkness can dispel darkness."[7] Jesus made the same point in rejecting "An eye for an eye" (Matthew 5: 38–42) as inadequate for redemption and reconciliation. Jesus advocates, as Gandhi notes, a law of meekness, mercy, and self-sacrifice: "if a man smote one on the right cheek, the left was also to be turned to him." Resolution and redemption and relationship are a function of practicing a duty that has no right correlated to it; they emerge from practicing a duty to merciful Soul Force not to retaliatory Body Force. Measured, then, by the difference between these two laws, "it seems modern civilization . . . is based not upon the human law of self-sacrifice, but upon the brutal law of the survival of the fittest (the fittest here evidently meaning physically the strongest), and that, therefore, it is inherently defective."[8] The brute force required by justice's demand for retaliatory symmetry "has been the ruling factor in the world for thousands of years," Gandhi goes on to say, "and mankind has been reaping its bitter harvest all along. . . . There is little hope of anything good coming out of it in the future, If light can come out of darkness, then alone can love emerge from hatred,"[9] the hatred manifest as brute, retaliatory justice.

Satyagraha, the truth of love, assumes that repaying evil for evil perpetuates evil; that darkness perpetuates darkness, that violence perpetuates violence, that retaliation reaps more retaliation, conflict more conflict in return.

It apprehends by faith the astonishing belief that only light dispels darkness, only soul force eclipses brute force, love overcomes hatred, peacemaking ends violence, mercy subverts injustice so that justice might. Indeed, he argues that to defeat oppression "nonviolence is infinitely superior to violence, forgiveness is more manly than punishment,"[10] benevolence and mercy are more powerful than intimidation and retribution. It is not that Gandhi preaches weakness and passive resignation, as if weakness and frailty is more powerful than might and violence. Instead he believes that mercy is in reality more potent than military might and violence, more "manly," as he puts it, and more certain of achieving freedom and reconciliation. But it takes faith, the conviction of things not seen to practice such benevolence. Gandhi realized that, given this matrix of opposites, Civil Disobedience was not only unavoidable but desirable. Noncooperation or "Civil Disobedience is not a state of lawlessness and license," he argues, "but presupposes a law-abiding spirit combined with self-restraint,"[11] of meekness. It is "rebellion without the element of violence in it. . . . [The resister] never uses [violent] force and never resists force when it is used against him. . . . Thus considered, civil resistance is a most powerful expression of a soul's anguish and an eloquent protest against the continuance of an evil state."[12]

But how is it that mercy is more powerful than justice? Why is it that the mercy of nonviolent civil disobedience is more powerful than the retaliatory force of violence? True strength, Gandhi argues, "does not come from physical capacity. It comes from an indomitable will. . . ." Indeed, if there is strength in sheer physical numbers, Gandhi points out, three hundred million Indians ought not be frightened by one hundred thousand Englishmen. India does have physical and material strength superior to England. India could very well justly punish England. But India possesses an even greater power, one that benefits it even more fully: ". . . waiving the right of punishment," superseding the symmetry of justice. "We have better work to do, a better mission to deliver to the world,"[13] namely, works of mercy that manifests themselves as nonviolent, civil disobedience. These two pillars, nonviolence and civil disobedience, are the duties of *satyagraha* to which correlate no British rights. Indeed, they benefit and are intended to benefit the British, vendors of injustice; not in order to preserve injustice, of course, but in order to establish self-determination and justice.

3. For Gandhi's benevolent community, several consequences follow from practicing *satyagraha*, namely, freedom, justice, and peace. These consequences are perhaps surprising to those who live by sight and not by faith, who employ body force and calculate just desserts; for moral reason cannot fathom the redeeming and reconciling fruits of granting unmerited benefits to undeserving enemies. Nevertheless one consequence of *satyagraha*, according to Gandhi, is liberation. The moral law guiding human relations is as compelling as nature's law of gravity. That law is *karma*: "Whatsoever we

sow, that shall we also reap," which properly understood is not a fatalistic, prescriptive law, but, like the law of gravity, a descriptive principle. In response to a reader, who asks why India, in seeking *swaraj* (self-rule or independence), should not use the same brute force against the British as the British use against India, Gandhi replies: ". . . by using similar means we can get only the same thing as they got [violence and oppression]. . . . Your reasoning is . . . saying we can get a rose by planting a noxious weed. . . . We reap exactly as we sow. . . ."[14] Gandhi's logic seems to be that so long as India tethers its quest for independence to the same justice, the same brute force used by the British, then it shall always remain, via the law of *karma,* enslaved to that same brute force and to its source, British imperialism. By so cooperating with the British in their project of oppression and violence, by playing according to the rules of *pax Romana,* India would capitulate to cycles of retaliatory violence and thus forfeit the very independence it seeks. But if India rejects the brute force to which it is enslaved; if it refuses to cooperate with it, then in the very act of doing so it bursts the bonds that bind it to British imperialism and asserts its independence, philosophically and practically. Rather than reifying and perpetuating the injustice of its bondage by repaying the evil of violence with the self-same bondage of evil, Gandhi argues that India should by its own indomitable will of noncooperation cut the tether of violence that binds it to the British and forge its own benevolent way of life through the use of nonviolent civil disobedience. By establishing its own rule, its own politics of mercy, India immediately and irrevocably in that very act liberates itself from the yoke of British oppression. "If India adopted the doctrine of love as an active part of her religion and introduced it into her politics, *Swaraj* [self-rule or independence] would descend upon India from heaven. . . ."[15]

A second consequence of *satyagraha* is justice, mutual respect, equality, and tolerance. To justify their colonialism, says Gandhi, Europeans often speak of the "White man's Burden:" "to dominate coloreds and blacks for their own good, to protect and civilize them." Raw "hypocrisy," replies Gandhi; the real "White Man's Burden" is simply to obey the central moral command of his own religion, namely, "Do unto others as you would they should do unto you," a command common to all world religions, a command that entails a more evolved moral character than embodied by British colonialism. "It is time white men learnt to treat every human being as their equal."[16] Mutual respect and equal justice is possible, says Gandhi, insofar as humans subscribe to the fact that "the cohesive force among animate beings is Love." Indeed, "mutual love enables Nature to persist. [Even] self-love compels regard for others. Nations cohere because there is mutual regard among individuals composing them." What results from *satyagraha*'s true Love, insists Gandhi, is not the imperialistic self-assertion of British justice but "voluntary interdependence."[17] What results is a moral and social order that requires both liberal and egalitarian justice. Gandhi puts it this way: "there shall be no high class or low class of people. . . .[a]ll communities shall live in perfect harmony . . . [Accordingly], women shall enjoy the same rights as men," and there shall be no distinction "between foreign and indigenous."[18] In short, Gandhi confirms part of what I am arguing, that only something like the mercy of *satyagraha* has the power to subvert injustice and bear the fruits of liberal justice and economic equality.

A third consequence of practicing *satyagrah*, according to Gandhi, is peace and with peace far fewer lives lost. In dutifully "holding to the Truth of Love," in sacrificing oneself nonviolently to the sword of violence, one would think that a greater loss of life would ensue, greater than if one resisted violence with equal violence. Not so, for Gandhi. A profound spiritual law underwriting most religious traditions asserts that in self-sacrifice the power of death is conquered and the vitality of life renewed. "As larger and larger numbers of innocent men come out to welcome death," Gandhi insists, "their sacrifice will become the potent instrument for the salvation of all others, and there will be a minimum of suffering."[19] Indeed, voluntary "Suffering in one's person is . . . the essence of nonviolence and is the chosen substitute for violence to others. It is not because I value life low that I can countenance with joy thousands voluntarily losing their lives for *satyagraha*, but because I know it results in the long run in the least loss of life, and what is more, it ennobles those who lose their lives."[20] Clearly, the burdens of mercy and the duties of *satyagraha* deviate from *pax Romana's* standard model of justice. The latter's notion of moral reason cannot comprehend the duties of nonviolence toward violent enemies; cannot comprehend asymmetrical duties to which no rights correlate, of seeking to benefit wrongdoers and undeserving, let alone the vulnerable. Accordingly, *satyagraha*, as the core of benevolent community, requires faith in the conviction of things not seen, the assurance of things hoped for; requires faith in Truth belonging to God, not humans; faith in the benevolence of love's mercy, a Love that belongs to Soul Force, not Brute Force. It is the former and not the latter that for the people of India made liberal and egalitarian justice a political and historical possibility as well as a reality. Who could even begin to guess the extent of brutality and human destruction (British and Indian) if India had tried to use Brute instead of Soul Force.

A case counter to Gandhi's campaign of *satyagraha* emerged in his own lifetime, a case against which the effectiveness of a politics of mercy can be compared. On August 14, 1947, the birth of the new Islamic Republic of Pakistan was completed. The next day India gained independence from British colonial rule. The British, in their colonial wisdom, partitioned India, founding Pakistan as an Islamic state and India as a secular state. The British assumed that there existed between Muslims and Hindus irreconcilable differences, based on religious differences and perceived intrinsic differences.

The Muslim leader Jinnah, in opposition to Gandhi, supported this British solution and in 1940 called for the establishment of Pakistan as an independent nation partitioned from India. Gandhi opposed this solution as inviting constant and continuing tension and conflict between the two nations and the two religions. And indeed, boundary issues (geographical, political, and religious) have contributed to several "wars" and ongoing strife and loss of life between the two nations.

Gandhi's *satyagraha* solution, in contrast, revolves around his notion of "civic nationalism," which is "based on the belief that it was possible to remain faithful to one's own religion and at the same time be respectful of the religion of others."[21] Politicians and citizens alike would have to, and indeed could, nurture relationships with persons of other faiths, having the same regard for other faiths as they have for their own.[22] In other words, Gandhi had faith that a politics of mercy and policies of benevolence were possible amongst Muslims and Hindus; that the citizens of India had internal resources to establish a civic nationalism and that its religious and ethnic and linguistic diversity was an asset and not a liability. Regrettably, this trajectory was not followed. Instead the British along with Muslim and Hindu politicians opted for the "realistic" solution of separation and partition, which simply fermented tensions and forwarded conflict, not solved them. Moreover, this "realistic" solution set a precedent for "realistic" solutions to other national and international tensions, especially Israel which demanded a separate homeland because of perceived irreconcilable differences between Palestinians and Jews.

From the perspective of Christian Realism the merciful benevolence of Gandhi's *satyagraha* campaign is fanciful idealism, an impossible possibility restricted in its application to private, personal matters, but otherwise powerless to bring about substantial political and global change. This view runs counter to facts. Realistic solutions to conflict have proven, as in the case of both Pakistan and Israel, both ineffective and tragic. Against all such skepticism, *satyagraha* possesses an integrity of character more powerful than the military might of Britain, liberating by means of a politics of mercy an entire nation from colonial injustice. And more recently, the Camp David Accords, employing policies of benevolence, provides further evidence, against realism, of mercy's power to bring a just peace from the ruins of injustice. Similarly, King's civil rights campaign exemplifies the power of a politics of mercy to establish justice in the midst of moral chaos and injustice.

MARTIN LUTHER KING JR.

Martin Luther King Jr., the charismatic leader of the Civil Rights Movement in the United States, embodies the power and passion of a benevolent community. He was very much influenced by Gandhi's life and teaching and was himself influential on international human rights movements, including on Nelson Mandela, Bishop Desmond Tutu and the South African Truth and Reconciliation Commission. He was born (1929) in Atlanta, Georgia, to a lineage of Baptist pastors and preachers. His grandfather served as pastor of Ebenezer Baptist Church from 1914 to 1931; his father served the same church from 1931, and Martin himself served with his father as co-pastor from 1960 until his death in 1968. He was educated at Morehouse College and Crozer Theological Seminary, graduating from the latter institution in 1951 with a BD degree. He then matriculated at Boston University and received his doctorate in theology in 1955. While in Boston he married Coretta Scott, a woman of exceptional intellectual and artistic ability.

King's role as a civil rights leader emerged in 1954 when he accepted the pastorate of the Dexter Avenue Baptist Church in Montgomery, Alabama. By this time he was already a member of the executive committee of the NAACP. In these positions, he was poised to lead the first nonviolent protest of the contemporary Civil Rights Movement, the Montgomery bus boycott (1955), a boycott sparked by Rosa Parks and lasting 382 days. By December 21, 1956, after the Supreme Court declared unconstitutional the laws requiring segregated seating on buses, blacks and whites rode the buses as equals. During these years Dr. King was arrested and imprisoned many times, subjected to personal abuse, his family threatened, and his home bombed. In 1957 he was elected president of the Southern Christian Leadership Conference, whose civil rights mission embraced a moral vision based on Jesus's teachings and operational techniques (nonviolent resistance and civil disobedience) derived from Gandhi's *satyagraha.* From 1957 until 1968, when he was assassinated, King traveled widely, spoke frequently, wrote five books and many articles. He was arrested many times, assaulted four times; he protested the Vietnam War, conferred with presidents (Kennedy and Johnson), and led numerous protests and boycotts against racial and economic injustice. King led, for example, a massive protest in Birmingham, Alabama, against policies and practices of segregation. This protest garnered international attention and inspired his well-known and provocative "Letter from a Birmingham Jail," a kind of manifesto of the civil rights movement and of benevolent communities. He led the peaceful march on Washington in 1963 at which he delivered his famous "I Have a Dream" speech. He was named *Time* magazine's "Man of the Year" in 1963 and at the age of thirty-five was the youngest person ever to receive the Nobel Peace Prize. On April 4, 1968, King, in Memphis, Tennessee, to lead a protest march in support of striking sanitation workers, was assassinated. His legacy lives on not only in the activities of organizations (NAACP, SCLC) he led but also in legislation (Civil Rights Act and Voting Rights Act) he inspired and in the programs of the Martin Luther King Jr. Center for Nonviolent Social Change, Inc. Consider, then, the aims, duties, and consequences of King's campaign and how mercy made liberal and egalitarian justice a historical reality in the United States.

1. The aim of King's Civil Rights Movement might be variously articulated. Its aim, some might say, is justice and freedom for all people, especially African Americans.[23] Others might say its aim was desegregation and others integration.[24] Still others might claim peace as the aim of King's campaign.[25] All of these, of course, are to some extent correct; but none of them adequately captures its full purpose. Each of these—desegregation, freedom, justice, equality, integration, and peace—is a virtue shaping King's philosophy. But none of them separately nor all of them collectively satisfactorily express the Movement's aim as articulated by King in his writings and speeches and indeed in his life. He identifies his aim sometimes in theological and sometimes in social-political terms: theologically his aim is often articulated as redemption; politically, his aim is articulated in terms of reconciliation and integration. King's notion of "integration," I argue, includes egalitarian as well as liberal justice and accordingly mercy and benevolence as indispensible means for achieving that aim. Desegregation and procedures of liberal justice although necessary are for him not sufficient. His frequent use of *agape*, especially, incorporates qualities of fair balance, something like the Distribution Principle, and a sustainable livelihood for all. *Agape*'s reconciliation and peace requires nothing less.

First, in theological terms, King writes: "May all who suffer oppression in this world reject the self-defeating method of retaliatory violence and choose the method that seeks to redeem."[26] Even though "redeem" involves "unearned suffering"[27] and unearned benefit he would settle for nothing less than redemption and full reconciliation of races. In "An Experiment in Love," King says that nonviolence "does not seek to defeat or humiliate the opponent, but to win his friendship and understanding. . . . The end is redemption and reconciliation. The aftermath of nonviolence is the creation of the beloved community, while the aftermath of violence is tragic bitterness." The justification for practicing *agape*'s merciful benevolence and "turning the other cheek" is "the realization that unearned suffering is redemptive. Suffering . . . has tremendous educational and transforming possibilities";[28] under conditions of injustice sacrifice is often unavoidable if justice and reconciliation are to triumph. In socio-political terms, King dreams of "integration," of a social order approximating the "fair balance" of egalitarian justice and not merely the equal opportunity of liberal procedural justice. And to secure such egalitarian integration, King acknowledges, requires projects of compassion and mercy that the power of *agape* alone can provide. In "Letter from a Birmingham Jail," for example, he locates the aim of his campaign as a mean between two extremes. In response to accusations that his activity in Birmingham is "extreme," King sees himself "in the middle of two opposing forces in the Negro community." On the one extreme are the forces of "complacency" those who because of oppression have been "so drained of self-respect and a sense of 'somebodiness' that they have adjusted to segregation," they have resigned themselves to a social (dis)order imposed by white government and to the unjust status quo of that order. They have lost any hope of redeeming the powers and of reconciling with them. On the other extreme are the forces of Black Nationalists and Black Power, whose "bitterness and hatred . . . [come] perilously close to advocating violence" and vengeance. Accordingly, they advocate the imposition of a separate, independent, and nationalistic political, social, and moral order that despises as weak and demeaning any campaign that aims at redeeming the powers that be and reconciling with them. In other words, King tolerates neither the status quo that aims to live with injustice and segregation, "the 'do-nothing-ism' of the complacent"; nor does he tolerate the "hatred and despair of the black nationalists" who aim at "separate but equal." "The more excellent aim 'of love and nonviolent protest' is integration, the reconciliation of people and not just compliance with the Constitution and the law, the wholeness of a world truly belonging to God." In short, "integration" implies for King not only liberal, procedural justice but also necessarily the fair balance of egalitarian justice, of sustainable livelihoods that in the midst of gross injustice require a politics of mercy and the redemptive power of benevolence.

Put differently, King's concern is not only with Rawls' Liberty Principle but also with a Distribution Principle. When he famously says, in "Letter from a Birmingham Jail," "Injustice anywhere is a threat to justice everywhere," he articulates his concern for human and civil rights, a concern for a fair juridical relationship between people and the state's law. But his dream of justice entails more than this. His concern is with the relationship between people and with God, a concern for finding some kind of social and economic equilibrium. The problem with segregation and unjust laws, according to King, is not just that they violate human law and moral order, but that they insult God and the image of God in which all humans are created.

> An unjust law is a human law that is not rooted in eternal law and natural law. Any law that uplifts human personality [the image of God] is just. Any law that degrades human personality is unjust. All segregation laws are unjust because segregation distorts the soul and damages the personality. It gives the segregator a false sense of superiority and the segregated a false sense of inferiority.[29]

Injustice not only violates human codes of justice; more profoundly it transgresses God's eternal law and insults God and persons created in the image of God; it subverts the relationship humans properly are to have with God and with each other. Injustice undermines proper interhuman relationships by damaging and distorting the image of God essential to human personality. It is this twofold relationship, communion with God and fellowship with other humans that is the primary concern of King's campaign. He hopes that along with civil rights his campaign will have a power to raise people ". . . from the dark depths of prejudice and racism to the majestic heights of understanding and brotherhood."[30] For King, broken divine and human relationships are even more fundamental than broken legal relationships.

Injustice and segregation, to use the terminology of the Jewish philosopher Martin Buber, substitutes an "I-it" relationship for an "I-thou" relationship and ends up regulating persons to the status of things. Hence segregation is not only politically, economically, and sociologically unsound, it is morally wrong and sinful. Paul Tillich has said that "sin is separation. Is not segregation an existential expression of man's tragic separation, his awful estrangement, his terrible sinfulness?"[31]

For King, I-it embodies a strictly legal procedural relationship, whereas I-thou requires something more, requires a reconciliation and integration of persons that *agape*'s compassion and mercy alone makes possible. Enforcing the Constitution and just laws addresses the relationship between people and the state; but it does not treat and heal relationships amongst people. Liberal justice addresses broken legal relationships but is not equipped to redeem and reconcile inter-racial relationships. Justice secures a measure of civil and social order, but it cannot restore and reconcile and redeem interpersonal relationships. Only a politics of mercy, or as King puts it, only *agape* (divine love) is powerful enough to accomplish that.

This contrast between the aim of liberal justice and the aim of mercy's benevolence (i.e., egalitarian justice) is addressed explicitly by King in chapter 2 of *Where Do We Go from Here?* Differences emerged between King and Stokely Carmichael, a leader of SNNC. Carmichael for some time had participated in King's campaign of nonviolent civil disobedience. His commitment to benevolence's aim of reconciliation with whites, however, began to shrink and his insistence on justice as separate and equal power swelled. The discrepancy seems to have emerged in 1966 during the Mississippi Freedom March. A participant, James Meredith, was shot in the back. King and Carmichael, along with others, hastened to Memphis to visit Meredith in the hospital and promptly joined the Freedom March in solidarity with Meredith and the other marchers. It was during this march that a rift between competing aims emerges. Some on the march, including Carmichael, begin to express dissatisfaction with King's aim of reconciliation with whites and to insist instead on sheer justice, on equal and separate power for blacks. For them the justice of desegregation, of separate and equal, was enough and preferable. They began to eschew King's vision of redemption and reconciliation implicit in integration. On the freedom march, one manifestation of this shift was a controversy over singing the civil rights anthem "We Shall Overcome." Some on the march declared to King that ". . . we do not sing those words any more. In fact the whole song should be discarded. Not 'We Shall

Overcome,' but 'We Shall Overrun'";[32] we shall exact equal vengeance, equal justice. Other indications of shifting aims included the demand that civil rights marches and protests be "all-black."

Along with this shift in aim was a call for a shift in tactics from nonviolence to use of force and violence, a shift from King's politics of mercy (*pax Christi)* to a politics of force and retaliatory justice (*pax Romana*). Stokely came to believe that the question of violence and nonviolence was irrelevant to achieving justice. Securing Black Power requires *lex talionis*, an eye for en eye, repaying evil with evil. The real issue is ". . . the need for black people to consolidate their political and economic resources to achieve power. 'Power,' [Stokely] said, 'is the only thing respected in this world, and we must get it at any cost,'"[33] including the use of vengeful and violent justice. And thus, the Black Power Movement was born as an intentional alternative to the Civil Rights Movement: strict retaliatory justice instead of merciful benevolence; separate and equal social order instead of mutual integration and reconciliation. Perhaps King was tempted at times, but apparently not seriously. His commitment to benevolent community, to Christian love and a politics of mercy, was too profound for him to capitulate to the easy hate, bitterness, and despair implicit in Black Power. Christian love's insistence on redemption and reconciliation was too powerful for King to travel the well-worn path of least resistance, of equal, retaliatory justice. Indeed, King reaffirms his commitment to "Mahatma Gandhi's movement in India . . . [that] mounted a revolution of hope and love, hope and nonviolence."[34]

2. Like Jesus and Gandhi, King's politics of mercy advocates duties that have no correlative rights. This moral thread woven into the fabric of King's campaign embodies, for example, Jesus's command to practice the meekness of turning the other cheek. Tactically, he was convinced of the power and efficacy of nonviolent protest and civil disobedience. Unlike Black Nationalists, he committed to *agape*'s duty of mercy, to granting unmerited benefits to the white oppressor, benefits they had no right to: namely, justice for all, for example, without vengeful bigotry and centuries of retaliatory oppression. Inspired by Socrates, Hebrew prophets, Jesus, as well as the strategic methodology of Gandhi, King practices a faith in things unseen and the assurance of things hoped for. To those whose moral matrix is simple, rational justice, mercy, and benevolence makes no sense; to them treating an enemy with generosity, acting benevolently out of love's duty to mercy, granting benefits of amnesty to oppressors who have no rights to them, is irrational, impotent capitulation. But King makes clear that he is committed not simply to duties of liberal justice to which certain rights correlate (i.e., desegregation), but to certain duties of *agape*'s mercy without which the Distribution Principle's fair balance and sustainable livelihood is impossible. In fact, he assumes that civil and economic integration is not likely to materialize unless the Movement is willing to practice mercy's benevolence, that is, the nonvio-

lence of civil disobedience. In "An Experiment in Love," for example, King identifies the duties of mercy with *agape*. "Along the way of life, someone must have sense enough and morality enough to cut off the chain of hate. This can only be done by projecting the ethic of love to the center of our lives. . . . *Agape* means understanding, redeeming good will for all men. It is an overflowing love which is purely spontaneous, unmotivated, groundless, and creative. . . . Therefore, *agape* shows no partiality toward friends and enemies; it is directed toward both."[35] It is "Spontaneous, unmotivated, groundless"; a kind of unmerited, unjustifiable merciful love benefiting even those who have no entitlement to it. That is the kind of benevolent love without which justice devolves into cycles of retaliation and forecloses on restorative reconciliation and integration.

In a speech in 1962, "The Ethical Demands for Integration," King distinguishes the demands of desegregation from the demands of integration. The demands of desegregation (liberal justice) he argues, are "enforceable demands while the demands of integration [egalitarian justice] fall within the scope of unenforceable demands." The enforceable demands of desegregation are duties of liberal justice to which certain rights correlate, such as equal opportunity of education and employment, equal access to public transportation and services, due process, and so on. These duties of liberal justice and desegregation "are regulated by the codes of society and the vigorous implementation of law-enforcement agencies. Breaking these obligations, spelled out on thousands of pages of law books, has filled numerous prisons." In contrast, *agape*'s duties of mercy "are beyond the reach of the laws of society" and reason's obligation to justice. To integrate according to the demands of egalitarian justice requires the assurance of faith and not the sight of reason. Indeed, to establish justice in a fallen, unjust world requires faith in the power of mercy's benevolence. Otherwise society spirals into the inescapable entropy of just, retaliatory violence. The duties of mercy ". . . concern inner attitudes, genuine person-to-person relations, and expressions of compassion which law books cannot regulate and jails cannot rectify." Such duties underwrite genuine reconciliation and integration and "are met by one's commitment to an inner law, written on the heart. Man-made laws assure justice, but a higher law [mercy's duties of benevolence] produces love."[36] King recognizes that duties of mercy entail a more highly evolved human ethic that lies beyond the rational vision and capacities of liberal justice itself. Practicing duties of benevolence requires faith, trust in the asymmetrical power of compassionate incarnation, and merciful redemption. The Christian community specifically is called to act mercifully, to obey unenforceable duties to which no rights correlate, granting thereby unmerited benefits to the undeserving: in this case, generosity of a sustainable livelihood for the poor who have no power of access to one; and amnesty for the white majority who otherwise deserve centuries of just punishment for oppressing minorities. Benevolent communities, inspired by *agape*, are equipped, according to King, to practice such merciful generosity and amnesty.

King famously summarizes, in "Letter from a Birmingham Jail," the duties of mercy, of nonviolent civil disobedience, to which the Civil Rights Movement is and benevolent communities should be, committed. He articulates his belief that genuine, egalitarian justice is impossible without *agape*, without the compensatory power of nonviolent, creative, benevolent acts of faith. He identifies himself with Jesus's injunction to live meekly and mercifully. "Was not Jesus an extremist for love": King explains, "Love your enemies, bless them that curse you, do good to them that hate you, and pray for them that despitefully use you, and persecute you." Clearly to do so requires the grace of mercy and faith in the conviction of things not seen. It obligates one to grant benefits to those who by definition are wrongdoers (i.e., oppressors, enemies) and have no right to them. Only then, as he goes on to quote Amos, will "justice roll down like waters and righteousness like an ever-flowing stream."[37]

In King's campaign of nonviolent, civil disobedience, the first duty of mercy, like *satyagraha,* is the truth: facing the reality of injustice, collecting facts and understanding conditions as they are. In Birmingham, for example, King notes that it "is probably the most thoroughly segregated city in the United States," and he goes on to catalogue some of the facts substantiating that truth. The second duty of mercy, according to King, is "negotiation." This too is an act of faith and not reason. The standard model of moral order, in King's day as well as today, is that those who suffer the wrong of injustice do not talk to let alone negotiate with wrongdoers, with terrorists. So dictates the symmetry of moral reason; advocates of strict justice are horrified, as were the Black Nationalists, even at the thought of negotiating with wrongdoers. But faith in the power of love's mercy emancipates a community from the "things seen" of moral reason and empowers it to freely converse and negotiate, even with the unjust evildoer. And so in Birmingham, when the occasion arises, King negotiates with the enemy, "the leaders of the economic community." But the racist leaders negotiate in bad faith; breaking promises (e.g., removing from stores humiliating racial signs) so that the black community is twice victimized, oppressed by racism and deceived by broken promises.

If and when negotiations fail to secure equal justice for victims, then the benevolent community engages in two additional, extraordinary duties of mercy, self-purification, and direct action. "Self-purification" is an idea King derives from Gandhi, who saw his own campaign as "a sacred fight"; accordingly, the community must prepare for it "with an act of self-purification" in which all people suspend their business . . . and observe the day as one of fasting and prayer."[38] King adapts this notion to the specific needs and circumstances of his Civil Rights Movement. Before undertaking direct action, protesters are to engage in "a process of self-purification" that includes "workshops on nonviolence" in which protesters asked themselves "'Are you able to accept blows without retaliating?' 'Are you able to endure the ordeal of jail?'"[39] Are you able to perform duties of mercy to which no rights correlate? Are you willing and able to benefit the undeserving wrongdoers for the sake of egalitarian justice? Undertaking such a process of Socratic self-examination is crucial to the success of nonviolent, civil disobedience or direct action. The power and success of direct action depends on the character and integrity of the people engaging in it. Any retaliation, any vengeful violence by the protesters would undermine the integrity of the movement and defuse the explosive power of nonviolent, civil disobedience.

"Direct action" is King's phrase for nonviolent acts of civil disobedience; these too are in the spirit not only of Gandhi's *satyagraha* movement but of Jesus's deliberate violation of Jewish Sabbath laws. So, what is the purpose of direct actions, such as sit-ins, marches, boycotts, and desegregating spaces like waiting rooms, rest rooms, and lunch counters? King makes clear that the purpose is not to resolve conflicts but to persuade the opponent to return to the negotiating table. "Nonviolent action seeks to create such a crisis and foster such a tension that a community which has constantly refused to negotiate is forced to confront the issue." Direct action seeks to generate a kind of constructive tension. "Just as Socrates felt that it was necessary to create a tension in the mind . . . , so must we see the need for nonviolent gadflies to create the kind of tension in society that will help men rise from the dark depths of prejudice and racism to the majestic heights of understanding and brotherhood." Creating such a social crisis, King believes, will "inevitably open the door to negotiation."[40] Nonviolent direct action is a duty and work of mercy, a duty that correlates with no rights because it does not seek to retaliate against or destroy perpetrators of injustice. Rather it seeks to persuade those perpetrators to return to negotiations, so that not only can issues be peacefully resolved but the benefits of friendship and community can be delivered mercifully to unjust wrongdoers.

3. What of the consequences of King's campaign of mercy? At least three can be identified: suffering, freedom and justice, and peaceable community. King was not naïve about the consequences of engaging in a campaign of nonviolent civil disobedience. Suffering is an inevitable result, he knew, but so also is freedom, justice, integration, and the peace of mutual friendship.

First, what about suffering? King institutes the practice of self-purification because he is fully "Mindful of the difficulties involved," fully aware, like Gandhi, of the likelihood of persecution, "that we would present our very bodies as a means of laying our case before the conscience of the local and the national community."[41] The phrases "present our very bodies" and "laying our case before" invoke religious imagery from King's own Judeo-Christian heritage in which there is no redemption without self-sacrifice and "the shedding of blood." King insists that there is no mercy and redemption without a benevolent Christian community being willing, like Jesus, to undergo unmerited suffering. Unmerited suffering is voluntary, suffering that the benevolent community willingly endures, suffering that sometimes results from delivering to the wrongdoer unmerited benefits. "Not my will," prays Jesus, "but yours." At times King made explicit this Christian dimension of his campaign. Why undertake a campaign that embodies meekness, the "political application of the ancient doctrine of turning the other cheek," King asks? His answer is that "unearned suffering is redemptive. Suffering . . . has tremendous educational and transformative possibilities." He goes on to quote Gandhi, who explains that "Things of fundamental importance to people are not secured by reason alone. . . ." Such things must be apprehended by people of faith and "purchased with their suffering. . . . Suffering is infinitely more powerful than the law of the jungle for converting the opponent. . . ."[42] Elsewhere King insists that "suffering becomes a powerful social force when you willingly accept that violence on yourself, so that self-suffering stands at the center of the nonviolent movement and the individuals involved are able to suffer in a creative manner, feeling that unearned suffering is redemptive, and that suffering may serve to transform the social situation."[43] Although King is reluctant to speak of his own suffering,[44] he does claim with the Apostle Paul that through suffering "I bear in my body the marks of the Lord Jesus Christ."[45] In an unjust and evil world, suffering is often a dimension of merciful benevolence, of turning the other cheek, of nonviolent civil disobedience. Mercy's unmerited suffering itself, King is convinced, possesses the power to redeem and restore. When a community apprehends by faith this asymmetrical truth and by faith is willing to appropriate mercy's unmerited suffering, then a culture of justice can displace habits and structures of injustice.

A second consequence of King's nonviolent campaign of mercy is justice, integration, equal freedom, and self-determination. This expectation parallels Gandhi's notion of *swaraj* or self-rule, which he rightly predicted for India if it practiced *satyagraha*. Similarly, King argues that by practicing the duties of mercy, such as nonviolent resistance, the Civil Rights Movement redeems and reconciles broken relationships and restores human dignity, restores justice and freedom. A basic fact about "nonviolent resistance," King argues, "is that it is based on the conviction that the universe is on the side of justice." Consequently, the benevolent community, "the believer in nonviolence has deep faith in the future";[46] has a conviction of things not seen, so that the mercy and suffering of turning the other cheek will assuredly yield the hoped-for fruits of justice (see Hebrews 11: 1–2). King, furthermore, locates the "Negro American" struggle within the context of a "profound longing for freedom that motivates oppressed peoples all over the world. . . . [W]hen oppressed people rise up against oppression there is no stopping point short of full freedom." The "democratic ideal of freedom and equality for all will be fulfilled for all"[47] or for none at all. Either all are free and equal or none are; no one is free and equal in a society where some are not. But the way to freedom and justice is a straight and narrow path: the path of merciful nonviolence. Freedom and justice are realized, according to King, neither by passively accommodating the status quo nor by retaliatory violence. "Freedom is not won by passive acceptance of suffering."[48] Nor is freedom won by the violence implied in "We Shall Overrun."[49] To acquiesce complacently to oppression is to reify it. To retaliate justly and violently to oppression merely subjugates the oppressed even further by chaining them yet again to the very methodology of evil and violence by which they already are oppressed. "The third way open to oppressed people in their quest for freedom," according to King, is mercy, "is the way of nonviolent resistance."[50] Justice and freedom for all results not from complacency nor from retaliatory justice but only from the persuasive power of merciful, nonviolent resistance. "Freedom is won by a [nonviolent] struggle *against* suffering."[51] Such a campaign of nonviolence frees the oppressed from cycles of retaliatory violence that undermined the efforts of Black Nationalists.

For King, the church as benevolent community has a central role in securing freedom and justice. "The broad universalism standing at the center of the gospel makes segregation morally unjustifiable. Racial segregation is a blatant denial of the unity which we have in Christ; for in Christ there is neither Jew nor Gentile, bond nor free, Negro nor white." In fact, King identifies two ways the church and its ministers can help secure freedom for Blacks. By teaching and practicing "the principle of brotherhood" (which relationship is the aim of mercy) the church can "[free] the Negro from the bondage of segregation but also . . . his white brothers from the bondage of fears concerning integration."[52] Toward the end of his "Letter from a Birmingham Jail," King expresses his "disappoint[ment] with the church. . . . In deep disappointment, I have wept over the laxity of the church."[53] Too often ministers preach and churches practice a gospel of disunity and segregation, not peace and reconciliation; too often they forget the mercy of their gospel and preach a pseudo-gospel of justice that eagerly stereotypes and demonizes whoever is "other": Blacks, and immigrants, and terrorists, and gays, treating them precisely as the enemies they feel they are, instead of making oneself neighbor to them, as Jesus commanded. "There was a time," observes King, "when the church was very powerful. It was during that period when the early Christians rejoiced when they were deemed worthy to suffer for what they believed. . . . Things are different now. The contemporary church is often a weak and ineffectual voice with a dim and distinct sound. It is so often the arch-supporter of the status quo."[54] Because it fears the unmerited suffering that accompanies mercy the church often fails to act in accordance with the very same mercy whereby it receives its identity and orientation in the first place. In so doing it forfeits its identity and mission, its moral integrity, and public credibility.

A third consequence of King's nonviolent campaign of mercy is reconciliation of enemies and creation of a fellowship of peace. *Agape* "seek[s] to preserve and create community. It is insistence on community even when one seeks to break it. *Agape* is a willingness to go to any length to restore community. It doesn't stop at the first mile, but it goes the second mile to restore community."[55] Merciful love, for King, manifests itself in nonviolent resistance, and "the way of nonviolence leads to redemption and the creation of the beloved community."[56] King agrees with Gandhi's simple logic that violence inevitably breeds violence and nonviolence breeds the nonviolence of peace. He recognizes that using violence to gain freedom has its temptations because it "brings about momentary results . . . [and] temporary victories." He agrees that justice itself is not a solution but the result of mercy's benevolence which *is* the solution. Yet, violence "never brings permanent peace. It solves no social problems; it merely creates new and more complicated ones."[57] Peace and a community of peace are created only by peaceful means, only by nonviolent resistance. "We adopt the means of nonviolence," argues King, "because our end is a community of peace,"[58] including economic, social, and racial integration. But what about segregation? Do black and white live largely at peace with one another as a result of Jim Crow segregation? Indeed, some whites complained that the Supreme Court's decision in *Brown v. Board of Education* (1954) was regressive in its effects because it disrupted otherwise peaceful relations among blacks and whites: "people of different races who had long lived in peace have now been turned against each other."[59] But this is a Pyrrhic peace, won at a price, the oppression of an entire race of people, which is no peace at all. Genuine peace requires mutual freedom and egalitarian justice for all people. So, the aim of nonviolence "is redemption and reconciliation." And the "aftermath of nonviolence is the creation of the beloved community, while the aftermath of violence is tragic bitterness."[60]

The Civil Rights Movement envisioned in King's dream is a success story that is nevertheless incomplete. As of yet, even liberal justice for minorities is not fully realized: Jim Crow treatment of African American males in the criminal justice system, for example. Nor is the ideal of integration, egalitarian justice, and a sustainable livelihood for all, even nearly realized. But one wonders what would have been the fate of African Americans and other minorities in the United States if King had opted for the trajectory of violence and retaliatory justice practiced by Black Nationalists. I suspect the apartheid of Jim Cow would have flourished and that Black Nationalists and White Nationalists would find themselves strange moral bed-fellows, mutually practicing their violent, retaliatory agendas; apartheid and alienation radiating from and to each.

Although Americans and many around the world lift up Gandhi and King as faithful disciples of a politics of mercy and leaders of benevolent communities, their visions are actually practiced by few. Most lack the moral spiritual courage to do so. Most lack the courage to practice the politics of mercy required by egalitarian justice to retrieve the harmony embedded in God's original Created Order, an Order constituting at the same time the horizon of expectation toward which Jesus and all prophets call benevolent communities. But Gandhi, King, and others were not lacking spiritual courage; as a result, their movements altered for good the lives of millions in the twentieth and twenty-first centuries. They are not the only ones. Examples of benevolent communities are plentiful: Mother Teresa and the Sisters of Charity, for instance; Nelson Mandela, Desmond Tutu and the South African Truth and Reconciliation Commission, and other such commissions they inspired; the Dalai Lama's community in exile; the Amish community of Lancaster Pennsylvania. Even more powerful are the many lives of Christians and devotees of diverse religious and humanist communities who in unheralded and innumerable ways daily practice a politics of mercy and perform works of benevolence.

Regrettably, many of these Christian devotees in the United States are bewitched by Capitalism's prohibition of benevolence in public and political life. Ironically, very often they abandon in public and political life the incomparable grace of *pax Christi* that they gladly claim, proclaim, and maintain and which otherwise identify them as Christian. Indeed, they often default in public life to the very values of fallen self-interest, pride, and greed that they claim their gospel is meant to redeem. What Christian community *qua* Christian could deny to any human, created by God in God's image, the well being of egalitarian justice; could relinquish to the vicissitudes of self-interest a "fair balance" of economic goods and resources? But Christian communities who live truly by the courage of Eucharistic gratitude, who live in gratitude for the unmerited mercy received through Christ's death and resurrection will practice in private and public life this self-same mercy and benevolence. They will not surrender public life to the self-interest of fallenness; they will practice the meekness they preach and not permit the positive evil and violence self-interest inflicts on the vulnerable; they will promote and practice a quality of peacemaking that distinguishes itself from the kind of peace *pax Romana* offers. Those who have so lived, like Amos, Jesus, the apostles, Gandhi, Mother Theresa, King, and anonymous multitudes, turn the world upside down.

NOTES

1. Gandhi, of course, was Hindu and not Christian. He was, however, familiar with and influenced by certain Christian ideas, especially those contained in Jesus's Sermon on the Mount. His Hindu principle of *satyagraha* parallels the notion of *pax Christi*, by advocating and practicing values of grace, mercy, benevolence, and peace.

2. Gandhi, *Satyagraha in South Africa*, chapter 12, 172–173, in *The Essential Gandhi: His Life, Work, and Ideas: An Anthology*, edited by Louis Fischer (New York, NY: Vintage Books, Random House, 1962), 87.

3. Gandhi, *The Story of my Experiments with Truth*, II.8., 93–94, in *The Essential Gandhi*, 41.

4. *Young India*, September 29, 1927, in *The Essential Gandhi*, 211.

5. *Harijan*, November 26, 1938, in *The Essential Gandhi*, 329.

6. *Indian Opinion*, July 1913, in *The Essential Gandhi*, 89.

7. *Ibid.*, 90.

8. *Ibid.*, 89–90.

9. *Satyagraha in South Africa*, chapter 24, 289, in *The Essential Gandhi*, 90

10. *Young India*, August 11, 1920, in *The Essential Gandhi*, 157.

11. *Young India*, November 17, 1921, in *The Essential Gandhi*, 165.

12. *Young India*, November 10, 1921, in *The Essential Gandhi*, 165.

13. *Young India*, August 11, 1920, in *The Essential Gandhi*, 157.

14. *Hind Swaraj*, chapter 16, 52–52, in *The Essential Gandhi*, 124.

15. *Hind Swaraj*, chapter 1, 12, in *The Essential Gandhi*, 119.

16. *Harijan*, June 30, 1946, in *The Essential Gandhi*, 323.

17. *Young India*, July 17, 1924, in *The Essential Gandhi*, 193.

18. *Young India*, September 10, 1931, in *The Essential Gandhi*, 196–197.

19. *Young India*, October 13, 1921, in *The Essential Gandhi*, 167.

20. *Young India*, October 1925, in *The Essential Gandhi*, 199.

21. Anthony J. Parel, *Gandhi's Philosophy and the Quest for Harmony* (Cambridge, UK: Cambridge University Press, 2006), 38.

22. See *The Collected Works of Mahatma Gandhi*, 100 Vols. (New Delhi Publications Division, Ministry of Broadcasting, Government of India, 1958–1994), 75, 147.

23. See for example, "Letter from a Birmingham Jail," *Why We Can't Wait, Where Do We Go from Here*? chapter 1.

24. See for example, "Letter from a Birmingham Jail," *Where Do We Go from Here*? chapter 2.

25. See for example, "A Christian Sermon on Peace," in *A Testament of Hope: The Essential Writings of Martin Luther King Jr.*, edited by James Melvin Washington (New York, NY: Harper & Row Pub., 1986).

26. "Nonviolence and Racial Justice," in *A Testament of Hope: The Essential Writings of Martin Luther King Jr.*, edited by James Melvin Washington (New York, NY: Harper & Row, Pub., 1986), 9.

27. "An Experiment in Love," in *A Testament of Hope*, 18. In the same anthology see also "Suffering and Faith," 41–42.

28. King, "An Experiment in Love," in *A Testament of Hope: The Essential Writings of Martin Luther King Jr.*, edited by James Melvin Washington (New York, NY: Harper & Row, Pub., 1986), 18.

29. "Letter from a Birmingham Jail."

30. *Ibid.*

31. *Ibid.*

32. See *Where Do We Go from Here*? chapter 2.

33. *Ibid.*

34. *Ibid.*

35. "An Experiment in Love," 19.

36. "The Ethical Demands for Integration," in *A Testament of Hope*, 123.

37. "Letter from a Birmingham Jail," see Amos 5: 24.

38. *The Story of My Experiment with Truth*, V.30., in *The Essential Gandhi*, 147.
39. "Letter from a Birmingham Jail."
40. *Ibid.*
41. *Ibid.*
42. "An Experiment in Love," in *A Testament of Hope*, 18. In the same anthology see also "Suffering and Faith," 41–42.
43. "Love, Law, and Civil Disobedience," in *A Testament of Hope*, 47.
44. He explains that "A person who constantly calls attention to his trials and sufferings is in danger of developing a martyr complex and of making others feel that he is consciously seeking sympathy." See "Suffering and Faith," *Ibid.*, 41.
45. "Suffering and Faith," *Ibid.*, 42.
46. "An Experiment in Love," 20.
47. *Stride toward Freedom*, chapter 11.
48. *Where Do We Go from Here*? chapter 1.
49. *Ibid.*, chapter 2.
50. *Ibid.*
51. *Ibid.*, chapter 1.
52. *Stride toward Freedom*, chapter 11.
53. "Letter from a Birmingham Jail."
54. *Ibid.*
55. "An Experiment in Love," in *A Testament of Hope*, 20.
56. "My Trip to the Land of Gandhi," in *A Testament of Hope*, 25.
57. *Stride toward Freedom*, chapter 11.
58. *Ibid.*
59. *Where Do We Go From Here*? chapter 1.
60. "Nonviolence and Racial Justice," *A Testament of Hope*, 8.

Chapter Eight

Benevolence and a Politics of Mercy

"Not everyone who says 'Lord, Lord,' shall enter the kingdom of heaven, but he who does the will of my Father who is heaven." In the passage immediately preceding, Jesus warns his followers of false prophets, "who come to you in sheep's clothing but inwardly are ravenous wolves." And how do you distinguish true from false prophets? "By their fruits," whether the fruits they bear are "good" or "evil," whether they yield benevolence, as we might say, or malevolence. Coincidently, in the passage immediately following, Jesus identifies the wise as those who not only hear but do God's will and the foolish as those who hear but do not do the will of God (Matthew 7: 15–27). Not all Christian communities that claim God's mercy for themselves are willing to grant it to others. Not unlike the self-righteous hypocrisy of the servant in Jesus's parable, they withhold in public life the very merciful benevolence that they eagerly accept for themselves. Like the servant, they gladly but disingenuously express gratitude for God's mercy while stubbornly denying it for others. This amounts to a version of "cheap grace"[1] in which Christians gratefully receive God's mercy for themselves but are unwilling to pay the same sacrificial cost of purchasing mercy for others. Christian communities often diffidently defer to secular versions of liberal justice and laissez faire economics, which in themselves are not evil, but whose fruits often yield a harvest of evil; when communities permit, for example, poverty and hunger and illiteracy and ill health and other real and positive evils that policies of benevolence otherwise would prevent. Jesus (Matthew 25: 31–46) warns that human destiny is a direct function of how life is lived; whether by faith and grace it is lived mercifully and benevolently or not; whether "the least of these" are cared for or not.

Although Jesus sometimes speaks of judgment (e.g., Matthew 25), in the Gospel narratives, he rarely speaks of justice *per se*. Not that he is indifferent to justice and injustice; indeed, in his discourses and parables and ministry, in his death and resurrection, Jesus compassionately confronts the reality of an unjust and malevolent world. By boldly, lovingly engaging with people and society he situates himself as a moral agent in a way that stands in stark contrast to the hypothetical disengagement of Rawls' "veil of ignorance" and to the distance of Smith's "impartial third party." Compassionate, interpersonal engagement is a distinctly Christian (religious) way of confronting the injustice of a malevolent world with policies of benevolence and a politics of mercy.

Just as in Christian theology injustice is subverted and justice established by the sacrificial mercy of Christ's passion, so also in public and political life injustice is subverted and justice established by the sacrificial mercy implicit in policies of benevolence. Very often in an evil and unjust world benevolence is the sacrificial price that must be paid for the purchase of justice. In a fallen, unjust world there is no justice, no liberation and redemption, no reconciliation and restoration without something like *agape*'s sacrificial mercy. So, for Christian communities to on earth "bind" in public life the very mercy that is "loosed" in heaven (Matthew 16: 19) is cowardly hypocrisy. If government can be evil and malevolent, then it can also be good and benevolent, if only citizens summon the courage and will. Americans in general and Christian communities in particular can pout like the elder son in Jesus's parable and complain that the younger son does not merit the benefits of his father's mercy and benevolence, or they can like the father with great joy lavish on others the same benefits of mercy that God has bestowed on them.

ECONOMICS AS MORAL SCIENCE

It is widely thought that the more self-interested and unregulated markets are the more likely they are to produce economic conditions that are free and fair. The current economic crisis (2007–2014) has unceremoniously and abruptly buried this belief for all but the most fanatical. Such markets, as Western societies have discovered, may appear somewhat free in form and procedures, but for the majority they are in practice a menace to both freedom and fairness; they produce freedom and fairness for only a relative few who have managed to monopolize for themselves the bulk of market resources. For the many whose share of the market is minimal to modest to begin with, their economic bulk and power is too frail and fragmented to attract available resources; ironically, in the reality of allegedly free markets they find themselves co-dependent on those few who monopolize economic resources. The self-interested free market, in other words, is analogous to a solar system in which the magnetic power of the few bodies with greater mass attract and bind to themselves bodies of lesser mass.

Why this is so should be no surprise, least of all a surprise for Christians, whose theology predicts that the self-interested greed of human fallenness, in which Smith's roots his free market economics, subjugates and enslaves. What else could be expected? Smith's law of unintended consequences mistakenly predicts that benefits of self-interest will inadvertently ripple centrifugally to others. But in truth forces of self-interest are centrifugal, as the phrase itself would lead one to believe. They entice resources inward toward each individuated axis, and especially disproportionately toward those who already have much. In so doing each individual is increasingly alienated economically from each. What results is encapsulated in *the principle of progressive inequality*: all being equal, those with greater economic mass attract to themselves at ever-increasing rates larger proportions of available goods; resources that thereby become increasingly unavailable to those with lesser economic mass. This at least is what recent research shows. In a twenty-five-year study titled "The Roots of the Widening Racial Wealth Gap: Explaining the Black-White Economic Divide,"[2] researchers traced the economic profile of the same households over twenty-five years (1984–2009). The findings show that households that begin with a greater mass of wealth attracted over the years a larger proportion of available resources than households that begin with a lesser mass. For an African-American household, for example, a $1 increase in average income generates $0.69 in additional wealth compared with $5.19 in additional wealth for a white household. The total wealth gap between African-American and white households nearly tripled in twenty-five years, increasing from $85,000 in 1984 to $236,500 in 2009. The study notes that the causes of this progressive wealth discrepancy include years of homeownership, household income, unemployment discrepancies, college education, inheritance, and preexisting family wealth. Moreover, equal achievements, such as increased income, results racially in unequal "wealth rewards."

What forces contribute to these progressive economic inequalities? "Public policies play a major role in widening the already massive racial wealth gap, and they must play a role in closing it. We should be investing in prosperity and equity, but instead we are advancing toxic inequality. A U-turn is needed," according to Dr. Thomas Shapiro, director of the institute and study.[3] What is needed to make an economic U-turn, I am arguing, are policies of benevolence and not simply policies of fairness; a politics of mercy and not simply a politics of liberal justice. Curiously, "The dramatic increase in the racial wealth gap has accelerated despite the country's movement beyond the Civil Rights era into a period of legal equality and the election of the first African-American president."[4] Indeed, government and its institutions are partly to blame, according to Shapiro, because they enforce almost exclusively policies of liberal, procedural justice, and largely neglect benevolent policies that address matters of egalitarian, economic justice. "[T]he dramatic gap in household wealth that now exists along racial lines in the United States," according to the study, "cannot be attributed to personal ambition and behavioral choices, but rather reflects [government] policies and institutional practices that create different opportunities for whites and African Americans."[5] Given conditions of inequality, in other words, the liberal, procedural justice of Civil Rights is itself incapable of subverting economic injustice and establishing the egalitarian justice required of a fully free and fair society.

Contrast self-interest, as a basis of free market economics, with "natural sympathy." Hume's humanistic argument is commensurate with biblical narratives that envision an original, created goodness on the basis of which alone human endeavors should properly flourish. Creation's primal goodness in general and humanity's original divine image in particular infer the "naked" goodness of natural sympathy as the intended basis for endeavors like politics and economics. Natural sympathy and its implied policies of benevolence, accordingly, should guide moral judgments regarding the distribution of economic goods. In short, liberal political procedures (Rawls' Liberty Principle) aligned with the Distribution Principle yields an open political process and a "fair balance" of economic and social goods that together constitute not only good theology and ethics, but, I think, a compelling framework for open and just societies.

The recent work of British economist Adair Turner in *Economics after the Crisis* is a case in point that challenges the main planks of the standard free market platform or what he calls "instrumental conventional wisdom." Turner believes that "the crisis [of 2008] *should* prompt us to challenge fundamental assumptions and to raise issues that go beyond those directly raised by the impact of the crisis itself." He argues that the theory and practices and policies that generated the financial system's crisis were a function of "a wider set of simplistic beliefs about the objectives and means of economic activity that dominated policy thinking. . . ."[6] Three assumptions were presupposed by "a dominant political discourse about economic objectives and a conventional wisdom about the means with which to pursue them," all of which Turner rejects. He challenges, first, the assumption that "the objective of successful policy is more rapid growth in measured policy," that is, in Gross National Product per capita; secondly, that the best way to deliver "more rapid growth" is "by creating freer markets—freeing entrepreneurs from red tape, unleashing incentives through lighter income taxes and capital-gains taxes, extending markets by means of privatization and liberalization"; and thirdly, that "a significant degree of inequality is both the inevitable consequence of and necessary to the operation of free markets, and that increased inequality is acceptable because and to the extent that it helps deliver superior growth."[7] I do not intend here to rehearse Turner's reasons for challenging these failed assumptions, but I do want to sketch a few features of his constructive argument delivered at the end of his book.

A first pertinent feature assumes, against "the instrumental conventional wisdom" and with John Maynard Keynes, that economics is essentially a moral science. This claim is commensurate with J. S. Mill's analysis, discussed in chapter 3, that although the laws of economic production are scientific the laws of economic distribution and consumption are moral, a matter of volition. No matter how scientific or mathematical economists want to make their discipline, it nevertheless embraces a moral dimension that science and mathematics cannot domesticate. Indeed, Turner concludes with Lionel Robbins that "There is nothing in economics which relieves us of the obligation to choose."[8] It seems to me that for the morally mature sympathy, compassion, and mercy are more persuasive than self-interest as a basis for making moral judgments regarding the distribution of economic goods. Even though Turner himself argues that economic freedom renders "some significant inequality . . . unavoidable," he does admit that "the degree of inequality" is a moral and political matter and, unlike the instrumental conventional wisdom, should not be avoided or neglected.[9]

A second feature of Turner's argument that contributes importantly to my project is his insistence that economic growth be tied to income redistribution, a position commensurate with the Distribution Principle: that economic and social inequalities are to be addressed by policies that directly and primarily benefit the least advantaged members of society, while at the same time minimizing burdens and/or maximizing benefits for the more advantaged. Although Turner rejects growth as an "crucial objective" of economic policy,[10] he does argue that "economic growth is relevant to the position of the poorest only and to the extent that it could, at least in theory, help ameliorate relative deprivation." So growth is justifiable and "valid only if it is combined with action to address the relative position of the least well off."[11] The laws of economic distribution as matter of moral science, Turner seems to be saying, ought to benefit most directly and intentionally those in society who suffer the greatest from economic deprivation; addressing economic deprivation, in fact, is an instrumental justification for free market growth. Nonetheless, Turner's vision here seems to fall short of St. Paul's vision of economic "fair balance": that those that have much do not have too much and that those who have little do not have too little. Nowhere that I am aware of does Turner suggest that in order to address deprivation it might be necessary, whether through progressive taxation or redistribution, to limit the individual accumulation of wealth.

A third way Turner contributes to the project of this book involves his discussion of economic freedom, although I think his view again falls short. Turner helpfully distinguishes economic freedom on "the production side" and freedom on "the consumption [distribution] side." Procedural freedom on the "production side" is, of course, crucial and inviolable; "freedom to innovate, to improve productivity, to set up new businesses, and to compete," for example, are critical for growth and progress and for avoiding economic regression.[12] Moreover, "'the freedom of people to act as they like in deciding where to work, what to produce, what to consume,' quoting Sen, is in and of itself an important aspect of freedom."[13] Procedural freedoms in the processes of production are crucial, certainly, to maximizing outcomes. But the economic outcomes themselves and their distribution and consumption are not what matters, for when left to freedom they should be left to freedom alone; and in so doing they are abandoned, as Smith himself admits, to the vicissitudes (in theological terms) and pride of fallenness and (in economic terms) to the greed of selfish interests. To act according to self-interest is not the same as acting freely; indeed, self-interest is a form of moral and social bondage; it corrupts freedom in the same way that self-deception corrupts truth: just as the "truth one speaks" to others is falsified by one's own self-deception, so the "freedom one exercises" in competing with others for resources enslaves one to one's own self-interestedness and falsifies the natural sympathy that defines "human." Ultimately and finally Turner apotheosizes freedom, in both of its modes, as production and as consumption. He views freedom "as a desirable objective in and of itself, not because of any prosperity it delivers."[14] But this is practical nonsense for all except those who have not suffered the pain of economic deprivation. Few cherish economic freedom in and of itself, whether it brings the prosperity of a sustainable livelihood or not; indeed, it is desired precisely because it brings prosperity or at least sustainable livelihood. And that freedom brings prosperity to so precious few in the world is in biblical narratives a damnable curse and not a blessing. Nevertheless Turner permits himself to argue that "inequality, rather than being instrumentally justifiable because and to the extent that it delivers growth, is justifiable because it is the unavoidable concomitant of economic freedom."[15] Fashioning freedom into an idol in this unmitigated way is, of course, no comfort to the vast majority of people in the world who suffer deprivation; nor should it be for those moral agents lucky enough not to suffer deprivation.

But what if compassion (mercy, benevolence, justice) along with freedom, constitutes a moral matrix for crafting a framework for politics and economics? I think it must be for Christian communities and for devotees of all religious traditions? What if freedom, for all its great worth, is an associate value in politics and economics instead of sovereign master? What if in social and political matters policies of benevolence and egalitarian justice are encouraged along with policies of liberal justice? What if Christian and all benevolent communities understand themselves not as propagandists for a parochial, partisan political agenda but as prophets of a transnational, peaceable Kingdom? What change of heart and mind is necessary?

TRANSFORMING HEART AND MIND

How must benevolent communities position themselves today so that public projects of benevolence are possible? What transformations of heart and mind are needed? First, there needs be a transformation from a human to a divine perspective, from the symmetry of reason to the asymmetry of faith, from legalism to law of liberty. St. Paul said it succinctly: "By the mercies of God . . . present your bodies as a living sacrifice, holy and acceptable to God, which is your spiritual worship. Do not be conformed to this world, but be transformed by the renewing of your minds, so that you may discern what is the will of God—what is good and acceptable and perfect." (Romans 12: 1–2). Paul's injunction culminates by rejecting the law of retaliatory justice and reaffirming mercy's law of liberty: "Never avenge yourselves, but leave room for the wrath of God; for it is written, Vengeance is mine, I will repay, says the Lord. No, if your enemies are hungry, feed them; if they are thirsty give them something to drink; for by doing so you will heap burning coals on their heads. Do not be overcome by evil, but overcome evil with good" (Romans 12: 19–21). This is a prime example of transforming human into divine mind, of "conforming" not "to the world" but to "the will of God," of conforming one's mind not to the world's patterns of just retaliation but to righteous patterns of merciful benevolence. Indeed, the very next thing St. Paul does, in his Epistle, is apply this transformed and transforming mind to governing authorities, who are endowed by God with authority to enforce moral and social order, overcoming evil with good and not evil with evil. (Romans 13: 1–7)

St. Paul understood that and how God in Christ alters "the basic way . . . humans view themselves and their experience," as Robert Kysar puts it. He suggests that if the kind of love that Christ practiced (i.e., mercy) guides a community then that community will "regard no one [including Christ] from a human point of view" but from a divine point of view, a point of view of one who is a "new creation," a point of view in which "the old has passed away" and the power of a new way of seeing and living freely by faith has been by God's grace granted (II Cor. 5: 61–17).[16] This new way includes viewing merciful benevolence as necessary for justice to roll down like waters, for the peace of God's kingdom to triumph. This divine perspective includes, Jesus instructs his disciples (Mark 10: 42–45), a new, creative way of ruling, not by exercising a power and authority of domination, but by the kind of sacrificial service and suffering often required by mercy. Genuine moral leadership, in other words, aims not at the just retribution and reward practiced by the Gentiles but aims at the merciful benevolence whose precondition is the power of grace. Such is the Christian life that is a "living sacrifice holy and acceptable to God," a life that is fruit and proof of a mind so "transformed" and "renewed" by grace that ultimately it will "rejoice with those who rejoice [and] weep with those who weep," living humbly, "associating with the lowly" and, insofar as conditions depend upon the Christian community, living peaceably with all; never avenging but showing mercy even to enemies, even to the vulnerable, to the hungry and thirsty, not allowing evil to triumph but "overcoming evil with good," injustice with mercy. Why? In so doing, in so acting with benevolence a community overcomes wrongdoers and makes itself neighbor to enemies, drawing them into love's transforming power (Romans 12: 1–2, 14–21).

Secondly, there needs be a transformation, especially in the United States, from benevolence as largely a private, disestablished virtue to practicing it as a public, established virtue. The moral/social order for which government is divinely ordained requires benevolence as well as justice; requires the Distribution Principle's economic goal of "fair balance" along with the Liberty Principle's political goal of equal liberty and rights. Already I have made a great deal of this transformation historically, philosophically, and theologically. Hume's "natural sympathy" as a distributive force is preferable to Smith's "self-interest." This transformation is admittedly difficult for some Christian communities; not merely because they might find themselves in concord with the "infidel" Hume, but because Smith's laissez faire formula is so firmly and finely woven into the fabric of the American consciousness. Sympathy is nevertheless preferable; not only because as motive it more nearly reflects the persuasion of biblical narratives than does Smith's motive of self-interest; but because its power is more likely to achieve justice's liberal and egalitarian freedoms at which government aims. What is needed, in other words, is a transition from Smith's disestablishment of economics and benevolence to a creative re-establishment of benevolence as normative for distributing economic goods.

Thirdly, there needs be a transformation from liberal, procedural justice alone to embracing egalitarian, economic justice as well. Not only are both necessary to establishing equal freedom but both are essential to moral integrity and civility. The evolution of ethics, in biblical narratives, from justice to mercy requires a maturing of Christian character that obligates benevolent communities to practice moral reciprocity, to practice what they preach in public as well as private life. One mantra of my argument, accordingly, is that in an unjust world and under conditions of inequality policies of benevolence and projects of mercy are required; otherwise it is unlikely that genuinely moral and civil order will be restored and creation redeemed. With minimal public commitment in the United States to a politics of mercy it is not surprising that crime is rampant and prisons overflowing; it is not surprising that moral disorder and social chaos, fear and violence persist; for they largely result from economic deprivation and social displacement: poverty, hunger, inadequate health, education, employment, and wages, and other forms of marginalization. But benevolence is crucial not only to social order, it is also vital to freedom and self-determination. Economic justice is as essential to freedom and self-determination as is political justice. The lack of self-sustaining economic resources diminishes freedom and independence as much as the lack of self-sustaining political rights. Inhumane and gross injustices are the direct result, as the author of *The Epistle of James* insists, of "earthly, unspiritual, and devilish" wisdom, of "selfish ambition" and resentment. "But the wisdom from above is first pure, then peaceable, gentle, open to reason, full of mercy and good fruits, without uncertainty or insincerity. And the harvest of righteousness is sown in peace by those who make peace" (3: 15–18). There is every reason and motive to treat this wisdom from above as normative for public order and peace as well as for private; there is every reason to think that a fair balance of economic and social goods are indispensable to establishing that freedom and peace.

Accordingly and fourthly, there needs be a transformation from something like Rawls' aristocratic Difference Principle to the populist Distribution Principle; social and economic inequalities should be addressed by policies that directly and primarily benefit the least advantaged members of society, while at the same time minimizing burdens and/or maximizing benefits for the most advantaged. Presupposed by this transformation is a concomitant transition from Rawls' abstract, hypothetical "veil of ignorance" and the distance of Smith's impartial third spectator to a direct, candid engagement with reality inspired by compassion's "vale of tears." This shift from alleged neutrality to engrossed care requires the benevolent community to forsake the habit of objectification, of subjugating the deprived to the distance of abstract object, and to cultivate habits of compassion for "the least of these," as Jesus puts it. Indeed, the Distribution Principle would establish in public policy something like St. Paul's "fair balance," in which those who have much do not have too much, and those who have little do not have too little. If society is not willing to undertake as a public policy some such transformation, I do not see how it can in fidelity call itself humane and civil.

Finally, there needs be a transformation from political ideology to moral integrity. The argument for "institutionalizing" merciful benevolence in public policies and programs is not an argument for partisan political agendas and party idolatry. Instead, benevolence establishes a normative guide for cooperative action that with integrity shapes and reshapes political discourse and practice. In this sense, the commitment of faith communities is to the Kingdom of God not to kingdoms of this earth. For a politics of mercy and policies of benevolence establish a moral axis whereby communities might educate and inspire each generation to sacrifice social status, privilege, and self-interest for the sake of God's Kingdom, for the sake of the "least of these," for the sake of "fair balance," for the benefit of being neighborly to all humans. A politics of mercy establishes, in other words, a criterion whereby the selfish-ambition of brutish Darwinian "survival of the fittest" economics is condemned as inflaming injustice and not squelching it. As normative, benevolence takes a moral stand and stance against any economic and social agenda that subjugates human persons and personality to the idols of individualism, license, and selfish interests. The belief that such vices are inevitable and indispensible to social and economic success is cynical, superstitious, and idolatrous. It forfeits moral courage and integrity for a fabricated, regressive belief, namely, that a vibrant and lively economy inevitably requires self-interest, beastly greed, and the advantage of a few over many. The faith promoted by biblical narratives, in contrast, envisions a power of grace, of compassion, mercy, and benevolence, that redeems, reconciles, and restores the harmony of God's primal, created order.

These transformations map an evolving spiritual journey toward moral integrity. They map a pilgrimage from Just to Righteous Community; an evolution from fear to faithfulness, from Fallen Order to Redeemed Order, from justice to mercy, from reason to faith, from law to grace, from self-interest to benevolence; an evolving consciousness and spiritual pilgrimage in which the faith one practices in private life expresses itself in public life as a politics of mercy.

BENEVOLENCE AS POLITICAL ECONOMY

What then do such transformations mean for benevolent societies? For civil societies? Many Americans fancy the United States as a nation committed to freedom and justice. But although freedom and justice may constitute its form, for many they are not prominent features of experience. Political and financial power brokers construct ever more complex bureaucracies that often obscure the fact that, although preached, the actual experience of freedom and justice is for many indefinitely deferred and denied. Michelle Alexander, for example, chronicles the massive, unfair incarceration of African American males, a gross injustice obscured by the bureaucracy of a criminal justice system whose procedural form is justice but whose prominent feature is a vast wasteland of Jim Crow prejudices and practices.[17] In fact, the system is a function of the economic injustices America has been unwilling with candor to face. The narcotic haze of American Capitalism hypnotizes many, obscuring the fact that although the form of Capitalism may include the rhetoric of freedom and justice its actual practices often do not. Banks, corporations, and government have fabricated such a maze of inscrutable, bureaucratic corridors that even the plutocrats inventing them often do not have sufficient crumbs to find their way home to the vaunted values of freedom and justice that belonged, allegedly at least, to the original promise of Smith's laissez faire economics. Many Americans and Christians soldier obediently albeit blindly on despite economic ill omens: a real estate crash, two unfunded wars, a banking collapse, unpunished financial fraud, a global economic recession (2007), and much more; in so doing sowing seeds of its own destruction; not unlike Sopholces' Oedipus. Recall that although Oedipus solves the Sphinx's riddle Sophocles' focus is not on this accomplishment but on the consequences; how Oedipus strives to stave off ill omens that loom over his kingdom; unwittingly he does unthinkable things; he marries his mother; long ago he has murdered his father; in despair he gouges out his eyes and in darkness exiles himself.

What can be done? No doubt, there is as vital a role for public policy in achieving economic "fair balance" as there is a role for private enterprise. Although policies of benevolence are not a panacea, they are and, along with free enterprise, should be a substantial stretch of the horizon. To a modest extent they are progressively shaping the policy horizon in the United States, with the Affordable Healthcare Act stumbling into place and a somewhat progressive tax structure, modest though it may be; with much more to be done. These recent policies, in fact, are part of a growing span of a horizon envisioned in 1944 by Franklin D. Roosevelt in his so-called second "Bill of Rights." During his State of the Union Address[18] he suggests that the people of the United States had come to see that along with the Constitution's original political "Bill of Rights," which itself was controversial, there should now be an "economic bill of rights." Roosevelt argues that these rights should guarantee:

Employment, with a living wage
Freedom from unfair competition and monopolies
Housing
Medical care
Education
Social Security

Roosevelt insists that implementing these rights would not only guarantee freedom and security for Americans domestically but also a secure, prominent role for America globally. Later, a Czech judge, Karel Vasak, would label this list a "second generation" of rights that are indispensable for civilizing modern societies.[19]

Roosevelt intended to implement this economic Bill of Rights as a series of benevolent public policies; and indeed during his own tenure as president he began to secure approval and implement some of them, most notably Social Security. He articulated in several speeches that supporting such policies is a matter of human rights and dignity and that protecting them is a matter of justice and freedom. Since Roosevelt, the U.S. Congress sometimes engages these social and economic rights, sometimes submits legislation addressing them, and even at times passes "bills of benevolence" that move American society incrementally closer to realizing its ideal of a just and free nation. In his January 11, 1944, State of the Union speech Roosevelt addresses the specifics of this economic Bill of Rights, as indicated in the following few excerpts.

1. Roosevelt addresses matters of political rights, of liberal, procedural justice:

> This Republic had its beginning, and grew to its present strength, under the protection of certain inalienable political rights—among them the right of free speech, free press, free worship, trial by jury, freedom from unreasonable searches and seizures. They were our rights to life and liberty.

2. Roosevelt addresses also substantive economic rights, matters of egalitarian justice:

> As our nation has grown in size and stature, however, as our industrial economy expanded—these political rights proved inadequate to assure us equality in the pursuit of happiness.
>
> It is our duty now to begin to lay the plans and determine the strategy for the winning of a lasting peace and the establishment of an American standard of living higher than ever before known. We cannot be content, no matter how high the general standard of living may be, if some fraction of our people—whether it be one-third or one-fifth or one-tenth—is ill-fed, ill-clothed, ill-housed, and insecure.
>
> We have come to a clear realization of the fact that true individual freedom cannot exist without economic security and independence. "Necessitous men are not free men."[20] People who are hungry and out of a job are the stuff of which dictatorships are made.
>
> In our day these economic truths have become accepted as self-evident. We have accepted, so to speak, a second Bill of Rights under which a new basis of security and prosperity can be established for all—regardless of station, race, or creed.

Among these are:

The right to a useful and remunerative job in industries or shops or farms or mines of the nation;

The right to earn enough to provide adequate food and clothing and recreation;

The right of every farmer to raise and sell his products at a return which will give him and his family a decent living;

The right of every businessman, large and small, to trade in an atmosphere of freedom from unfair competition and domination by monopolies at home or abroad;

The right of every family to a decent home;

The right of adequate medical care and the opportunity to achieve and enjoy good health;

The right to adequate protection from the economic fears of old age, sickness, accident, and unemployment; and
The right to a good education.

All of these rights spell security. And after this war is won we must be prepared to move forward, in the implementation of these rights, top new goals of human happiness and well-being.
America's own rightful place in the world depends in large part upon how fully these and similar rights have been carried into practice for all our citizens.
For unless there is security here at home there cannot be lasting peace in the world.

Roosevelt gets it largely right when he argues that the practice of justice and individual freedom, of fairness and self-determination depend on guaranteeing not only political rights but certain economic rights as well. He correctly envisions his second "Bill of [Economic] Rights" as the natural culmination and fulfillment of a promise implicit in the constitution's political "Bill of Rights": that America's vaunted freedom and justice requires guaranteeing economic rights as well as political. Roosevelt's social and moral sensibilities are commensurate, I think, with biblical sensibilities; he seems to have a keen sense of the fallenness of humanity and the need for grace, for extraordinary acts of public benevolence if the original justice and peace of God's creation is to be restored. He sees, as so many political leaders today do not, the implicit interdependence of liberal and egalitarian justice, of political and economic rights. He sees that they are reciprocal, so that the promise of the one quite naturally evolves toward and is realized in and by the other; he sees, as Rawls does not, that the possibility of realizing Rawls' Principle of Liberty is interdependent not with Rawls' Difference Principle but with something like a Distribution Principle in which a "fair balance" of economic justice is guaranteed along with liberal justice: "Necessitous men are not free men"; ". . . true individual freedom cannot exist without economic security and independence." Guaranteeing egalitarian economic justice along with liberal justice constitutes mercy, not only by granting benevolence to the vulnerable who otherwise have no power of access to a sustainable livelihood, but also by granting amnesty instead of just retaliation to those who for centuries have unfairly advantaged themselves and unfairly oppressed the vulnerable and poor in their societies.

What can be done? What path forward? Christian communities interested in leading the way must nurture specific spiritual habits of Remembrance and Gratitude: remembering mercy and the benefits of mercy that God in Christ freely delivers to undeserving humans; gratitude for the grace of mercy that empowers communities, as recipient of such a gift, to deliver to others the same mercy it has received. Failure of a community to cultivate in its members spiritual habits of Eucharistic Remembrance and Gratitude not only renders incoherent and impractical an ethics and politics of mercy, but forfeits the community's claim to its identity as Christian. Too often, in making moral/political judgments, Christians neglect their spiritual family of origin and default to their culture's mores and attitudes. In doing so, they undermine their original, unique identity and moral orientation in such a way that although in theory a politics of mercy sounds good in practice, they claim, it seems quite unrealistic. Partly this is because in public and political life many Christians eagerly and uncritically take moral cues from political parties and partisan agendas, or from fashionable theories of economics or from popular self-help psychologies. Christians, of course, are obligated to interact with and evaluate ancient and current moral/political orientations. But if the orientation they develop is to be genuinely Christian, it must begin and end with its own primary, indigenous spiritual sources: namely, remembrance and gratitude for Christ's compassion, mercy, and benevolence. When a student writes a research paper she must begin and end with primary sources and empirical evidence in support of her thesis. Of course, she is obligated as well to interact with and evaluate alternative sources and orientations. But she undermines her first duty and forfeits her scholarly integrity when she neglects her own primary sources and empirical evidence, in terms of which alternative claims are judged. In short, Christian communities *qua* Christian are obligated to begin eucharistically, with remembrance and gratitude.

What benevolent policies characterize such a politics of mercy? A sustainable livelihood entails the necessities for human survival and minimal well-being. This is the goal of a politics of mercy and of benevolent policies. By practicing something like the Distribution Principle, benevolent public policies can realistically and significantly reduce if not eliminate the "least of these" locally, nationally, globally. Roosevelt's economic Bill of Rights targets issues of sustainable livelihood, including self-sufficient resources, enduring employment, adequate food, shelter, clothing, healthcare, education, wages, due process, and equal protection under the law. These are issues addressed by the Distribution and Liberty Principles together.

MORAL ENTROPY, MORAL INTEGRITY

The most profound moral struggle of our day, I have argued, is not a conflict of cultures or civilizations; nor a struggle of good and evil. Rather it is a struggle between two goods, between habits of justice and habits of benevolence. How and why this is so I have tried to show in this book. I have tried to unpack the paradox that the cure for the disease of injustice cannot be justice itself; justice is not *sui generis;* it requires the power of mercy and policies of benevolence. In a fallen world, mercy and benevolence are the moral means whereby injustice is subverted and egalitarian justice established. The ramifications of mistaking justice instead of mercy as the cure for injustice are considerable. Energies and resources are accordingly diverted from the remedy (policies of benevolence) to an oligarchy of market plutocrats who promote liberal justice and liberal, laissez faire economics from which they almost exclusively benefit. Urgently needed, if humanity is to cure the evils of economic injustice, are organizations, religious and secular, local and global, dedicated to the values of both liberal and egalitarian justice. Few communities have greater local and global presence and power than those rooted in religious traditions. Not even the United Nations, for all its extensive and constructive work around the world, can claim a local and global reach as expansive and powerful as religion.

Moral entropy, as argued in chapter 1, measures the degree of order or disorder in a moral system. The Christian assumption is that moral entropy in *pax Dei* (Created Order) is nil although possible. God originally created and creates all things good and orderly. The disobedience of the Fall inaugurates a process of relatively low moral entropy that, like physical systems, tends toward ever higher states of moral disorder, depicted in Genesis, for example, from Adam until the time of Noah. As in physical systems so in moral systems moral states tend always toward higher entropy; this is because there are more ways for humans to fall into moral disorder than there are ways to create a moral order. Fallen humans tend toward self-interest, injustice, and higher moral entropy. The energy and thrust of this tendency can be transformed and reversed only by an intentional exercise of free will, only by the choices and actions of moral agents. In chapter 1, I traced how in the history of ancient Israel an evolving moral system endeavors through various phases to reverse the fallen human tendency toward high moral entropy. Israel's covenantal system establishes an evolving culture of moral integrity toward lower states of moral entropy. First, by establishing tribal common law and the notion of "corporate personality," which evolves eventually into *lex talionis* and higher forms of justice wherein moral duties are correlated with certain individual and human rights. Finally we find evolving in the Hebrew prophets and in the ministry of Jesus an even higher measure of moral integrity in which the relatively modest entropy of justice is transformed into the relative low moral entropy of compassion and mercy. Whether contemporary civilizations possess the wisdom and courage to pilot successfully the rough waters of this transformation from entropy to integrity, from justice to mercy, is uncertain. The moral undertow of justice conspires to subvert the high tide of mercy. The church has been especially susceptible to this undertow, even though it is endowed by God with the awful grace and power of mercy. The church diffidently defers to the symmetry of secular versions of justice and their tendencies, in a fallen world, toward moral entropy. This is not surprising; the law of moral entropy predicates that moral systems left to drift on their own momentum degenerate into ever more vicious cycles of avenging violence. Jesus understands this law of moral entropy when he commands his disciples to supersede justice's "eye for an eye"; he knows that in an unjust world justice by itself decays and is arrested and reversed only by compassion and projects of mercy's benevolence; by the meekness of turn the other cheek and loving enemies.

One might object that what I am advocating is the establishment of religion, some Christian or religious theocracy. Absolutely not! What I am advocating is that benevolent communities, inspired by their own personal, local, spiritual dialect, speak and practice in public life the universal language of compassion and mercy. Indeed, it is important not to invent Christian states and Islamic empires and Socialist regimes. Nevertheless, as Shailer Mathews rightly argues, the gospel embedded in biblical narratives "demands a choice between a policy that is selfish and one [that is not] selfish, between one that seeks to give justice and one that seeks to maintain privilege."[21] I have argued that any society that seeks justice must do so by practicing a politics of mercy and policies of benevolence. Moreover, transforming the Fallen Order requires the collaboration of all traditions, religious and secular, for whom the grace of compassion and mercy are supreme values, as indeed they are in Judaism, Islam, Hinduism, Buddhism, Jainism, Sikhism, Bahaiism, and various forms of Humanism. The entropy of the Fallen Order is diverse and varied; so then also must be the cultural and religious tools of transformation. Although my argument in this book is articulated in terms of the local dialect of my own religious community, it is an argument that can and should be made in the local dialect of many religious and secular tongues. Without that proliferation of tongues, a global culture of compassionate mercy is unlikely to materialize.

My final question, then, is: How can societies rescue themselves from the moral entropy of our present age. What will it take for Christians and devotees of all faiths to reverse moral entropy and nurture the integrity of compassion and mercy? Two deceptions threaten to fog the Christian (and I suspect all religious) vision. These two deceptions in Christianity, ironically, are falsifications or fallacies of Eucharistic faith itself and, accordingly, are falsifications that for Christians something like Eucharistic worship alone can redeem. The first fallacy involves a failure of Eucharistic remembrance the results of which cloud the community's vision; and the second is a failure of Eucharistic gratitude that cowers its will. These two Eucharistic fallacies are interrelated as is their remedy; the first is rectified *prophetically* and the second is rectified *pastorally*. How so?

The fallacy of remembrance is not a failure of Christian theology, nor a failure of liturgical form or practice; rather, it is a failure of sight, of hindsight, of remembrance and therefore foresight and vision. Although virtually all versions of Christianity scattered along the continuum from conservative to liberal, from East to West, from Orthodox to Catholic and Protestant, profess a theology of mercy and redemption, and although the Eucharist's liturgical utterances are beautifully and correctly rendered, many Christian communities, like the unforgiving servant in Jesus's parable, falsify that worship and forfeit its blessing by failing too often in personal and political life to remember what they revere, to practice what in worship they preach. In all versions of Communion the command "remember" is central. And what the faithful community is to remember and in remembering practice is something dangerous and provocative, namely, that in his passion, death, and resurrection Jesus, and *a fortiori* the Christian community, absorbs on behalf of humanity the pain and sacrifice and suffering embedded in a fallen world. Remember that it is not justice itself but the grace of mercy that redeems and justifies; remember it is mercy that transforms sin into salvation, injustice into justice; and remember that faithful communities *qua* Christian are thereby called and empowered to practice the self-same grace of mercy for which Christ liberates them. So for Christian communities all occasions private and public are occasions for faithful remembrance, for practicing the very grace of mercy that identifies who they are and what they are to do. Christian communities too often default to the status quo of self-interest and a toxic notion of freedom as license; too often they forget to "love doing mercy" and thereby falsify their own Eucharistic faith. They often do this by prescribing the placebo of liberal justice that perhaps for a time appeases doctors and tranquilizes patients; but that placebo finally has no actual power to heal injustice. In contrast, a politics of mercy fosters a "fair balance" of political and economic benefits without which is impossible the longed for harmony of *pax Dei*.

This failure of remembrance often results from muffling the community's prophetic voices. The prophet is one who situates herself paradoxically in relation to her own community and speaks candidly to it. The prophet is without honor in her own community, not some alien one. The prophet declares to her own community, on the one hand, the secret maladies in its own heart, a knowledge without which the community withers and dies. On the other hand, the prophet prescribes a remedy that heals, but not without sacrifice and pathos. As prophetic, Eucharistic remembrance is a retrieval of moral integrity. It inspires Christian communities with vision to see and with voices to speak: vision to see the transformative power of mercy and the courage to proclaim to power that the justice it seeks requires a politics of mercy.

Concomitant with the fallacy of remembrance is the fallacy of gratitude. Whereas the fallacy of remembrance is a failure of vision the fallacy of gratitude is a failure of will that defaults to the moral entropy of human fallenness. Although the servant in Jesus's parable gratefully receives the unmerited benefits of his master's mercy he does not have the courage of will in turn to show the same mercy toward his fellow servant. He is grateful, but not that grateful. He pleads for and receives a gift of mercy but is too cowardly to grant it to another. Instead he flinches like the craven cad he is, captured by the lure and lair of justice where not only his fellow servant but he himself reaps the fair penalty of his moral cowardliness. And thus it is so often with Christian communities when they cower before ideologies and governments, before *pax Romana*, accommodating if not sanctifying machinery of inequality, of poverty, discrimination, and war that protects freedom for a few at the expense of the many.

This falsification of Eucharistic gratitude results from neglecting a pastoral role. Pastoring requires a community to practice the sweat equity of compassion and mercy and forgiveness and not just utter it earnestly in worship. If Christian communities are to emulate the King, in Jesus's parable, and not the unforgiving servant, then Eucharistic gratitude will inspire them to grant in private and public life the same magnificent power of mercy, not only to neighbor but to the vulnerable and enemy as well. Like Jonah, Christian communities often excuse themselves and flee their moral and spiritual calling. As Jonah confesses to God "That is why I made haste to flee to Tarshish; for I knew that thou art a gracious God and merciful, slow to anger, and abounding in steadfast love, and repentest of evil" (4: 1–2, KJV). Like Jonah, Christian communities often prefer justice's condemnation to love's mercy; they forsake public life, abandoning it and their responsibilities for it to the corruption of self-interest and license and greed; they flee to Leviathans of sentimentality and parochialism and eschatological fantasies. Would that Christian communities were as honest with themselves as was Jonah.

These two Eucharistic fallacies are inseparable symptoms of a single illness, just as their prophetic and pastoral prescriptions are solutions of a single cure. If the Christian community is to rescue itself from spiritual bankruptcy and the world from barbarity, if it is to really fulfill the teaching of Christ, if it is to deliver to the world what it promises, if it is to be prophetic and pastoral, then it must devote itself single-mindedly to *pax Christi,* to a compassionate, benevolent politics of mercy. To the wisdom and values of *pax Romana* Christian communities must be willing to seem, as the Apostle Paul eloquently puts it, foolish and weak and low and despised and "not" (I Corinthians 1: 18–31). For Moses, Jesus, and Paul the die is cast: choose life and prosperity or death and adversity (Deut. 30: 15–20); choose the wisdom of worldly reason or the foolishness of faith; choose the power of *pax Romana* or the promise of *pax Christi;* the limits of law or the liberty of grace; the gloss of liberal justice or the gospel of merciful benevolence. Which will it be? "For it is written," Paul says, quoting the prophet Isaiah (29: 14): "'I will destroy the wisdom of the wise, and the cleverness of the clever I will thwart.' . . . . For the foolishness of God is wiser than men, and the weakness of God is stronger than men" (I Cor. 1: 19, 25). Which will it be: the wisdom and strength of justice alone or the foolishness and weakness of mercy; moral entropy or moral integrity? Yahweh, the God of Jonah says, "Enough of justice, grant mercy!" For Christians today, there is no better way than to declare with the Psalmist, "According to Thy mercy . . . !" According to the ancient, awful grace of God.[22]

NOTES

1. Dietrich Bonhoeffer famously distinguishes "costly grace" and "cheap grace" in his book *Cost of Discipleship.*
2. See *Institute on Assets and Social Policy* (Brandeis University), Research and Policy Brief (February 2013).
3. "Heller study finds public and institutional policies widen racial wealth gap," *Brandeis-NOW*, brandeis.edu/now/2013/February/wealthgap.html, 1.
4. *Ibid.*, 1.
5. *Ibid.*, 1.
6. Adair Turner, *Economics after the Crisis: Objectives and Means* (Cambridge, MA: MIT Press, 2012), x.
7. *Ibid.*, xi.
8. *Ibid.*, 96.
9. *Ibid.*, 73–74.
10. *Ibid.*, xi.
11. *Ibid.*, 70.
12. *Ibid.*, 71.
13. *Ibid.*, 73.
14. *Ibid.*, 72.
15. *Ibid.*, 73.
16. Robert Kysar, *Called to Care: Biblical Images for Social Ministry* (Minneapolis, MN: Fortress Press, 1991), 113.
17. Michelle Alexander, *The New Jim Crow: Mass Incarceration in the Age of Colorblindness* (New York: The New Press, 2010, 2012).
18. Roosevelt's Address was delivered by radio and filmed for later broadcast. The film was thought to be lost until it was recovered in 2008 by Michael Moore while he was conducting research for his film *Capitalism: A Love Story.*
19. Karel Vasak was the secretary-general of the International Institute of Human Rights. The "second generation" of rights refers to "The International Covenant of Economic, Social and Cultural Rights," section of the United Nation's *International Bill of Rights*, 160 countries ratified this "Covenant"; an additional 7 countries, including the United States, signed but did not ratify it.
20. This phrase is in the old English property law case, *Vernon v. Bethell* (1762), 28 ER 838, according to Lord Henley LC
21. Matthews, *Jesus on Social Institutions*, 144.
22. The phrase, "the awful grace of God" comes from Edith Hamilton's translation of "Agamemnon," lines 179–182, in Aeschylus's *Oresteia* cycle of plays. See Edith Hamilton, *Three Greek Plays: Prometheus Bound, Agamemnon, the Trojan Women* (New York: W. W. Norton & Co., Inc., 1937).

Bibliography

Abe, K., et al. "Observation of Large *CP* Violation in the Neutral *B* Meson System." *Physical Review Letters* 87, 091802, Issue 9–27, August 14, 2001.

Abela, Andrew. "Adam Smith and the Separation Thesis," *Business and Society Review 106*, 3 (2001): 187–199.

Adair, Douglas. "'That Politics May Be Reduced to a Science': David Hume, James Madison, and the Tenth Federalist," *Hume: A Re-evaluation*. ed. by Donald Livingston and James King. New York: Fordham University Press, 1976: 404–417.

Agresti, James D. "Social Spending, Constitutional History," *Just Facts* (December 5, 2007).

Alexander, Michelle. *The New Jim Crow: Mass Incarceration in the Age of Colorblindness*. New York, NY: The New Press, 2012: 200.

Appadurai, Arjun. *Modernity at Large: Cultural Dimensions of Globalization*. Minneapolis, MN: University of Minnesota Press, 1996.

Aquinas, Thomas. *Summa Theologica*. II–II, Q. 66; aa. 1–7.

Aubert, B., et al. "Observation of *CP* Violation in the *B* 0 Meson System," *Physical Review Letters*, 87, 091801, Issue 9–27, August 14, 2001.

Beckley, Harlan. "A Christian Affirmation of Rawls's Idea of Justice as Fairness," I-II, *Journal of Religious Ethics*, I, 13, 2, 1985: 210–242; II, 14, 2, 1986: 229–246.

Blomberg, Craig L. *Matthew*, in *The New American Commentary* series. Nashville, TN: Broadman Press, 1992: 22.

Blum, Lawrence. "Compassion," *Explaining Emotions*. ed. Amelie O. Rorty. Berkeley, CA: University of California Press, 1980: 507–517.

Bonhoeffer, Deitrich. *Cost of Discipleship*. New York, NY: Macmillan Co., 1959.

Butkus, Russell. "Dangerous Memory and Social Justice Education," *Religious Education* 82 (1987): 426–446.

Camenisch, Paul F. "Gift and Gratitude in Ethics," *Journal of Religious Ethics* 9 (Spring 1981): 1–34.

Canon, Katie. *Katie's Canon: Womanism and the Soul of the Black Community*. New York, NY: Continuum Pub., Co., 1995.

Cather, Katherine. *Religious Education through Story-telling*. New York, NY: Abingdon Press, 1925.

Corbett, Julia and Michael Corbett. *Politics and Religion in the United States*. New York: Garland Publishing, Inc., 1999.

Childs, Brevard. *Memory and Tradition in Israel*. New York, NY: Alec R. Allanson, 1962.

Close, Frank. *Lucifer's Legacy: The Meaning of Asymmetry*. London, UK: Oxford University Press, 2000.

Dale, Leigh. "This Nineteenth Century of Progress and Humanity: The Life and Times of Frederick Weld," in *Burden or Benefit? Imperial Benevolence and Its Legacies*. Bloomington: Indiana University Press, 2008.

Davies, Paul. *God and the New Physics*. New York: Touchstone Books, Simon & Schuster, 1984.

Edwards, Jonathan. *Religious Affections*. Portland, OR: Multnomah Press, 1984.

Fletcher, Joseph. *Situation Ethics: The New Morality*. Philadelphia, PA: Westminster Press, 1966.

Freire, Paulo. *Pedagogy of the Oppressed*. New York: Continuum Pub., Co., 1993.

Fleischacker, Samuel. "Adam Smith's Reception among the American Founders, 1776–1790," *The William and Mary Quarterly* 59, 4 (October 2002): 916.

Gadamer, Hans-George. *Truth and Method*. Second edition. New York, NY: Crossroads Press, 1989.

Gandhi, Mohandas. *The Collected Works of Mahatma Gandhi*. New Delhi Publications Division, Ministry of Broadcasting, Government of India, 1958–1994.

———. *The Essential Gandhi: His Life, Work, and Ideas: An Anthology*, ed. and trans. Louis Fischer. New York, NY: Vintage Books, Random House, 1962.

Gide, André. "André Gide," *The God That Failed*, ed. Richard Crossman. Chicago, IL: Regnery Gateway, 1949, 1983: 169.

Gilman, James E. *Fidelity of Heart: An Ethic of Christian Virtue*. New York, NY: Oxford University Press, 2001.

Greene, Brian. *The Fabric of the Cosmos: Space, Time, and the Texture of Reality*. New York, NY: A Vintage Book, Random House, 2005.

Greenspan, Patrica. *Emotions and Reasons: An Inquiry into Emotional Justification*. New York, NY: Routledge, 1988.

Grimshaw, Jean. *Philosophy and Feminist Thinking*. Minneapolis, MN: University of Minnesota Press, 1986.

Gullaci, Giovanni. "On the Moral Conception of the Enlightenment," *Journal of Value Inquiry* 27 (1993): 391–402.

Gustafson, James. *Can Ethics Be Christian?* Chicago, IL: University of Chicago Press, 1975.

Hamilton, Alexander. "Report on Manufactures" (December 5, 1791).

Hanley, Ryan Patrick. *Adam Smith and the Character of Virtue*. Cambridge, UK: Cambridge University Press, 2009.

Hauerwas, Stanley. *After Christendom: How the Church Is to Behave if Freedom, Justice, and a Christian Nation are Bad Ideas*. Nashville, TYN: Abingdon Press, 1991.

Hays, Richard B. *The Moral Vision of the New Testament: Community, Cross, and New Creation*. San Francisco, CA: Harper, 1996.

Himmelfarb, Gertrude. *The Roads to Modernity: The British, the French, and the American Enlightenments* New York: Vintage Books, 2005.

Hobbes, Thomas. *Leviathan*. New York: Penguin Classics, 1982.

Horne, Herman Harrell. *The Teaching Techniques of Jesus*. Grand Rapids, MI: Kregel Publications, 1920.

Hume, David. *A Treatise of Human Nature*, ed. L. A. Selby-Bigge. London, UK: Oxford at the Clarendon Press, 1888, 1948.

———. *An Enquiry Concerning the Principles of Morals*. Oxford, UK: Clarendon Press, 1975.

———. *The History of England: From the Invasion of Julius Caesar to the Revolution of 1688*. Philadelphia, PA: McCarty & Davis, Pub., 1832.

———. "Perfect Commonwealth," *Essays Moral, Political, and Literary* (1758).

Hunter, Archibald M. *The Parables Then and Now*. Philadelphia, PA: Westminster Press, 1971.

Jensen, Hans E. "John Stuart Mill's Theories of Wealth and Income Distributiion," *Review of Social Economy* 59, 4 (December 2001): 491–507.

Keenan, James F. T*he Works of Mercy: The Heart of Catholicism*. New York, NY: Rowman & Littlefield, 2005.

Kierkegaard, Soren. *Uplifting Discourse in Various Spirits*, ed. and trans. Howard V. Hong and Edna H. Hong. Princeton, NJ: Princeton University Press, 1993.

———. *Soren Kierkegaard's Journals and Papers*, ed. and trans. Howard V. Hong and Edna H. Hong. Princeton, NJ: Princeton University Press, 1967–1978.

Kilsdonk, Edward. "Benevolent Organizations, and American Pluralism;" http://are.as.wvu.edu/kilsdonk.htm.

King, Martin L., Jr. *A Testament of Hope: The Essential Writings of Martin Luther King, Jr.*, ed. James Melvin Washington. San Francisco, CA: Harper & Row, 1986.

———. *Stride Towards Freedom*. San Francisco, CA: Harper & Row, 1986.

———. *Where Do We Go From Here*? San Francisco, CA: Harper & Row, 1986.

———. *Why We Can't Wait*. San Francisco, CA: Harper & Row, 1986.

Kysar, Robert. *Called to Care: Biblical Images for Social Ministry*. Minneapolis, MN: Fortress Press, 1991.

Jensen, Hans E. "John Stuart Mill's Theories of Wealth and Income Distribution," *Review of Social Economy* 59, 4 (December 2001): 491–507.

Jordan, W. K. *The Development of Religious Toleration in England: From the Convention of the Long Parliament to the Restoration, 1640–1660*. Gloucester, MA: Peter Smith, 1965.

Jordan-Smith, Paul. "Man's Justice and God's Justice," *Parabola* 16, 4 (1991): 71–72.

Locke, John. *A Letter Concerning Toleration*. Indianapolis, IN: Bobbs-Merrill Company, Inc., 9th Printing, 1975.

———. *First Treatise of Civil Government*. New Haven, CT: Yale University Press, 2003.

———. *Second Treatise of Civil Government*. New Haven, CT: Yale University Press, 2003.

Long, Edward LeRoy, Jr. *Facing Terrorism: Responding as Christians*. Louisville, KY: Westminster/John Knox Press, 2003.

Lyon, K. Brynolf. "The Unwelcome Presence: The Practical Moral Intention of Remembering," *Encounter* 48 (Winter 1987): 139–148.

MacPherson, C. B. *The Political Theory of Possessive Individualism*, Oxford, UK: Oxford University Press, 1972.

Marciano, Alain. "Benevolence, Sympathy, and Hume's Model of Government: How Different Is New Political Economy from Classical Political Economy," *History of Political Economy* 37 (2005): 40–67.

Matthews, Shailer. *Jesus on Social Institutions*. Philadelphia, PA: Fortress Press, 1971.

McKnight, Scott. "The Mary We Never Knew," *Christianity Today* (December 2006).

Metz, Johann B. *Faith in History and Society: Toward a Practical Fundamental Theology*, trans. David Smith. New York, NY: Seabury Press, 1980.

Mill, John Stuart. *Principles of Political Economy*. New York, NY: Colonial Press, 1899.

Miller, Perry. *Roger Williams and His Contribution to the American Tradition*. New York: Atheneum, 1962.

Moore, Mary E. M. *Teaching from the Heart: Theology and Educational Method*. Minneapolis, MN: Fortress Press, 1991.

Morgan, Edward S. *Roger Williams: The Church and the State*. New York: Harcourt, Brace & World, Inc., 1967.

Morrison, Toni. *Beloved*. New York, NY: Penguin Books, Inc., 1988.

Mott, Stephen C. *Biblical Ethics and Social Change*. New York, NY: Oxford University Press, 1982.

Nielsen, Kai. *Equality and Liberty: A Defense of Radical Egalitarianism*. Savage, MD: Rowman & Littlefield, 1985.

Noddings, Nel. *Caring: A Feminine Approach to Ethics and Moral Education*. Berkeley, CA: University of California Press, 1984.

Nussbaum, Martha. *Cultivating Humanity: A Classical Defense of Reform in Liberal Education*. Cambridge, MA: Harvard University Press, 1997.

———. "Equity and Mercy," *Journal of Philosophy and Public Affairs* 22, 2 (1993): 83–125.

———. *Loves Knowledge: Essays on Philosophy and Literature*. New York, NY: Oxford University Press, 1990.

Nygren, Anders. *Agape and Eros*, trans. Philip S. Watson. Philadelphia, PA: Westminster Press, 1953.

Outka, Gene. "Universal Love and Impartiality," *The Love Commandment: Essays in Christian Ethics and Moral Philosophy*, eds. Edmund Santurri and William Werpehowski. Washington, DC: Georgetown University Press (1989): 1–103.

Parel, Anthony J. *Gandhi's Philosophy and the Quest for Harmony*. Cambridge, UK: Cambridge University Press, 2006.

Pemberton, Prentiss L. and Daniel R. Finn. *Toward a Christian Economic Ethic: Stewardship and Social Power*. Minneapolis, MN: Winston Press, Inc., 1985.

Pence, Gregory. "Can Compassion be Taught," *Journal of Medical Ethics* 9 (1983): 189–191.

Phillips, Anthony. *Deuteronomy: The Cambridge Bible Commentary*. Cambridge, UK: Cambridge University Press, 1973.

Piper, Adrian. "Impartiality, Compassion, and Imagination," *Ethics* 101 (July 1991): 726–757.

Plato. *Republic*, trans. H. D. P. Lee and Desmond Lee. New York: Penguin Classic, 3rd edition, 2007.

Prior, William J. "Compassion: A Critique of Moral Rationalism," *Philosophy and Theology* 2, 2 (1987): 167–197.

Rawls, John. *A Theory of Justice*. Cambridge, MA: Belknap Press of Harvard University Press, 1970.

Roberts, Robert C. "Emotions as Access to Religious Truth," *Faith and Philosophy* 9, 1 (January 1992): 83–94.

Sacks, Jonathan. *The Dignity of Difference: How to Avoid the Clash of Civilizations*. New York, NY: Continuum Pub., 2002.

Schactel, Ernest G. *Metamorphosis*. New York, NY: Basic Books, 1959.

Scheler, Max. *The Nature of Sympathy*. Hamden, CT: Archon Books, 1970.

Sen, Amartya. *The Theory of Moral Sentiments*, by Adam Smith. New York: Penguin Books, 2009.

Shapiro, Thomas, et al. "The Roots of the Widening Wealth Gap: Explain the White-Black Racial Divide," from the Institute on Assets and Social Policy, Brandeis University. Research and Policy Brief (February 2013).

Shriver, Donald, Jr. *An Ethic for Enemies: Forgiveness in Politics*. New York, NY: Oxford University Press, 1995.

Smith, Adam. *An Inquiry into the Nature and Causes of the Wealth of Nations*. Oxford, UK: Clarendon Press, 1976.

———. *The Theory of Moral Sentiments*. New York, NY: Penguin Books, 2009.

Smith, Jean Edward. *FDR*. New York, NY: Random House, 2007.

Snow, Nancy. "Compassion," *American Philosophical Quarterly* 28, 3 (July 1991): 195–197.

Soloman, Robert. *A Passion for Justice: Emotions and the Origins of the Social Contract*. New York, NY: Addison-Wesley Pub., Co., 1990.

———. *The Passions*. Notre Dame, IN: University of Notre Dame Press, 1976.

Stassen, Glen. *Just Peacemaking: Transforming Initiatives for Justice and Peace*. Louisville, KY: Westminster/John Knox Press, 1992.

Stith, Richard. "Generosity: A Duty without a Right," *Journal of Value Inquiry* 25, 3 (1991): 203–216.

Taylor, Charles. *A Secular Age*. Cambridge, MA: Belknap Press of Harvard University Press, 2007.

Taylor, Vincent. *Forgiveness and Reconciliation: A Study in New Testament Theology*. London: Macmillan, 1956.

Tiflin, Chris. "Benevolence, Slavery, and the Periodicals," *Burden or Benefit: Imperial Benevolence and Its Legacies*. Bloomington: University of Indiana Press, 2008.

Toulmin, Stephen. *Cosmopolis*. Chicago, IL: University of Chicago Press, 1992.

Turner, Adair. *Economics after the Crisis: Objectives and Means*. Cambridge, MA: MIT Press, 2012.

Unamuno, Miguel de. *Tragic Sense of Life*, trans. J. E. Crawford Flitch. New York, NY: Dover Publications, Inc., 1954.

Van Til, Kent A. *Less Than Two Dollars a Day: A Christian View of World Poverty and the Free Market*. Grand Rapids, MI: William B. Eerdmans Pub., Co., 2007.

Vanderpool, Rudolph. "Hume on the 'Duty' of Benevolence," *Hume Studies* 16, 1 (April 1988): 93–110.

Verburg, Rudi. "Adam Smith's Growing Concern on the Issue of Distributive Justice," *European Journal of the History of Economic Thought* 7, 1 (Spring 2000): 23–44.

Walton, Craig. *Hume: A Re-evaluation*, ed. Donald Livingston and James King. New York, NY: Fordham University Press, 1976: 389–403.

Weber, Max. *Ancient Judaism*. New York: The Free Press, 1952.

West, Traci C. *Disruptive Christian Ethics: When Racism and Women's Lives Matter*. Louisville, KY: Westminster/John Knox Press, 2006.

Wilson, Catherine. "A Humean Argument for Benevolence to Strangers," *The Monist* (July 2003): 454–468.

Wink, Walter. "'Neither Passivity nor Violence': Jesus's Third Way." *Forum* 7, 1 & 2 (March/June, 1991): 5–28.

Winthrop, John. "Journals, I," *The History of New England*, ed. James Savage. Boston: James Savage, 1825.

Yoder, John Howard. *The Politics of Jesus*. Grand Rapids, MI: Eerdmans Pub., Co., 1972.

Zouboulakis, Michel. "On the Social Nature of Rationality in Adam Smith and John Stuart Mill," *Cahiers d'economie politiqu, Eeditions L'Harmattan* (2005): 51–63.

Index

About the Author

James E. Gilman is professor emeritus of philosophy and religion at Mary Baldwin College. He is the author of *Fidelity of Heart: An Ethic of Christian Virtue*, *Faith, Reason and Compassion: A Philosophy of the Christian Faith*, and many scholarly articles. He is an ordained deacon in the Episcopal Church, a volunteer mediator, and works with those who are mentally ill. He has two children, Ian and Caitlin, and lives with his wife, Rosemary, in Seattle, Washington.

Lightning Source UK Ltd.
Milton Keynes UK
UKOW01n0649160217
294541UK00010B/182/P

9 780739 186855